Winning the Unwinnable War

Winning the Unwinnable War

America's Self-Crippled Response to Islamic Totalitarianism

Edited by
Elan Journo

LEXINGTON BOOKS
A division of

ROWMAN & LITTLEFIELD PUBLISHERS, INC.
Lanham • Boulder • New York • Toronto • Plymouth, UK

Published by Lexington Books
A division of Rowman & Littlefield Publishers, Inc.
A wholly owned subsidiary of The Rowman & Littlefield Publishing Group, Inc.
4501 Forbes Boulevard, Suite 200, Lanham, Maryland 20706
www.lexingtonbooks.com

Estover Road, Plymouth PL6 7PY, United Kingdom

British Library Cataloguing in Publication Information Available

Library of Congress Cataloging-in-Publication Data

Winning the unwinnable war : America's self-crippled response to Islamic totalitarianism
/ edited by Elan Journo.
    p. cm.
  Includes bibliographical references and index.
  ISBN 978-0-7391-3540-2 (cloth : alk. paper) — ISBN 978-0-7391-3541-9 (pbk. : alk.
paper) — ISBN 978-0-7391-3542-6 (electronic)
  1. September 11 Terrorist Attacks, 2001. 2. War on Terrorism, 2001– 3. Jihad.
4. United States—Foreign relations—Middle East. 5. Middle East—Foreign relations—
United States. I. Journo, Elan, 1976–
  HV6432.W564 2009
  909.83'1—dc22   2009025628

Printed in the United States of America

⊗™ The paper used in this publication meets the minimum requirements of American
National Standard for Information Sciences—Permanence of Paper for Printed Library
Materials, ANSI/NISO Z39.48-1992.

Contents

INTRODUCTION

———◆———

An Unwinnable War?

Elan Journo

"I don't think you can win it. . . . I don't have any . . . definite end [for
the war]"

—President George W. Bush[1]

The warriors came in search of an elusive Taliban leader. Operating in the
mountains of eastern Afghanistan, the team of Navy SEALs was on difficult
terrain in an area rife with Islamist fighters. The four men set off after their
quarry. But sometime around noon that day, the men were boxed into an impossible situation. Three Afghan men, along with about one hundred goats,
happened upon the team's position. What should the SEALs do?

Their mission potentially compromised, they interrogated the Afghan herders. But they got nothing. Nothing they could count on. "How could we know,"
recalls one of the SEALs, "if they were affiliated with a Taliban militia group
or sworn by some tribal blood pact to inform the Taliban leaders of anything
suspicious-looking they found in the mountains?" It was impossible to know for
sure. This was war, and the "strictly correct military decision would still be to
kill them without further discussion, because we could not know their intentions." Working behind enemy lines, the team was sent there "by our senior
commanders. We have a right to do everything we can to save our own lives.
The military decision is obvious. To turn them loose would be wrong."

But the men of SEAL Team 10 knew one more thing. They knew that
doing the right thing for their mission—and their own lives—could very well
mean spending the rest of their days behind bars at Leavenworth. The men

vii

were subject to military rules of engagement that placed a mandate on all warriors to avoid civilian casualties at all costs. They were expected to bend over backward to protect Afghans, even if that meant forfeiting an opportunity to kill Islamist fighters and their commanders, and even if that meant imperiling their own lives.

The SEALs were in a bind. Should they do what Washington and the military establishment deemed moral—release the herders and assume a higher risk of death—or protect themselves and carry out their mission—but suffer for it back home? The men—Lt. Michael Murphy; Sonar Technician 2nd Class Matthew Axelson; Gunner's Mate 2nd Class Danny Dietz; and Hospital Corpsman 2nd Class Marcus Luttrell—took a vote.

They let the herders go.

Later that afternoon, a contingent of about 100–140 Taliban fighters swarmed upon the team. The four Americans were hugely outnumbered. The battle was fierce. Dietz fought on after taking five bullets, but succumbed to a sixth, in the head. Murphy and Axelson were killed not long after. When the air support that the SEALs had called for finally arrived, all sixteen members of the rescuing team were killed by the Islamists. Luttrell was the lone survivor, and only just.[2]

The scene of carnage on that mountainside in Afghanistan captures something essential about American policy. What made the deadly ambush all the more tragic is that in reaching their decision, those brave SEALs complied with the policies handed down to them from higher-ups in the military and endorsed by the nation's commander-in-chief. Their decision to place the moral injunction to selflessness ahead of their mission and their very lives encapsulates the defining theme of Washington's policy response to 9/11.

Across all fronts U.S. soldiers are made to fight under the same, if not even more stringent, battlefield rules. Prior to the start of the Afghanistan War and the Iraq War, for instance, the military's legal advisors combed through the Pentagon's list of potential targets, and expansive "no-strike" lists were drawn up.[3] Included on the no-strike lists were cultural sites, electrical plants, broadcast facilities—a host of legitimate strategic targets ruled untouchable, for fear of affronting or harming civilians. To tighten the ropes binding the hands of the military, some artillery batteries "were programmed with a list of sites that could not be fired on without a manual override," which would require an OK from the top brass.[4] From top to bottom, the Bush administration consciously put the moral imperative of shielding civilians and bringing them elections above the goal of eliminating real threats to our security.

This book shows how our own policy ideas led to 9/11 and then crippled our response in the Middle East, and makes the case for an unsettling conclusion: By subordinating military victory to perverse, allegedly moral constraints, Washington's policy has undermined our national security. Only by radically rethinking our foreign policy in the Middle East can we achieve victory over the enemy that attacked us on 9/11.

But from the outset the Bush administration had insisted that we're in a new kind of war—an unwinnable war. To scale back people's expectations, it told us not to wait for a defeated enemy to surrender, in the way that Japan did aboard the USS *Missouri* in 1945.

This much is true: the "war on terror" is essentially different from our actions in World War II. Back then, we brought Japan to its knees within four years of Pearl Harbor—yet eight years after 9/11, against a far weaker enemy, we find ourselves enmeshed in two unresolved conflicts (Iraq and Afghanistan) while further mass-casualty attacks and new flashpoints (such as Pakistan) loom. Why?

It is not for lack of military strength and prowess; in that regard America is the most powerful nation on earth. It is not for a lack of troops, or planning, or any sort of bungled execution. Our soldiers have amply demonstrated their skill and courage—*when* they were allowed to fight. But such occasions were deliberately few; for as a matter of policy Washington sent them, like the SEALs in Afghanistan, into combat but prohibited them from fighting to win. This underscores how Bush's war indeed differs from the triumphant, all-out military campaign against Japan—and how it is far from a new kind of war. It is in fact an eerie replay of Vietnam.

The philosopher Ayn Rand observed, at the time, that in the Vietnam War "American forces were not permitted to act, but only to react; they were to 'contain' the enemy, but not to beat him." Nevertheless Vietnam—like the fiascos of today—was seen as discrediting military action, even though (as Rand observed) U.S. soldiers in Vietnam were thrust into *"a war they had never been allowed to fight.* They were defeated, it is claimed—two years after their withdrawal from Vietnam. The ignominious collapse of the South Vietnamese, when left on their own, is being acclaimed as an American *military* failure."[5]

For good reason Vietnam was called a "no-win" war. Rand properly laid the blame for the disaster at the feet of American politicians and their intellectual advisors. The entire "war on terror" is likewise a no-win war. His words redolent of the Vietnam era, President Bush told an interviewer on NBC's "Today" show that "I don't think you can win [the war]," and that he blithely envisioned no definite end for it (see the epigraph). His words have been self-fulfilling. In the current conflict—as in Vietnam—the disaster is due not to a military failure. We are in an unwinnable war, but only because of the ideas setting the direction of our foreign policy.

Irrational ideas have shaped the Mideast policy not just of George W. Bush, but also of earlier administrations that had to confront the Islamist movement—from Jimmy Carter on. And although President Obama glided into office as the candidate of "change," his administration brings us full circle to the appeasing policies that characterized the run-up to 9/11 (see chapter 1). The irrationality of American policy all but guarantees that the Islamist movement will continue to menace the American public and that this conflict will figure prominently in foreign-policy thinking for years to come.

But the overarching message of this book—that certain dominant ideas about morality subvert American policy—should not be taken as a rejection of the need for morality, per se, in foreign policy. Far from it. Trying to implement a foreign policy unguided by the *right* moral principles is like trying to cross an eight-lane freeway blindfolded and with your ears plugged. Seat-of-the-pants amoral temporizing does not a policy make, and practically it is inimical to achieving U.S. security. What we demonstrate in the following pages is that the United States needs to challenge the specific morality that currently dominates our policy—and instead adopt better, more American, ideas.

To that end, we offer a new vision and specific policy recommendations for how to address ongoing problems and threats deriving from the Middle East. Those suggestions—and, broadly, all the critiques offered in this book—originate neither from a liberal, nor a conservative, nor a libertarian, nor a neoconservative outlook. Their frame of reference, instead, is the secular, individualist moral system defined by Ayn Rand. Taking U.S. policy in this new direction would enable us properly to conceptualize and achieve America's long-range self-interest: the safeguarding of our lives from foreign aggressors.

No one can predict with certainty what will unfold in the interval between the writing of this book and your reading of these words. But given the entrenched policy trends described in these pages, the lessons of the last eight years will likely go unlearned—much to the detriment of our security. My hope is that this book will counteract those trends by awakening Americans to the actual nature of the war we are in, and that in fact, if we're guided by the right ideas, the war against Islamic totalitarianism is winnable.

———•◆•———

The book's central argument is developed across seven essays. Although each essay is self-contained, I encourage you to read them all in sequence because they are parts of a thematic whole. To aid the reader in integrating the steps of the argument, I offer the following outline of the topics covered and their logical progression.

Part 1 considers the nature of the Islamist threat, its origin, and the role of U.S. policy in empowering that menace. Chapter 1 demonstrates how unprincipled U.S. policy—from Carter through Clinton—worked to galvanize the enemy to bring its holy war to our shores on 9/11. Chapter 2 explores the widely evaded nature and goals of the enemy, and indicates how that should figure in America's military response.

Part 2 focuses on the change in policies that were the impetus for Washington's military operations in Iraq and Afghanistan. Chapter 3 exposes the nature of Bush's crusade for "democracy"—sometimes called the Forward Strategy for Freedom—and the destructive moral ideas that informed it. Chapter 4 identifies the ruinous impact on U.S. self-defense of "Just War Theory"—the widely accepted doctrine of morality in war. Chapter 5 brings out the profound opposition between neoconservative thought (a major ideological influence on Bush's war policy) and America's true national interest in foreign policy.

Taken together, what these three chapters argue is that America effectively renounced the fully achievable goal of defeating the enemy—for the sake of a welfare mission to serve the poor and oppressed of the Middle East. With the goal of victory abandoned, war certainly becomes unwinnable.

Part 3 looks at what Bush's policies have wrought in the Middle East—and what the Obama administration should do. Chapter 6 surveys Afghanistan, post-surge Iraq, and the broader Islamist threat emanating from Pakistan, Iran, and elsewhere. Bush's policy, it is argued, has actually left the enemy stronger than before 9/11. The enduring threats we face and the depressingly inadequate policy options being considered underline the pressing need for a real alternative to the conventional mold in foreign policy. Although the enemy grows stronger, chapter 7 argues that victory remains achievable. The way forward requires that we adopt a radically different approach to our foreign policy in the Middle East—one founded on a different moral framework.

A word on the genesis of the essays in this collection. All but three of the essays originally appeared, in somewhat different form, in *The Objective Standard* between 2006 and 2007. The exceptions are chapters 1, 6, and 7. These were written in winter 2008–09, and are published here for the first time.

Elan Journo
The Ayn Rand Institute
May 2009

PART I

———◦◦◦———

THE ENEMY

What exposed America, militarily and economically the most powerful nation on earth, to the aggression inflicted on us on 9/11? Who or what are we up against? Why did this enemy come after us? What can we do to end this threat? The goal of victory presupposes knowing whom we must target, demoralize, and kill, so that we can judge when we have in fact defeated the enemy. There is no hope of successfully defending ourselves from its predations, without a clear definition of the enemy and a grasp of its motive.

To arrive at that necessary understanding, we must begin with history. The enemy's war against us began decades before 9/11. That campaign is distinguished not by a particular tactic—terrorism—but by the ideological goal motivating it: the establishment of a global, totalitarian Islamic regime. The following two essays consider the nature of the Islamic totalitarian movement, its ideological goal and inspiration—and how our policymakers have responded to the jihad on America.

CHAPTER ONE

———◆◆◆———

The Road to 9/11

Elan Journo

No Stone Left Unturned?

One evening about eight years ago, a group of men sat lounging around their camp in the forbidding mountains of Afghanistan. Their leader had told the men to expect something big, soon. Among their few possessions the men had a satellite dish and television set. That night they tried to pick up a broadcast signal, but couldn't get much more than static. One of them fiddled with a radio and tuned in the BBC World Service in Arabic. They sat, and they listened.

"A newscaster was just finishing a report when he said there was breaking news: A plane had struck the World Trade Center in New York! The members of Al Qaeda, thinking that was the only action, cried in joy and prostrated themselves. But bin Laden said, 'Wait, wait.'" Moments passed. Another jet had rammed into the World Trade Center. The leader wept and prayed to Allah. Then, before "his incredulous companions, bin Laden held up three fingers. . . . When news came of the Pentagon strike, bin Laden held up four fingers to his wonder-struck followers" signifying United 93 (which crashed into a Pennsylvania field, rather than its intended target, the U.S. Capitol).[1]

Add to this macabre scene a few items from the paper trail—notably the passport photos of the nineteen suicide-hijackers and the airport security footage—and you have many people's idea of the force behind 9/11. The hijackers, a kind of vanguard, were minions of the reclusive master-terrorist, Osama bin Laden. It's a straightforward picture of what we're up against—but is it right?

3

The landmark investigation into the attacks, the 9/11 Commission, definitely left that impression. The commission was celebrated for its bipartisan make-up: five Republicans, five Democrats. The panel correctly felt itself obligated to leave no stone unturned. And above all things it was painstaking, if crudely undiscriminating in its focus. The investigation sucked in an ocean's worth of facts about the attacks: some 2.5 million pages of documents were sifted, and there were interviews and testimony from more than 1,000 individuals, including scores of officials from intelligence, aviation, border control, and a host of other government agencies. Practically every significant bureaucrat, cabinet member, and elected official was hauled in to be drilled with questions.

In its tone and attention to the tiniest details, the commission's final report suits the approach you might expect from a police crime-scene investigation. CSI teams painstakingly sweep for finger prints, scrape up bloodstains for DNA sampling, and calculate a bullet's angle of entry. So, from the commission's report we learn—to take some examples at random—the biography of each hijacker, where he went to school, what he majored in; we learn about Al Qaeda's hopscotching from one base in Sudan to another in Afghanistan; we are offered a by-the-minute recounting of the flight path of each jet, with diagrams, from take-off to crash; we learn how the FAA and Norad handled the crisis. On it goes, for pages—585 to be precise, including three appendices and 119 pages of source notes.[2]

The report offered many concrete policy recommendations on sharing data between U.S. intelligence agencies; on biometric identification of travelers at border checkpoints; on disrupting the flow of money to terrorist groups; on fortifying homeland security; on locating and shutting down terrorist sanctuaries; on funding emergency preparedness for future terrorist atrocities; on public diplomacy (to name just a few). In Congress the enthusiasm to act on this advice was palpable. And why not? Laid out before the nation, in legalistically specific detail, we had an official yet bipartisan account of what happened, and what we must do next.

Except that the commission skirted the fundamental issue, the one on which our security crucially depends.

An investigation into the events leading up to 9/11 is essential. We need to understand the origin and identity of the enemy that carried out the attacks against us. Without that knowledge, we cannot tell what to do going forward; how we define the enemy (or neglect to define it) necessarily shapes the actions we should take in response. If we classify the attackers as criminals, for example, the obvious implication is to round them up, along with any accomplices, and put them all on trial (the remedy taken after the 1993 car bombing of the World Trade Center). By contrast, the attack on Pearl Harbor in 1941 was recognized as an act of war carried out by the imperialist Japanese regime. So the United States responded—on the waves, in the air, and on the land—with a devastating retaliatory war.

The cardinal responsibility of the 9/11 Commission was to figure out the nature of the force that struck us. But the panel's investigation occupied itself with microscopic details—to the exclusion of the most important object of inquiry. That is evident in the commission's focus on Al Qaeda as the chief foe and in the blinkered view of 9/11 as occurring in a historical vacuum. In the commission's report we learn that Al Qaeda had carried out a few attacks prior to 2001, and that the organization proved itself a formidable threat with the 1998 bombings of U.S. embassies in Kenya and Tanzania. But missing is a recognition of the much longer progression of attacks predating even the formation of Al Qaeda in the early 1990s. Missing also is an assessment of the U.S. policy response to three-plus decades of persistent aggression—and the effect of that policy on the morale of the aggressors.

These conspicuous omissions reflect a kind of cognitive myopia. It's symptomatic of a prevalent approach to the formulation and practice of U.S. foreign policy, afflicting both conservatives and liberals, Republicans and Democrats. This myopic outlook spurns any serious concern for the past—on the idea that no lessons from the past can have a bearing on the new situation, event, or crisis of the moment. Each crisis stands apart from what came before, and it is dealt with in isolation. This approach yields conclusions that ignore deep-rooted problems while grasping for surface-level fixes. And so, true to form, the 9/11 Commission told us that America's intelligence agencies had failed to piece together their data and recognize that an attack was imminent. The solution adopted was to unify them under the new Cabinet-level Department of Homeland Security. But the ones ultimately culpable for failing to recognize the long-standing threat against us were our political leaders and their advisors.

This charge goes way beyond the damning fact that prior to 9/11 President George W. Bush shrugged off intelligence briefings warning of imminent Al Qaeda attacks on U.S. soil. It also goes beyond the bitter recriminations against President Bill Clinton for failing to bring bin Laden to justice when attractive opportunities presented themselves (e.g., capturing him when he was within grasp in Sudan). When we consider the attacks of 9/11 in context, it becomes clear that they were a part of a trend, an escalating pattern of attacks. They were salvos in a war—a war prosecuted by a particular enemy.

The abdication of our leaders today correctly to identify that enemy is in keeping with the ingrained practice of U.S. foreign policy. Since

America's first confrontation with that enemy, it has gone unidentified and therefore unopposed.

But connect the dots, and the enemy comes into sharp focus: Islamic totalitarianism, an ideological-political movement seeking a global regime under Islamic law (or sharia). Its modern origins lie in Egypt, with the Muslim Brotherhood; the movement's paramount exponent, financial backer, and intellectual inspiration is the Islamic Republic of Iran. The Islamist movement holds that achieving its moral-political ideal requires a holy war, or jihad. The regime in Tehran exemplifies this totalitarian ideal in its domestic rule and in its militant quest to export the rule of sharia internationally. Islamists have long been hostile to the United States (reviled by Iran as the "Great Satan") and they attacked us as part of their jihad. (We will return to examine the motives of Islamic totalitarianism in chapter 2.)

Facing the Islamist onslaught, our policymakers aimed, at most, to manage crises with range-of-the-moment remedies—heedless of the genesis of a given crisis and the future consequences of today's solution. Running through the varying policy responses of Jimmy Carter, Ronald Reagan, George H.W. Bush, and Bill Clinton there is an unvarying motif. In the four major episodes that we will explore (one in the tenure of each president), our leaders failed to recognize that war had been launched against us and that the enemy is Islamic totalitarianism. This cognitive failure rendered Washington impotent to defeat the enemy. Owing to their myopic policy responses, our leaders managed only to appease and encourage the enemy's aggression.

Fueling a Spiral of Aggression

Episode one began on a November morning in 1979. The diplomats and guards at the American embassy in Tehran saw a crowd gathering outside the gates, chanting. The vehemently anti-American slogans were commonplaces in revolutionary Iran. Some in the crowd wore placards, suspended with string around their necks, bearing pictures of Ayatollah Khomeini. Khomeini was the wildly popular spiritual leader of the Islamist movement in Iran. It looked like yet another demonstration, no different from the many previous ones, a run-of-the-mill affair. But on this occasion the crowd of demonstrators stormed the embassy compound. Breaching the gates and security fence, they engulfed the grounds and got into the office buildings. They took the diplomats and guards hostage.

To invade an embassy is to flout a bedrock convention of diplomacy. It is tantamount to invading the sovereign territory of a foreign country. It is an act of war. To hold more than fifty Americans in captivity and subject them to torment is unconscionable. The hostages endured a living hell. They were, by turns, humiliated, threatened, beaten, terrorized.

Take just one incident. The captors dragged a group of male hostages into a room, lined them up against a wall, forced them to pull down their pants and stand before a firing squad. They were made to stand there, waiting, wondering if the next few breaths would be their last. Would the firing squad follow the gruesome practice of some groups in the Middle East? Would they spray the hostages with bullets, starting from the feet and working upward slowly—to prolong the agony of the victims as they bleed out to a certain death? Imagine standing, waiting for the bullets to pierce your flesh, waiting for the gunmen to take aim, waiting—until, suddenly, instead of a burst of gunfire, the guns are put away. This was a mock execution. The terror was real. [3]

The hostage-takers justified their actions, in part, as reprisals for America's past support for the deposed Shah. For many years Washington had worked to keep the Shah in power. The regime was brutal, but it was also aligned with Washington, and backing the Shah appeared to some policymakers to be a useful, even if morally questionable, arrangement. After leaving Iran, the Shah was allowed to enter the United States for medical treatment, and the militants demanded his expulsion. Yet they evidently had a larger agenda for which the Shah served as a pretext. It may well be true that they chafed under his oppressive regime, but the cause animating their violence was not liberty but the quest for an even worse form of tyranny: Islamic theocracy. Whether the militants invaded the embassy at Khomeini's explicit command remains open to question. But it was clear that Khomeini, who was working to solidify clerical rule, gave the hostage-takers his blessing and reaped benefits from the crisis.

How did Washington respond to this outrage? If there were any truth in the critique of U.S. policy as assertive and calculatingly self-interested, the Iranian hostage situation, if it had arisen at all, would have ended within days. Who, after all, would dare affront a fearsome giant capable of squashing your cause underfoot; who would venture to magnify the insult by rubbing Washington's nose in the dirt as the hostage-takers did? A nation single-mindedly committed to protecting the lives of its citizens would be expected to have immediately threatened, and if necessary deployed, military force to release the hostages. Taking such action would affirm its reputation as a nation that none dare menace. But what America in fact did had the opposite effect.

The response from Washington was foreshadowed by orders given to the American guards on the day of the embassy takeover. Facing the invading militants, the guards were instructed not to fire their weapons—lest they anger the mob.[4] Such reluctance to stand up to aggression pervaded the response of Carter's administration. When Carter took office, America was still reeling from the unhealed wounds of the war in Vietnam. That trauma, a painfully drawn-out campaign lacking a clear purpose, had demoralized the nation, sapped its self-confidence, and left many in government with the fallacious conclusion that military self-assertion, as such, should be taken off the table as an option. With the specter of Vietnam looming in the background, the Carter administration quickly sidelined military options.

The prevailing fear was that a self-assertive military operation would upset the Iranians. A rescue mission, reports one of Carter's policy advisors, was deemed to involve unacceptably high risks of civilian casualties, and might prompt the Iranians to kill the hostages. (Not taking this step, as history would show, cost far more American lives in the following decades.) The worry was that a retaliatory strike might be seen as punitive, rather than simply a means of releasing the hostages (as if retaliating against such aggression were an illegitimate goal). There was talk of mining Iranian harbors and even imposing a military blockade. But these and similar steps were to be held in reserve as "sticks" that might be brought out, if and only if all non-military avenues were exhausted. The main thrust of the administration's approach was to tempt Iran with diplomatic "carrots."[5]

Diplomatic engagement is one name for that policy; a more honest name for it is appeasement.

Laying the groundwork for that appeasement, Carter assured the Iranians that "the United States has done nothing and will do nothing that could be used to justify violence or imprudent actions by anyone."[6] What followed was an embarrassing game in which America acted on the (self-deluded) premise that its adversary was not an aggressor, that it had not committed a flagrant act of war, and that it could be bought off. The administration would not denounce Iran or commit itself publicly to any retaliatory steps, beyond meekly repeating its expectation that Iran live up to its assurance to release the hostages unharmed. Even from Carter, known for his submissive foreign policy, one would have expected at least the expulsion of Iran's ambassador, in protest and in rebuke. But that was far too bold a step: Carter's administration requested that Iran reduce the size of its staff (it was deemed desirable to keep this line of communication open). Months would pass before the United States broke off official diplomatic relations. Carter did freeze some Iranian funds in U.S. banks, and impose some trade sanctions, such as an embargo on shipments of military products—but not on food.[7]

Carter's team of advisors and strategists scrambled to come up with proposals to give Iran a face-saving way out of the crisis. In the initial stages,

Washington took the astonishing step of reaching out to the Palestinian Liberation Organization for assistance. Yasir Arafat's terrorist group, which had ties to Khomeini, was asked to serve as a go-between. The PLO, it must be remembered, was an outlawed organization in the United States stained with the blood of American victims. Why should it help? There was apparently no formal quid pro quo offered to the PLO, but it was winkingly understood that Washington would remember this favor later, when it was time to pressure Israel to make concessions to the PLO. Thus Carter's team sought to bribe this band of killers to open doors for us so that we could then bribe Tehran. This conduit to Iran, however, proved fruitless. Another proposed idea entailed asking the U.N.'s secretary-general, Kurt Waldheim, to approach television networks and have them film a one-hour presentation by the militants, effectively giving them an international stage from which to denounce the West and justify their aggression. Fortunately this scheme did not get far.[8]

The back-room negotiations, for a while through the PLO and later other intermediaries, went in fits and starts. Predictably, with time Iran's position hardened. There was even, late in the game, an abortive U.S. military rescue mission. It was a failure and an embarrassment. Soon the diplomats returned to the negotiating table. And after the fifty-two American hostages had endured imprisonment in Iran for 444 days, the crisis finally ended without bloodshed. They were released as part of a diplomatic bargain.

This seemed like a win-win resolution. We got what we wanted—the hostages back, alive. The Iranians got what they wanted—the unfreezing of some $7 billion in funds held in U.S. banks; respect for their new theocratic regime; a promise to revoke American economic sanctions; a promise to drop legal action against Iran for damages or breaches of contract resulting from the revolution (an international tribunal would handle such claims).

Advocates of engagement saw this as a triumph. The diplomats, not the Marines, had carried the day! Warren Christopher, the secretary of state at the time, wrote to the Algerian foreign minister who mediated the final settlement, celebrating the resolution: "You and your government have demonstrated an inspiring commitment to humane values, and have provided the world with a singular example of the art of diplomacy." Harold H. Saunders, who served in the administration's crisis group, echoed that sentiment: "Indeed, the entire experience had 'provided the world with a singular example of the art of diplomacy.'"[9] Carter had wanted to demonstrate the superiority of solving crises through non-violent means. Behold the proof.

But it was Khomeini and his underlings who drew the correct lesson. Like all acts of appeasement, the vaunted triumph of diplomacy was a total victory for the aggressor, Iran.

Washington followed a pseudo-sophisticated policy calibrated to send Iran the right carrot-and-stick message. Our people would dangle just enough carrots while also mumbling empty hints at the presence of a stick—even as they went out of their way to accommodate Iran. Epitomizing that sham toughness, Carter feebly warned that "the authorities in Iran should realize, . . . that the availability of peaceful measures, like the patience of the American people, is running out"—this, after the hostages were in captivity for *five months*.[10] Such timid threats were abundantly refuted as the coward's bluff by the fact that our willingness to appease never ran out.

Iran forcibly kept American citizens hostage, it extorted from Washington a ransom—and we capitulated. The financial cost: roughly $154 million for each of the remaining fifty-two hostages (counting funds in U.S. banks that were unfrozen and doled out to the new regime as part of the settlement). But that price pales in comparison to the moral meaning and destructive consequences of Washington's surrender. Our first response to Iran's act of war was to assure the aggressor that we had no intention of taking military action in retaliation; afterward, the settlement acquitted Iran from any guilt and required Washington to abjure any retribution. So Iran was to be held blameless. And by condescending to negotiate with Iran at all, we conferred on it the undeserved status of a civilized, moral equal. The Algiers Accord, spelling out the terms of the U.S.–Iranian settlement, runs to fourteen pages of legal prose. But its import can be summed up simply: it was a license and invitation to further aggression.

Speaking of the hostage crisis, Khomeini famously observed that America cannot do a damn thing. He was half-right: we could, but our policymakers advised otherwise.

Khomeini had additional reasons to rejoice. By the time that crisis was winding down, the Islamist transformation of Iran was building momentum. The rule of clerics took root in the universities and in government. Sharia, or Islamic holy law, crept in. Islamists undertook murderous purges to rid themselves of political rivals.[11] Khomeini and his followers were bringing into reality what other elements of the Islamist movement in Egypt, in Pakistan, and elsewhere had never achieved: an actual regime founded on the principles of Islam as a total state. Iran thus embodied the movement's ideological vision, it proved the feasibility of the political ideal for which jihad was a means, and it provided a model of what the pious could achieve even when taking on better-armed infidels. After having slapped the vastly stronger United States in the face, how potent the Islamic Republic now looked!

The new Iran not only inspired hope of future advances; it was committed to hastening them. Its 1979 constitution states that the army and the

Revolutionary Guards Corps "will be responsible not only for guarding and preserving the frontiers of the country, but also for fulfilling the ideological mission of jihad in God's way; that is, extending the sovereignty of God's law throughout the world."[12] In the ensuing years, Iran has made good on this mission of exporting its Islamist revolution by means of jihad.

A major target of that holy war is America. If Iran could collect a reward for taking Americans hostage, why not try something even more aggressive? In the streets of Tehran the crowds chanted "Death to America": the time was now ripe to strike at what Khomeini had vilified as the "Great Satan."

Eager to be seen as the standard bearer of a global jihad, the Iranian regime was emboldened to escalate from taking Americans hostage to taking American lives.

<hr />

Episode two unfolded during Ronald Reagan's watch. The hostages in Iran were released on the day of his inauguration in January 1981. Many hoped that Reagan would restore America's reputation by standing up to aggressors. He was contemptuous of Carter's appeasement of Iran, arguing that we should not make deals with "barbarians" who take our people hostage.[13]

Once in office, Reagan conveyed that he held a black-and-white view of morality, and that this should inform U.S. policy. In a famous speech about the Soviet threat, the president admonished his audience not to give in to the "temptation of blithely declaring yourselves above it all and label both sides equally at fault, to ignore the facts of history and the aggressive impulses of an evil empire, to simply call the arms race a giant misunderstanding and thereby remove yourself from the struggle between right and wrong and good and evil."[14] (Many people sharply criticized Reagan for this mild intimation of moral absolutism, betraying their degraded conception of what a tough foreign policy looks like.)

Was this professed commitment to U.S. security, seemingly on moral principle, the real thing? On April 18, 1983, one month and ten days after that controversial "evil empire" speech, the Reagan administration was put to the test. The scene: Beirut, Lebanon.

The roar sounded like thunder, but there were no storm clouds in the sky; it sounded like the dynamite used by fishermen working the waters off the nearby coast, but far louder and closer. When the explosive-laden truck rammed the building and blew up, the blast tore away much of the building's facade. A fine dust of glass and debris clouded the air. Broken pipes spewed out jets of water. Employees inside the U.S. Embassy in Beirut felt the entire building sway; they were the lucky ones. The guards at the front entrance were obliterated by the force of the explosion. Sixty-three people died, seventeen of them Americans.[15]

For the driver of the truck, a jihadist, this was a suicide mission. The attack had been orchestrated on the ground in Lebanon by Hezbollah, an Islamic totalitarian outfit that Iran had helped organize, train, direct, and finance. Hezbollah's mandate was to establish an Iran-style regime in Lebanon. It was Tehran's proxy force, part of the jihadist vanguard, working to expand the Islamic revolution. But Washington did nothing to retaliate against or deter Iran. So this attack became merely a prelude.

Six months later, on October 23, what seemed to be a water-delivery truck making a routine visit approached the barracks in Beirut where U.S. Marines were sleeping. At a little after 6 a.m., the truck sped past the perimeter barrier and into the compound. Ismalal Ascari, an Iranian, was at the wheel. The resulting explosion, according to experts who testified in court,

> was the largest non-nuclear explosion that had ever been detonated on the face of the Earth. The force of its impact ripped locked doors from their doorjambs at the nearest building, which was 256 feet away. Trees located 370 feet away were shredded and completely exfoliated. At the traffic control tower of the Beirut International Airport, over half a mile away, all of the windows shattered. The support columns of the Marine barracks, which were made of reinforced concrete, were stretched, as an expert witness described, "like rubber bands." The explosion created a crater in the earth over eight feet deep. The four-story Marine barracks was reduced to fifteen feet of rubble. [16]

The carnage was unspeakable. Murdered were 241 servicemen. Many who lost their lives suffered in protracted agony before they succumbed. Hundreds were injured and maimed. (Almost simultaneously another suicide bomber struck the barracks of French armed forces in Beirut.)

Who was behind this atrocity? The sophistication of the attack outstripped what Hezbollah and other pro-Iranian Islamist groups could have pulled off by themselves: without material and technical help from Iran, the operation would have been a non-starter. Loaded in the truck-bomb was an explosive material (pentaerythritol tetranitrate, or PETN) in a form that was not commercially available in Lebanon, but was in production in Iran. The culpability of the Islamist regime in Tehran was confirmed by an intercepted kill-order sent by Iran to its ambassador in Syria. U.S. Naval intelligence intercepted a message instructing the ambassador to instigate Iran's proxies in Lebanon to strike against Western forces in Beirut, and to "take a spectacular action against the United States Marines" in particular.[17] (Iran has left little doubt about its role: at a cemetery in Tehran there stands a shrine honoring the "martyrs" responsible for the 1983 barracks attack.[18])

Washington had sent the Marines into Lebanon to "provide a presence" as peacekeepers in that country's civil war. Their mission was to help the Lebanese lift themselves out of anarchy and (as Reagan put it) determine their own destiny. That so-called humanitarian mission was reflected in the rules of engagement governing the Marines: They were forbidden from carrying weapons with live rounds in their chambers, and were not allowed to load the chambers unless ordered to do so by a commissioned officer (with the exception of being under immediate deadly attack). It has been observed that they were more restricted in their use of force than an ordinary U.S. citizen walking down a street of practically any American city. [19]

Seeing the U.S. Marines it had put in harm's way savaged by an Islamist act of war, how did Washington respond? This time around the tough-sounding Reagan, not Carter, was in the White House. Reagan's administration had previously committed itself to "swift and effective retribution" against terrorists. Whoever harbored such hopes about the administration was soon disappointed.

Conspicuously missing from Washington's response to the attacks was an explicit recognition of Iran's central role in the massacre—and that it was the motor of the Islamist proxies on the ground. Our leaders diligently avoided even the merest hint of using military force to punish Iran for massacring Americans. That option was off the table.

Instead, U.S. forces fired some inconsequential shells against Syrian forces that were besieging Lebanon. As Reagan explained at a press conference, however, "the most recent shelling was not because of attacks on the Marines at the airport [barracks]; it was because of shelling of our Embassy." Despite return fire, Reagan explained that "we have not responded, because we think this is a time for restraint and for hoping to cool things down." [20] Seeming resolute, Reagan had vowed that the attacks would not deter America from its mission. The Marines would stay in Lebanon, dauntless. But not long afterward, he ordered the "redeployment" of the Marines to the USS *New Jersey* off the coast of Lebanon. Reagan spun this as something other than "cutting and running," since they were just offshore, not back in America. But it was a transparent retreat.

Islamists wanted America out of Lebanon. We let their aggression go unopposed. And then we fulfilled their wish. New crisis, same appeasing outcome. To Khomeini this was an affirmation of the lesson drawn after the hostage crisis.

The American retreat only encouraged Iran and its Islamist brothers-in-arms across the world. Watching all this play out was Osama bin Laden. "We have seen in the last decade," he said in 1998, "the decline of the American government and the weakness of the American soldier who is ready to wage Cold Wars and unprepared to fight long wars. This was proven in Beirut when the Marines fled after two explosions."[21] Like Khomeini, bin Laden was half-right: it is not our brave soldiers who are weak, but our political leaders who send them into the line of fire, disarm them, and then refuse to retaliate after Americans are pulverized in their beds.

The grotesque spectacle of American military superiority but moral weakness spurred the jihadists to venture farther afield and to feel that they could operate with practical impunity.

In Lebanon, Iranian-backed Islamist militants went on a spree of abductions and murders of Westerners. The victims included Malcolm Kerr, president of the American University in Beirut (murdered in a drive-by shooting); William Buckley, the CIA's station chief in Beirut (abducted in 1984, murdered in captivity, his mutilated remains dumped by a roadside); Terry Anderson, a correspondent for the Associated Press (taken hostage in 1985 and held until 1991). In Europe, a jihadist group hijacked U.S. airliners. In West Berlin, a discotheque popular with off-duty American soldiers was devastated by a bomb. In Naples, the USO club was attacked with a car bomb. All sorts of opportunistic, anti-American militants also felt emboldened to pile on. Palestinian terrorists hijacked an Italian cruise ship in the Mediterranean Sea; the terrorists murdered Leon Klinghoffer, a wheelchair-bound American passenger, by rolling him overboard. It was open season on Americans.

Occasionally, Washington lurched from its passive mode of appeasement to fits of punch-drunk crisis management. The order of the day: to "do something," anything, in response to such outrages. In 1984 the Reagan administration put the Islamic Republic of Iran on the blacklist of terrorist-sponsoring states. That had all the retributive force of fining a mass murder for an overdue library book. Predictably, with time the problem worsened. The Reagan administration tasked the CIA for a study on what could be done about the wave of terrorism. Robert Gates, a CIA veteran and the Secretary of Defense under George W. Bush and Barack Obama, recounts the process of deliberation.

> We focused especially on Iran, the worst offender. The downsides of an attack on Iran, to everyone's regret, outweighed how much Iran deserved punishment. We pointed out that failure to hit Iran would ensure that Iranian-sponsored terrorism would continue and even grow, but terrorist-connected targets were near cities and attacks against them would, by themselves, have little impact. [22]

Despite regarding it as "the worst offender," analysts counseled against confronting Iran, and instead for selecting an alternate target. By a process of elimination, the CIA settled on Libya. Why? "[B]ecause it was in the poore position to sustain itself against U.S. actions—military or economic—it became the target for U.S. retaliation against all state-sponsored terrorism." [23] So in April 1986, American bombers fired on some military targets in Libya, and on one of Qaddafi's homes. The damage inflicted, Gates recalls, was less than hoped for, but made Qaddafi more cautious "and probably inhibited others as well—at least for a while." [24]

Yet unsurprisingly attacks against Western targets continued and so did abductions in Lebanon; within two years, Libya instigated the mid-air bombing of Pan Am 103 over Lockerbie, Scotland (killing 270). America's meaningless retribution was in itself encouraging to Iran and other Islamists. By taking on the weakest menace, Washington presumably hoped to send Iran and others a cautionary message. The actual effect of that token strike on Libya was to certify America's lack of self-confidence and its fear of confronting the chief enemy. More still: it certified Khomeini's belief that America was fundamentally impotent.

It is worth remembering that, as was uncovered later, the Reagan administration was then actively arming the regime in Tehran. Spectacularly myopic, this clandestine scheme was supposed to help extricate a number of American hostages held in Lebanon by Iranian-backed groups. In exchange for its "help" in freeing hostages, Iran received powerful U.S. missiles. This was exposed to the light of day in the so-called arms-to-Iran scandal. Here, then, we find America, a powerful and innocent victim, on its knees, appeasing and laboring to strengthen its own destroyer.

So much for standing up to the "barbarians."

———•••———

Episode three. In his inaugural speech in 1989, President George H.W. Bush made an overture toward Tehran. Alluding to the remaining American hostages held in Lebanon, he suggested that "Assistance can be shown here, and will be long remembered. Good will begets good will." [25] Translation: if Iran would be so kind as to give the order to release the hostages, Washington would reward it. Like Carter and Reagan before him, Bush conformed to the pattern of appeasement. And by the late 1980s, Islamists understandably came to feel licensed to make outrageous demands of us—and to expect us to comply.

They felt licensed do this in the open, flagrantly. That was evident in the international scandal over Salman Rushdie's novel, *The Satanic Verses*. The novel portrayed the prophet Muhammad in a manner that some Muslims felt was unflattering. A minor controversy over the book simmered for a while after its publication; it boiled over into a major crisis on Valentine's Day, 1989, when Ayatollah Khomeini issued a decree, or *fatwa*:

> I inform all zealous Muslims of the world that the author of the book *Satanic Verses*—which has been compiled, printed, and published in opposition to Islam, the Prophet, and the Qur'an—and those involved in its publication who were aware of its content, are sentenced to death.
>
> I call on all zealous Muslims to execute them quickly, wherever they may be found, so that no one else will dare to insult the Muslim sanctities. God willing, whoever is killed on this path is a martyr. [26]

This was not some shadowy plot to blow up Marine barracks; this was not some hidden contract-hit; this was a public, self-righteous call to *murder*.

Furthermore, this was a demand that America, and other nations, suspend a crucial principle of secular society: the freedom of speech. This right protects an individual's freedom to express his ideas—in whatever medium and regardless of what others feel or think of his ideas—without fear of physical retribution. Khomeini's edict commanded that the West totally nullify this freedom.

This fit with the broader goal of the Islamist movement: to establish the supremacy of its ideology upon all mankind. Khomeini had imposed Islamic law, sharia, within the frontiers of Iran. "The struggle will continue," he had stated, "until the calls 'there is no god but Allah and Muhammad is the messenger of Allah' are echoed all over the world."[27] By commanding us to bow in deference to the medieval notion of slaughtering whomever he accuses of offending Islam, Khomeini presumptuously asserted global jurisdiction for his moral-political ideal.

Did Washington declare that an individual's freedom of speech is sacrosanct, regardless of who finds it objectionable? Did Washington vow to hunt down and bring to justice anyone who dares to act on Khomeini's death decree? No, any suggestion that we might use military force to uphold our ideals and protect American lives—that would just irritate the Iranians even more.

Washington instead extended to Iran a token of our "good will." When President Bush finally commented publicly on the death-decree, he said: "However offensive that book may be, inciting murder and offering rewards for its perpetration are deeply offensive to the norms of civilized behavior." With that shameful statement, Bush implied that Khomeini and Rushdie were equally objectionable. He added the pro forma warning that America would hold Iran "accountable" should any action be taken against U.S. interests, a warning no one in Tehran had reason to tremble over.[28] Rather than take a stand, our leaders opted to keep their heads down, to show that they had no intention of flouting Khomeini's will, in the vain hope that Iran would back off and the issue would go away, somehow. By such appeasing passivity, however, Washington bowed in deference to a blood-lusting cleric and sacrificed the freedom of Americans.

Zealous Muslims had heard the fatwa. With bounties of $2.5 million on his head, Rushdie was driven into hiding under twenty-four-hour police protection; his American publishers were inundated with threats. His Italian translator was assaulted so badly he almost died; his Japanese translator was murdered. Two bookstores in Berkeley, California, were firebombed. In March 1989 alone, the FBI received word of more than seventy threats to bookstores; Waldenbooks received forty anonymous threats. The climate of fear led some stores to withdraw the book from display. A store at Dulles International Airport posted a sign, by way of an insurance against threats: "We Don't Stock the Satanic Verses." One American publisher canceled the contract for a book deemed too incendiary;[29] the number of other projects that publishers avoided out of fear of retribution is incalculable.

Unprotected by their government, many Americans were left with little choice but to submit and crouch in fear of Khomeini's fatwa. By the default of our leaders, that death-decree against a supposedly blaspheming author was a wholesale attack on the freedom of speech in America and across the world. Our leaders demonstrated that they did not believe we had a moral right to assert ourselves against those who seek to murder Americans and subjugate us under dictates of sharia. Yet again Washington handed Islamic totalitarianism a triumph—one that Islamists went on to exploit seventeen years later in the furor over Danish cartoons of Muhammad. (We explore aspects of that crisis in chapter 2 and chapter 6.)

For Islamists, having abducted, intimidated, and murdered Americans, the next step in the escalation was to bring the terror-war to our shores.

———◆———

Episode four opened with the *first* attack, in 1993, on the World Trade Center, an attack obviously meant to inflict catastrophic harm. The truck-bomb was supposed to topple one of the towers onto its twin. Though unsuccessful, the blast did manage to kill six and injure more than 1,000. Think of this as a rough draft of 9/11. Clues indicating that this was another salvo in the broader jihad against America went unexplored. The newly inaugurated Clinton administration dealt with the bombing as a criminal matter.

Then came a sequence of major attacks—in Saudi Arabia, Kenya, Tanzania, and Yemen—each inflicting serious casualties and probing to see how much aggression America would tolerate. The probing elicited from the

United States the familiar pattern. Clinton's time in office reflected all the salient aspects of that pattern: blatant appeasement—sporadic, toothless reprisals—evasive passivity.

Consider the bombing in 1996 of the Khobar Towers apartment complex in Dhahran, Saudi Arabia. The building housed U.S. forces involved in protecting that country from Iraq. The blast wave emitted by the truck bomb pummeled the eight-story building and killed nineteen Americans. Investigations revealed that the bombers had been trained by Iran in Lebanon's Bekaa Valley; they had been given passports at the Iranian embassy in Damascus, Syria; they had received $250,000 in cash to pay for the operation from an Iranian general; and afterward, some were living in Iran. According to Louis Freeh, who headed the FBI at the time, the Clinton administration purposely dragged its feet to slow down the investigation, lest it be revealed that Iran was behind the Khobar attack. Eventually, when that was established with certainty, Freeh reports that the administration's interest in the case "translated into nothing more than Washington 'damage control' meetings held out of the fear that Congress, and ordinary Americans, would find out that Iran murdered our soldiers."[30]

No action was taken against Iran, because that would endanger plans for improving relations with Tehran and pursuing a dialogue. Clinton had called for a genuine reconciliation between the U.S and Iran. Echoing that message, at the time that the Khobar investigation was being stonewalled, Secretary of State Madeline Albright offered that "As the wall of mistrust comes down, we can develop with the Islamic republic, when it is ready, a road map leading to normal relations."[31] To that end the administration progressively lifted previously imposed economic sanctions on Iran (piddling restrictions easily breached and often suspended through waivers). More goodies, Washington suggested, might be forthcoming.

Behind this appeasing maneuver was a rationalization that many found tantalizing. Within Iran, it was claimed, there was a new crop of leaders seeking "reform." Notable among them was Mohammad Khatami, who in 1997 became president of Iran. For a brief spell there seemed to be some kind of ferment, some modest loosening of social restrictions (e.g., men and women "felt freer to move about, to mix and mingle; university students of both sexes dared to address one another on campus"; women "did not hesitate to expose a bare wrist, ankle, painted toe, or even a bit of bare neck"; the regime licensed a few more newspapers).[32] In reality these superficial changes were evanescent, and soon there followed a crackdown. Khatami himself was uninterested in anything like "a secular government on the Western model," observe the scholars Patrick Clawson and Michael

Rubin. Rather, he "was dedicated to perfecting the Islamic Republic, not to replacing it."[33]

Nevertheless the Clinton administration desired a rapprochement with Iran, and to make that happen it pushed out of mind the reality of the regime's character and its ongoing proxy war against us. Thus after Khobar, the latest attack in that war, Washington went out of its way to refrain from retaliation, and busied itself with trying to purchase Iranian good will.

While our diplomats tried to coax the Islamists in Iran to dance a waltz, other Islamists pounded U.S. interests in Africa. In August 1998 massive bombs went off outside the American Embassies in Kenya and Tanzania. One of the explosions leveled a three-story building and incinerated dozens of passengers in a nearby bus.[34] Thousands were injured. The death toll climbed into the hundreds.

But on this occasion, Washington *did* take military action. Clinton told the nation that "There are no expendable American targets"—but this rhetoric was belied by his actions in the Khobar case and again in the meek retaliation that was about to unfold.[35] U.S. Navy ships in the Red and Arabian Seas sprinkled seventy-odd Tomahawk cruise missiles into Afghanistan and Sudan. Their targets were primitive boot camps for Islamist holy warriors in the Afghan wilderness and a purported chemical weapons factory in Sudan that turned out to be no such thing.[36] Far from seriously disrupting the Al Qaeda bases in those countries (as the administration claimed) these strikes were pinpricks. Just as in 1986 America opted to confront the runt among the threats before it, striking at Libya instead of Iran; so again Washington appeased Iran (which had helped train Al Qaeda's bombers) and gingerly wagged an admonishing finger at Al Qaeda.

The boot camps reconstituted, the training resumed, and the holy warriors marched on—galvanized at seeing America's timidity.

Hard on the heels of the bombings in Africa came the attempt to sink the USS *Cole* in Yemen. The warship had stopped at the port of Aden to refuel. Two suicide-bombers came alongside it in a small fishing boat loaded with explosives. The explosion opened up a forty-foot-by-forty-foot hole in the hull, and killed seventeen servicemen.[37] Neither Clinton, nor his successor, George W. Bush, deemed it worthwhile responding to that attack. They sat by passively.

A young man interviewed after the attacks at the port of Aden eloquently stated a view that, affirmed over and over by U.S. policy, had become gospel in the Middle East. Looking at the gaping hole in the side of the mighty USS *Cole*, he put it simply, with satisfaction and perhaps even pleasure: "You have big boats, and look, they are nothing!"[38] True enough. Lacking a conception of who the enemy is and lacking the certainty of our moral right to permanently eliminate that enemy, the United States *is* impotent.

Observe how, after the storming of an embassy in Tehran and the kidnapping of its personnel, we then faced the wholesale murder of Americans, blown up in their beds, at cafes, in night clubs, on airliners. Observe how continual appeasement served, not to diminish the enemy's ardor, but to inflame it—not to placate the enemy, but to infuse it with audacity, the audacity to put a bounty on the head of a novelist and his publishers. Observe how America's perpetual evasion of the enemy's nature empowered the jihadists.

Observe how this pattern paved the way from an attack on our embassy in Tehran one November morning, to a catastrophic morning in downtown Manhattan.

The Pattern

There is a common outlook in foreign policy that generates this pattern: "realism." Proponents of realism tell us that morality is a hindrance to achieving results in foreign policy. Getting hung up on moral distinctions (for example, between friends and foes) would mean severely constricting the range of actions open to our policymakers. Moral ideals and other broad principles, therefore, are pushed aside in the name of a hard-boiled commitment to "practicality." But the inexorable result of this aversion to principles is intellectual myopia.

The realist mindset shuns the need to sort through the data and discern the nature of events. It spurns the process of cognitively digesting past events and abstracting out the patterns and trend lines. The many distinct dots, in other words, are left unconnected and their significance unidentified. In this regard, recall how after the Beirut bombings, the Reagan administration secretly worked to bribe Tehran with missiles, in order to release American hostages in Lebanon. Or recall how following 9/11 Washington organized an anti-terrorism coalition and (in all seriousness) invited Iran, the arch-sponsor of Islamist terror, to join. On the realist outlook, each crisis, each problem, each situation is dealt with on its own perversely narrow terms.

This myopia also means that so-called realists cannot project the future consequences of actions taken in the present. And while proponents of this outlook profess a devotion to advancing the national interest, they cannot define what is in America's interest, since formulating that definition requires the long-range perspective that realists abandon. Take, for instance, the policy that began in Carter's administration, and continued under Reagan, of supporting jihadists in Afghanistan during the 1980s. Why do this? We were against the Soviets, who had invaded Afghanistan, and so were the holy warriors—even though they were equally anti-American. History has shown us the results of that scheme. We have suffered grievously at the hands of some of those holy warriors—a bearded, willowy man from Saudi Arabia being prominent among them.

Disaster is the inevitable result of following realist policy in the face of an enemy driven by a moral ideal and committed to fighting a generations-long struggle to realize that ideal. The operating assumption for realist policymakers is that (like them) no one would put an abstract, far-off ideal ahead of collecting some concrete, immediate advantage (money, honor, influence). So for realists, an enemy that is dedicated to a long-term goal— and thus cannot be bought off with bribes—is an enemy that must remain incomprehensible.

So it was and remains.

<hr>

In the wake of 9/11, proponents of realism moved to the sidelines. To a significant extent the policy of the Bush administration came to reflect the influence of neoconservative thinkers, particularly their idea that moral principles must inform U.S. foreign policy. In part 2, we will explore this brand of principled policy, one that proved no less destructive to our security.

CHAPTER TWO

———◆———

What Motivates the Jihad on America

Elan Journo

Fathoming the Atrocities

On that cloudless Tuesday morning in September, downtown Manhattan was engulfed by an eerie fog. It was a fog of dust and ashes. From the top floors of the Twin Towers of the World Trade Center plumes of smoke billowed, and inside an inferno raged. The courtyard at the foot of the towers was strewn with aircraft debris, shattered glass, and corpses. These were the bodies of suicides who had sought escape from the intense flames, fed by hundreds of gallons of airplane fuel, that were ripping through the towers. Hundreds of other desperate souls, hurrying down fire-escapes, were pulverized under tons of buckling girders and cement.

The massacre of September 11, 2001, claimed nearly 3,000 lives.

But it was calculated to kill many more. Of the other hijacked airplanes, one rammed into the Pentagon; the intended target of the fourth plane was the U.S. Capitol. By seeking to destroy the headquarters of the Department of Defense, the nation's legislature, and the global hub of financial markets—by striking at organs crucial to the security and prosperity of America—the attacks were an assault on everything that depended on those organs. The attacks intended to devastate the entire country.

The hostility unleashed against America on that day has extended also to our allies. On March 11, 2004, bombs on commuter trains in Madrid transformed the vibrant bustle of rush hour into a scene of unspeakable carnage. Human limbs and random chunks of flesh lay on the ground amid pools of blood. Nearly 200 individuals perished, but as with the attacks on American soil thirty months earlier, the killers had hoped for a higher death toll. Police found and safely detonated three further explosive devices. Then London, in the summer of 2005, was hit by suicide bombings on three Tube trains and a No. 30 bus in the center of town. On one of the trains, the explosion left remains so mutilated and burned that they were scarcely recognizable as ever having been human. Fifty victims died, and 700 were injured; some had massive burns, some had limbs blown off. (Three weeks later another team of bombers attempted to strike the Tube system again, albeit unsuccessfully.)

The hostility of the killers is fierce. They diligently toil for our destruction. Human life, to them, is cheap. Not merely the lives of their victims, but also their own. Unlike soldiers risking death in hopes of living to see their nation's army triumph, the attackers who strap on dynamite vests, who drive trucks laden with explosives into buildings, and who deliberately crash airplanes into skyscrapers, do so certain of their own annihilation. They have no hope of surviving to see the success of whatever goal they are working to achieve. This perverse willingness to kill themselves in order to kill Americans makes the atrocities all the more bewildering.

Who are these killers? What drives their gleeful slaughter of human beings? What motivates their rabid hostility to America? Putting an end to this threat entails knowing what impels our enemy.

One commonly accepted explanation blames U.S. policy in the Middle East. The massacres, on this view, are supposedly retaliation against what the killers regard as American hostility and "imperialism." Echoing statements by some of the killers, Western advocates of this notion paint them as rebels against America's "arrogant power," and its "sanctimoniously munificent support not only of Israel but of numerous repressive Arab" regimes.[1] The idea is that the killers are incensed and frustrated and desperate to break the U.S.-endorsed chains that oppress them; terrorism somehow expresses their fury.

The killers, it is true, do seek to overthrow certain regimes in the Arab-Islamic world, and they do want to transform their culture; but they are avowedly hostile to political freedom. Instead, they want to institute a form of religious servitude. The killers do regard themselves as avenging supposed injustices, but their implied or stated moral criterion derives from Islam. The killers are incensed that infidel American troops, by their mere presence, befoul the holy land of Islam (specifically, Saudi Arabia). They oppose America's support for the infidel state of Israel, which has usurped lands they believe ought to belong to Islam.

The killers believe that the West, led by America, is somehow leading a war on their religion. In a videotaped statement, the leader of the London bombings attested that "Our drive and motivation doesn't come from tangible commodities that this world has to offer. Our religion is Islam, obedience to the one true God Allah and following the footsteps of the final prophet messenger. This is how our ethical stances are dictated." His stated rationale for the attack was "protecting and avenging my Muslim brothers and sisters."[2]

Millions of people around the world despise U.S. policies, but they do not become mass murderers of Americans (and Westerners). Nineteen Muslims did on September 11—as did the London and Madrid bombers, and countless others. The hijackers deliberately chose a manner that assured their own "martyrdom." The ringleader of the 9/11 attacks wrote a detailed note instructing his warriors how to prepare themselves: "Remember that this is a battle for the sake of God. As the prophet, peace be upon him, said, 'An action for the sake of God is better than all of what is in this world.' . . . Either end your life while praying, seconds before the target, or make your last words: 'There is no God but God, Muhammad is His messenger.'"[3]

The key to understanding what impels the killers—and what can be done to stop them—is to listen to what they themselves confess as their motive.

What They Tell Us

The nineteen suicide-hijackers were part of an ideological movement. Followers of this cause proclaim themselves holy warriors in the path of Allah. They believe that there is a fundamental problem afflicting the world—and that they must solve it.

The problem: the dominion of Islam, like the rest of the world, has fallen into sordid impiety. Religious law, or sharia, no longer governs men's thought and action. Muslims in particular are failing to live up to the dictates of Islam; unbelief and godlessness abound across the face of the earth.

Sayyid Qutb, an intellectual leader of the movement, diagnosed the situation in stark terms. *Jahiliyya* is the state of supposedly barbaric ignorance that obtained in pre-Muhammadan times, and for Qutb, "Everything around us is *jahiliyya*—people's beliefs and ideas, habits and traditions, culture, art, and literature, rules and laws, to such an extent that much of what we consider Islamic culture, Islamic sources, Islamic philosophy, and Islamic thought are also constructs of *jahiliyya*!" But in the modern *jahiliyya* mankind is not merely ignorant of the truth, it has rejected universal subjugation to Allah's will. For Qutb, therefore, the modern world is even lower than the pre-Muhammadan barbarism; unlike that first *jahiliyya*, men now claim that "the right to create values, to pass laws and regulations, and to choose one's way in life rests with man, in disregard of what Allah has prescribed."[4]

The solution: Bring about a global sharia regime enveloping the totality of human life and society. The apt designation for this movement is Islamic totalitarianism (Islamist and jihadist are terms used interchangeably in this book to denote a member of the movement).

Instructing the faithful in how to realize that ideal, Qutb writes that "The establishment of Allah's kingdom on earth, the elimination of the reign of man, the wresting of sovereignty from its usurpers and its restoration to Allah, and the abolition of human laws and implementation of the divine law [sharia] cannot be only achieved through sermons and preaching."[5] The righteous fighters "must employ Jihaad."[6]

It is immaterial, Qutb argued, "whether the homeland of Islam—in the true Islamic sense, Dar ul-Islam—is in a condition of peace or whether it is threatened by its neighbors." The movement's goal is not merely to preserve one small corner of the world as a domain for Muslims; it is to ensure "that the obedience of all people be for God alone," everywhere.[7] For the "object of this religion is all humanity and its sphere of action is the whole earth."[8]

Prolific and articulate, Qutb served as a driving force behind the Muslim Brotherhood. This Egyptian group began in 1928, and mushroomed across the Middle East. It is the ancestor of Al Qaeda, Hamas, and many other jihadist outfits across the world. In Pakistan, another element of the Islamist movement sprang up; its theoretician and organizing impetus was Abul Ala Mawdudi.

Starting from the same moral-political ideal, Mawdudi came to the same practical conclusion. Society must be brought under a sharia regime, but it "cannot evidently restrict the scope of its activities. Its approach is universal and all-embracing. Its sphere of activity is coexistent with the whole of human life." And achieving it necessitates a sustained jihad to "destroy those regimes opposed to the precepts of Islam and replace them with a government based on Islamic principles . . . not merely in one specific region . . . but [as part] of a comprehensive Islamic transformation of the entire world."[9]

Ayatollah Ruhollah Khomeini, an enormously influential figure in the movement, was the architect—and until 1989, the supreme leader—of Iran's totalitarian regime. In his book *Governance of the Jurist*, Khomeini argued that anyone "who has some general awareness of the beliefs and ordinances of Islam will unhesitatingly give his assent to the principle of the governance of the *faqih* [cleric]"[10] as a self-evident necessity. The lamentable fact that this principle needs to be demonstrated, he observed, is due to the decadence prevailing in Muslim society, a society that has strayed from the path of Allah. The clerical regime that Khomeini envisioned—and established—would serve merely as an earthly conduit to the Almighty, for "in Islam the legislative power and competence to establish laws belongs exclusively to God Almighty. . . . In this form of government, sovereignty belongs to God alone and law is His decree and command."[11]

Many decades prior to the eruption of the ferocious Islamist revolution in Iran, Khomeini told audiences that "those who study *jihad* will understand why Islam wants to conquer the whole world. All the countries conquered by Islam or to be conquered in the future will be marked for everlasting salvation. For they shall live under [God's law]."[12]

The 9/11 hijackers understood the imperative of fighting a jihad to implement the rule of sharia. They were enforcers of that principle. If Allah is the only God and if His law is absolute, then unbelievers must be put to the sword. They must learn that their vices are hateful to Him. The razing of the World Trade Center was thus a grand-scale meting out of justice to the infidels who refuse to submit to the authority of Allah. There was no other way to correct the wickedness of those who made their careers reaping profits for themselves in the fields of finance and commerce.

And if killing infidels in Allah's name means forfeiting one's own life, that should not be regarded as a loss. Khomeini had observed:

> We do not fear giving martyrs. . . . Whatever we give for Islam is not enough and is too little. Our lives are not worthy. . . . Martyrdom is a legacy which we have received from our prophets. Those should fear death who consider the aftermath of death to be obliteration. We, who consider the aftermath of death a life more sublime than this one, what fear have we?[13]

Qutb lionized fallen jihadists: "Those who risk their lives and go out to fight, and who are prepared to lay down their lives for the cause of God are honorable people, pure of heart and blessed of soul."[14] He is here merely echoing Islamic sacred texts. "Allah has bought from the believers their soul and their possessions against the gift of Paradise; they fight in the path of Allah; they kill and are killed . . . and who fulfils his covenant truer than Allah? So rejoice in the bargain you have made with Him; that is the mighty triumph."[15] Martyrs are promised sumptuous rewards in the afterworld.

To varying extents, Islamic totalitarianism has gained power in parts of the world. The brutality of its rule has stunned many people, but there's a logic behind its notoriously harsh enforcement of sharia law. Its quasi-medieval political practices follow from its moral ideal. Massive coercion is necessary to ensure the public's total obedience to Islam. Consider the practice of sharia in Iran, Taliban-controlled Afghanistan, Saudi Arabia, and Nigeria.

With the advent of Islamist rule in Iran, taverns were destroyed and movie theaters closed. Khomeini noted that "We no longer allow boys and girls to undress and go bathing in the sea." Islam, he continued, "has put an end to means that lead our young men into corruption. Islam wants fighters to stand up to the unbelievers, to those attacking our country. Islam wants to create mujihad [holy warriors] . . . . Islam is a serious religion. There is no debauchery in Islam."[16] The Iranian regime banned music and poetry, and it censors films, books, and newspapers. Dissenters or critics of the regime are deemed enemies of Islam and their murder is considered justified. Iran forbids "prohibited acts"—a term so vague it can encompass simple association between two individuals of different sexes, such as walking in the park, sitting next to each other in a car, or anything the ruling clerics decide is irreligious, blasphemous, or somehow un-Islamic.[17]

Upon rising to power in Afghanistan, Taliban leaders pulled down satellite TV dishes and ordered such "corrupting" devices as televisions, radios, and VCRs "hanged" publicly. The Taliban's infamous "Department for the Propagation of Virtue and the Prohibition of Vice" patrolled the streets in search of Muslims violating moral law or otherwise engaging in un-Islamic behavior. Movie theaters were shuttered; the wearing of Western-styled suits and the playing of music were banned. Women were compelled to wear all-encompassing veils as a mark of their modesty and lest they provoke lust in the men around them. Women caught wearing robes that were deemed immodest were flogged (in one incident, an enforcer summarily ripped the antenna from a nearby car and thrashed a woman for her immodest attire). The draconian penalties prescribed by the sharia code included flogging for the consumption of liquor and stoning to death for adultery.[18]

Like Iran and the Taliban regime, Saudi Arabia also has its own government-sanctioned vigilante force to foster virtue. These shock-troops assault people for failing to attend mosques at the five daily prayer times. In one notorious case, the morality thugs prevented female students from leaving a burning school in Mecca, because they were insufficiently covered up when they tried to escape the flames; more than a dozen students burned alive.[19] Crimes like apostasy and blasphemy are punished by death, "often by stoning or beheading on a Riyadh plaza . . . popularly known as 'chop-chop square.'"[20]

Several years ago sharia was imposed in certain provinces of Nigeria, in a depressingly predictable way. The spread of sharia in that country began in Zamfara province, which "sexually segregated all buses and taxis. Men are not allowed to use most taxis and instead must get rides on motorcycles. Women are forbidden to ride these motorcycles, and some who have tried have been stoned." Alcohol was banned, women were forbidden to wear trousers, and vigilantes were licensed to enforce divine law. "Just beyond the boundary sign welcoming travelers to 'Zamfara, the home of farming and Sharia' are two burned out trucks whose drivers made the mistake of carrying beer over the border."[21]

And of course, true to the ideal of Islam's universal purview, the quest to subjugate people under sharia has spread beyond national borders. Iran and Saudi Arabia are infamous for exporting their ideology. Saudi Arabia has spent billions of dollars to build mosques worldwide, to publish tracts, and to dispatch missionaries that disseminate the regime's Wahhabi strain of Islamic totalitarianism. Saudi wealth helped build up the Taliban regime (which in turn hosted Al Qaeda) and has financed terrorist groups in the Balkans and across the Middle East.

"The Iranian revolution," declared Ayatollah Khomeini, "is not exclusively that of Iran, because Islam does not belong to any particular people. . . . We will export our revolution throughout the world because it is an Islamic revolution. The struggle will continue until the calls 'there is no god but Allah and Muhammad is the messenger of Allah' are echoed all over the world."[22] Iran's constitution commits the regime to expanding "the sovereignty of God's law throughout the world."[23] And for three decades Iran has sustained its jihad on America and other nations by means of a terrorist proxy war, spearheaded by Lebanese Hezbollah (see chapter 1).

Underwriting and inspiring such aggression serves a dual purpose: it is a means of ridding the world of unbelievers and of compelling wholesale submission to Allah's will.

What motivates the jihadists, if we judge by their words and deeds, is their belief in Islam.

Deviating from Islam?
Despite the decades of explicit statements, in books and speeches, by jihadist ideologues naming their political-cultural ideal—

> despite Osama bin Laden's praise of 9/11 as a righteous act in the path of God—
>
> despite the declaration by Ayman al-Zawahiri that the jihad against the West aims to "restore [the Muslim nation's] fallen caliphate and regain its lost glory"—
>
> despite the declaration by Sheik Omar Abdel Rahman, mastermind of the 1993 bombing of the World Trade Center, that Muslims "must terrorize the enemies of Islam and frighten them and disturb them and shake the earth under their feet"—

despite the unrepentant bloodlust of Zacarias Moussaoui, charged with complicity in 9/11, who told prosecutors of his desire to "inflict pain on your country," and of his willingness to kill Americans "any time, anywhere" in the name of Allah—

despite all this and more, we are asked to believe that the jihadists' motivation is decidedly *not* the religion of Islam. [24]

This notion came to the fore remarkably fast. Long before the torrent of editorials and books exculpating Islam, while the ruins of the World Trade Center were still blazing, President Bush invited a Muslim cleric to speak at the National Day of Prayer and Remembrance. A couple of months later he invited fifty Muslim ambassadors to the White House to break the fast of Ramadan. His purpose, evidently, was to underscore his belief that "the terrorists have no home in any faith."[25] Voicing the feelings of countless people, Bush insisted ardently that "The face of terror is not the true faith of Islam. That's not what Islam is all about. Islam is peace. These terrorists don't represent peace. They represent evil and war."[26]

Many serious scholars have labored, in print and on television, to distance Islam from terrorism. Bernard Lewis, an eminent historian and an advisor to the Bush administration, has argued that terrorist groups like Al Qaeda "sanctify their action through pious references to Islamic texts, notably the Qur'an and the traditions of the Prophet." But they are "highly selective in their choice and interpretation of sacred texts," and accept or reject texts "according to whether they support or contradict their own dogmatic and militant positions."[27]

Clearly, among Muslims there are differences on how to understand the Koran and the sayings attributed to Muhammad (or *hadith*). There are rival sects, most notably Sunni and Shiite, and multiple schools of thought on the body of laws known as sharia. Within the religion there are competing lines of doctrinal interpretation. It may well be true that the jihadists have an interpretation distinctive to them. But is theirs a "hijacking" of the religion, a rank perversion of it—or an interpretation understandably flowing out of Islam?

It is helpful to think about this from a wider perspective. In all of the major religions of the world there are disputes about interpretation. For example, devout Catholics and equally committed Protestants have disagreed violently on the meaning of Christianity (and of course Protestants are themselves splintered into countless subgroups). Catholics have denounced Protestants for deviating from the one true interpretation of the Bible; Protestants have denounced Catholics for losing sight of the authentic teachings of Christ. They have reviled each other as heretics and fought devastating wars over their beliefs.

Protestants and Catholics may wish to regard their line of thinking as truer to the faith, but from the outside looking in, there's no basis to anoint either side as hewing to the definitive interpretation. To say that one side or another has "hijacked" or "perverted" Christianity would mean that it advocates some view with manifestly no relevance to or intelligible basis in the religion's teachings and sacred books. That sort of charge might be plausible if, say, the Pope issued an edict that believers must henceforth emulate, not the humility of Jesus, but the pride of Zeus, and exalt, not the virginal purity of Mary, but the keen sensuality of Aphrodite. Such an edict would not intelligibly follow from, but flout two millennia of Church doctrine and practice. But, despite the many theoretical differences that separate Catholics and Protestants, it would be absurd to claim that the sermons of Pope Benedict XVI and those of evangelical pastor Rick Warren have no bearing on Christianity. Rather: they represent two groups differing over how to interpret Christianity.

The same argument applies to Islam. To say that jihadists have "hijacked" the religion would mean that their interpretation flies in the face of Islam. It would mean that Qutb, Khomeini, Mawdudi, bin Laden, and other Islamists embrace goals and means that are as alien to Islam as Zeus is to Christianity. That's essentially how President Bush has portrayed followers of the jihadist movement:

> Whatever it's called, this ideology is very different from the religion of Islam. This form of radicalism exploits Islam to serve a violent political vision: the establishment, by terrorism and subversion and insurgency, of a totalitarian empire that denies all political and religious freedom. These extremists distort the idea of jihad into a call for terrorist murder against Christians and Jews and Hindus and also against Muslims from other traditions, who they regard as heretics.[28]

Contained in this statement are three assertions: (1) that Islam and the creed of the jihadists are fundamentally dissimilar; (2) that their totalitarian political goal has no basis in the religion; and (3) that their conception of holy war is antithetical to Islam. Let's ponder each of these in turn.

Islam vs. Islamic totalitarianism

"Despite the rich diversity in Islamic practice," writes John L. Esposito, a noted scholar of Islam at Georgetown University, "the Five Pillars of Islam remain the core and common denominator, the five essential and obligatory practices all Muslims accept and follow." Esposito is rightly viewed as something of an apologist for Islam, and his widely-adopted college text, *Islam: The Straight Path*, is an openly sympathetic account of the religion. From his discussion of the Five Pillars, we can observe that the sum of these supreme values is to effect and demonstrate the believer's complete submission to authority.

The first pillar is the call upon a Muslim ("one who surrenders") to proclaim: "There is no god but the God [Allah] and Muhammad is the messenger of God." With this acknowledgement, "a person professes his or her faith and becomes a Muslim," writes Esposito.[29] This profession of absolute commitment is reaffirmed at daily prayers (the second pillar). Five times a day, every day, believers must drop whatever they are doing, face the direction of the holy city of Mecca in a mosque ("place of prostration"), at home, or elsewhere, and then pray—on their knees, bowing their heads to the floor.

A Muslim is obligated to make payments of *zakat*, a kind of tithe that goes to support the community, specifically orphans, widows, the poor; it also goes to support the spread of Islam (the third pillar). But this is not charity, because the giving is not optional; the money is regarded as a due owed to the poor and the suffering. The giver is not the rightful owner of the wealth, but merely the trustee of what Allah has deigned to provide from His bounty.

The fast of Ramadan is the fourth pillar. For one month every year, from dawn to dusk, Muslims must deprive themselves of the pleasures of food and drink and sexual intercourse. The fifth pillar is the duty to make a pilgrimage to Mecca, incumbent on males. At least once in his lifetime, the Muslim must set aside his work and any other responsibilities and invest time and money to make his way to Islam's holy city.[30]

Consider some of the implications of these tenets. The believer is duty bound to bow continually before Allah; he is duty bound to cross oceans and continents in pilgrimage to prove his unwavering submission; he is duty bound to sacrifice fruits of his labor for the sake of Muslims who suffer in his community; he is duty bound to efface his desires—for food, drink, and the pleasure of sex—in a show of devotion; he is duty bound to proclaim, by his words and deeds, that he subordinates himself to his supernatural master.

The belief that man must obey Allah rests only on faith—an emotionally induced belief in the absence of facts and evidence. The believer is commanded to will his mind to believe—based not on what he himself can see or hear, nor on what he himself can infer logically from the evidence of his perception. To believe, he must put aside his rational faculty and accept blindly the mystical revelations of Muhammad; he commits, on principle, to put the dictates of an authority—the Koran, the local cleric—above his own grasp of facts.

The believer's surrender must be complete. The moral principle of Islam (as of Christianity) demands the sacrifice not only of *mind*, but also of *self*. A Muslim's wealth, his own pleasures, his goals—none of these are important. The only will that matters belongs to God. Thus a believer is forbidden from "hoarding" goods or services that are in demand, and from lending money out on interest. Were he to charge interest, he would benefit by increasing his wealth, gaining the means to better serve his health and comfort. And were he to "hoard" water or rice, he would gain the means to survive a famine ("hoarding" carries an additional complication, since it might also betray his doubt in the unfailing providence of Allah to take care of His people). The believer's duty is to sow the money back into the Muslim community without gaining by it; likewise, if he has an abundance of water when it is scarce, he must surrender his claim to it for the sake of others in the community. The beneficiary of his sacrifice is always something or someone other than the believer himself—Allah or His divine law; his neighbors; the community. His own life is of no significance or value, except to the extent that he surrenders his mind and values obediently.

Morally, the believer must learn that he is not a sovereign individual; his life is not his own to dispose of as he sees fit; he belongs to Allah, who alone is sovereign. And he must serve the interests of his master. A believer's determination of what's true or false is inconsequential; he must accept unreservedly the ideas, beliefs, commandments handed to him—never questioning authority. What this moral code offers is guidance on how one can achieve the ideal of becoming a slave to Allah.

Now listen to Sayyid Qutb.

The theoretical foundation of Islam, in every period of history, has been to witness 'La ilaha illa Allah'—'There is no deity except God'—which means to bear witness that the only true deity is God, that He is the Sustainer, that He is the Ruler of the universe, and that He is the Real Sovereign; to believe in Him in one's heart, to worship Him Alone, and to put into practice His laws. Without this complete acceptance of 'La ilaha illa Allah,' which differentiates the one who says he is a Muslim from a non-Muslim, there cannot be any practical significance to this utterance, nor will it have any weight according to Islamic law.

Theoretically, to establish it means that people should devote their entire lives in submission to God, should not decide any affair on their own, but must refer to God's guidance through only one source, that is, through the Messenger of God—peace be on him. Thus, in the second part of the Islamic creed, we bear witness 'Wa ashhadu anna Muhammadar Rasul Allah'—'And I bear witness that Muhammad is the Messenger of God.'[31]

If the Five Pillars form the core of Islam, is not Qutb's one intelligible interpretation of their meaning and application?

Organizing Society and Government

Integrity to Islam's moral principles implies a certain kind of social order. Politically, believers must obey Islamic law, or sharia—a body of rules derived from the Koran and the *hadith*. Under such laws, Muslims can practice their faith without compromise; the laws that govern them protect and foster piety, while exacting punishments for offenses against Muslims—such as theft or murder—and against their creed.

Just as there must be a unity within the believer between his life and belief; so, politically, state and religion are one, indivisible. The concept of separating state and church is a distinctively Western innovation that was long unknown, and then shunned, in Islam. The purpose of such a barrier wall is to limit the scope of religion over life. Such a wall is a value if one regards man as a rational, sovereign being, and wishes to protect individuals from the imposition (or proscription) of ideas by religion. But if one holds that sovereignty belongs only to Allah, the state must be an extension of the authority of Islam.

The dominion of Islam, many Muslims hold, must encompass all of a believer's existence—but also the existence of all nonbelievers. Since the Koran is the Truth of Allah, as communicated by His final messenger, it purports to answer the universal needs of man. Islam's embrace therefore must span all of Allah's creations. The Koran states: "Fight those who believe not in Allah nor the Last Day, nor hold that forbidden which has been forbidden by Allah and His messenger, nor acknowledge the religion of Truth, [even if they are] of the People of the Book, until they pay the *jizya* with willing submission, and feel themselves subdued."[32]

Those who carry out this command, according to the Koran, rank highest among believers:

> Do ye make the giving of drink to pilgrims, or the maintenance of the Sacred Mosque, equal to [the pious service of] those who believe in Allah and the Last Day, and strive with might and main in the cause of Allah? They are not comparable in the sight of Allah: and Allah guides not those who do wrong. Those who believe, and suffer exile and strive with might and main, in Allah's cause, with their goods and persons, have the highest rank in the sight of Allah: they are the people who will achieve [salvation].[33]

On their interpretation, a boundless sharia regime is the organization of men and of society that Islam demands—and the one that Islamic totalitarians have made their mission to realize. Hassan al-Banna, founder of the Muslim Brotherhood, observed that "Islam is a comprehensive system which deals with all spheres of life.

> It is a country and homeland or a government and a nation. It is conduct and power or mercy and justice. It is a culture and a law or knowledge and jurisprudence. It is material and wealth or gain and prosperity. It is Jihad and a call or army and a cause. And finally, it is true belief and correct worship.[34]

Jihad

In their embrace of holy war, Islamic totalitarians consciously try to model themselves on the religion's founder and the figure who is held to exemplify its virtues, Muhammad. He waged wars to impose, and expand, the dominion of Islam.

The prophet told the faithful that he "was ordered to fight all men until they say 'There is no god but Allah.'"[35] Assuring Muslims that the "gates of paradise are under the shadow of the swords," Muhammad urged that "A morning or an evening expedition in God's path is better than the world and what it contains, and for one of you to remain in the line of battle is better than his prayers for sixty years."[36]

In the last nine years of his life, Muhammad is "recorded as having participated in at least twenty-seven campaigns and deputized some fifty-nine others—an average of no fewer than nine campaigns annually."[37] The successors of Muhammad embarked on further campaigns (occasionally vying with Christian holy warriors). Their expeditions, reports the historian Efraim Karsh, were considerable:

> Within twelve years of Muhammad's death in June 632, Iran's long-reigning Sasanid Empire had been reduced to a tributary, and Egypt and Syria had been wrested from Byzantine rule. By the early eighth century, the Muslims had extended their dominion over Central Asia and much of the Indian subcontinent all the way to the Chinese frontier, had laid siege to Constantinople, the capital of the Byzantines, and had overrun North Africa and Spain.[38]

They sought also to penetrate Europe, reaching as far as northwest France, but were then repelled.

Jihad, the armed striving in the path of Allah, became a fixture of Islamic culture. For centuries scholars have written treatises glorifying jihad and defining the proper conduct of such warfare—for example, the propriety of deploying certain weapons and the terms under which Muslims might be exempt from the duty of fighting in a jihad. (There is another conception of jihad—understood as an internal struggle against desires and temptations. Many Western apologists eager to whitewash Islam have trumpeted this notion. This essentially metaphorical meaning, advanced by some sects, is not the term's primary meaning. The dominant meaning of jihad throughout the substantial body of Islamic literature on the subject is that of religiously motivated war.)[39]

By means of the sword, an Islamic military empire arose. Some conquered peoples were forced to convert, others were left to choose among death, conversion, or a subhuman existence as subject-peoples. Those who chose the last were required to pay special taxes to their rulers and lived as humiliated inferiors of Muslims, subject to minimal legal protections and at times open persecution. The scholar Bat Ye'or, in *Islam and Dhimmitude*, and Andrew Bostom, in his comprehensive *The Legacy of Jihad*, have described the wretched fate of non-Muslim peoples in lands ruled by Allah's warriors. Whether converts or subjugated men, all were made to enslave their mind and life to Allah's authority.

In the fourteenth century, to take one example, Muslim forces launched a jihad on the Indian subcontinent. A chronicler at the time reports how the sultan leading the war "ordered the massacre of all the chiefs of Hindustan out of the pale of Islam, by his infidel-smiting sword, [and] that if in this time it should by chance happen that a schismatic should claim his right, the pure Sunnis would swear in the name of this Khalifa of God, that heterodoxy has no right."[40] Some years later the same author recounted: "The whole country, by means of the sword of our holy warriors, has become like a forest denuded of its thorns by fire. . . . Islam is triumphant, idolatry is subdued."[41] After a battle in 1305, the jihadists had laid waste to the land; so far "as human eye could see, the ground was muddy with blood." Muslim holy warriors were known on some occasions to celebrate their triumphs by erecting a pillar of pagan heads.[42]

Returning to the holy warriors that now confront the West, we hear Khomeini explaining: "Islam says: Whatever good there is exists thanks to the sword and in the shadow of the sword! People cannot be made obedient except with the sword!" And: "The great prophet of Islam in one hand carried the Koran and in the other a sword; the sword for crushing the traitors and the Koran for guidance."[43] In the view of Ali Benhadj, who led a jihadist campaign in Algeria, the enforcers of Allah's law must never shrink from the need of massacres and butchery. "If a faith, a belief, is not watered and irrigated by blood, it does not grow. It does not live. Principles are reinforced by sacrifices, suicide operations and martyrdom for Allah. Faith is propagated by counting up deaths every day, by adding up massacres and charnel-houses."[44]

Abdullah Azzam, an ideological mentor to Osama bin Laden, extolled slaughter in the path of Allah:

> History does not write its lines except with blood. Glory does not build its lofty edifices except with skulls. Honor and respect cannot be established except on a foundation of cripples and corpses. Empires, distinguished peoples, states and societies cannot be established except with examples. Indeed, those who think that they can change reality or change societies without blood, sacrifices, and invalids—without pure innocent souls—do not understand the essence of this din [Islam] and they do not know the method of the best of Messengers [Muhammad].[45]

In the jihadists' attempt to emulate Muhammad, their record of atrocities speaks for itself.

The warriors of Islamic totalitarianism are undeniably motivated by an interpretation of Islam. And it is this interpretation that leads Islamists to the notion that their archenemy is America.

Wrath against America

We have already noted how the Islamists decry the impiety of the Muslim world. Seeing decadence all about them, they claim that the House of Islam is a community besieged. The force assailing their society, according to this diagnosis, is the influence of Western secularism—a force that drives a political wedge between religion and life.

The contours of this alleged problem were identified long ago. Assorted Muslim traditionalists bewailed the oncoming of modern technology and secular ideas as threats to Islam. When the first telephone was introduced into the kingdom of Ibn Saud, in 1927, observes one historian, "there was a great theological debate before the *ulema* [religious scholars] were persuaded of the lawfulness of this infidel invention."[46] A gloomy mood beset some Muslim thinkers, for they felt that the foundations of the House of Islam were in peril. In the schools, the advent of a modern curriculum provoked fears about the piety of future generations. The teaching of science, which claims rationally knowable, demonstrable, objective truth, threatened to sideline Islam's revelations on the nature of man and of the universe. According to some, the teaching of Islam had become perfunctory; others believed that the innovation of teaching it as a distinct subject was anathema, because doing so reinforced the growing dichotomy between life and religion.[47]

The accelerated pace of life diluted piety, because as one thinker explained, "work hours hamper people from praying during the daytime [for lack of special time slots for it] and entertainment programs divert them from it at night."[48] In the economy, the introduction of both socialistic and vaguely capitalistic policies came as blows to Islam's traditions: The first asked Muslims to identify themselves with an economic class, rather than their religious community; the second brought with it infidel practices such as charging interest on loans. The coming of foreign laborers and investment threatened a further loosening of morals, through the influence of infidels on Muslims.[49]

For the totalitarians, there is no middle ground between Islam and secularism; Qutb asserted that "In any time and place human beings face that clear-cut choice: either to observe the Law of Allah in its entirety, or to apply laws laid down by man of one sort or another. In the latter case, they are in a state of jahiliyya."[50] The initial targets of Islamists were modernizing states in the Middle East. Because such regimes limited the scope of Islam over life, they were deemed complicit in the decadence of Muslims—and qua apostate regimes, they had to be overthrown.

The Muslim Brotherhood sought to topple Egypt's regime. Hassan al-Banna reviled the regime, because (in the words of one historian) it used the newly invented radio "to corrupt the minds and souls of ordinary Egyptians with songs about love and sex rather than to inculcate them with the virtues of death and martyrdom in the quest for Allah's universal empire."[51] Among Egypt's other evils, the Brotherhood held, was its espousal of socialist and Arab-nationalist policies. Such doctrines, though laced with Islamic ideas to make them palatable, frayed the bond of faith that subsumes all classes, sects, and national borders. By elevating loyalty to Arab nationalism above Islam, the regime compromised the principle of total submission to only one authority, Allah.

From the 1950s until the latter decades of the century, the obsession of Islamic totalitarian groups was combating apostate Muslim regimes. They focused particularly on those "poisoned" by the influence of former European colonial powers, such as Britain and France. But some Islamists recognized that the wellspring of poison lay elsewhere.

It was America that surpassed all the former colonial powers as an influence on global culture in general, and on the Middle East in particular. It had emerged as the only superpower. America, moreover, was the embodiment of what Islamic totalitarians abhor. It was the antithesis of their moral ideal.

Born with an act of audacious revolt against authority, America was the nation that accepted nothing as higher than the inalienable rights of the individual. Neither a monarch nor an established religion governed men. The laws and principles of America's government were defined not by clerics, but by men who shared the Enlightenment's reverence for reason. They created a system of government grounded in objective facts accessible to all men who chose to observe and think.

These laws protected each man's moral entitlement to pursue his own earthly happiness, as he deems proper and as conditioned by the principle of individual rights. The government was the servant of the people, not its master. If the government breached the defined limits of the powers delegated to it, the people recognized their right to dissolve such a government and establish one that better served their lives. Man was left free to advocate and practice any ideology, including religion, without fear of being forced to submit to the ideas of another. And to this day Americans are freer than any peoples. They are free to earn fortunes and to spend their wealth on their own chosen values.

The United States is the culmination of the Enlightenment's anti-authoritarian ethos and its concomitant esteem for the sanctity of man's rational mind. It was this legacy that enabled America's standard of living to skyrocket. Because men are free to invest their wealth, energy, and ideas as they see fit, the United States has become a nation unsurpassed at the task of producing values that sustain human life—that make it longer, safer, and more enjoyable. Across the globe people gaze up, far up, in admiration at the stunning luxuries and life-saving technologies that even the poorest American workers can afford.

Yet these are precisely the reasons that, for Islamic totalitarians, America is the embodiment of evil. With his signature perverseness, Osama bin Laden stated: "You are the nation who, rather than ruling by the Sharia of Allah in its Constitution and Laws, choose to invent your own laws as you will and desire. You separate religion from your policies, contradicting the pure nature which affirms Absolute Authority to the Lord and your Creator. . . . You are the worst civilization witnessed by the history of mankind."[52]

Obviously other nations embrace Western values—science, secular government, individual rights, economic freedom—to varying degrees. But what distinguishes America, and what fans the hatred of Islamic totalitarians, is that it has been so spectacularly successful. This makes it all the more objectionable, and singles it out as a focus of their hostility.

Islam teaches its followers that they are a chosen group, that their piety will be rewarded, and that in this world they will enjoy superiority over the infidels who reject Allah and his prophet. But in actuality, the Arab-Islamic world is weak and woefully poor, whereas infidel America is strong and fabulously wealthy.

This fact raises awkward questions.

The twentysomethings who dropped out of grad school to launch Google and reaped billions in wealth—were they right to have studied computer science rather than memorizing the Koran? Can the middle-class American parents who buy their teenager a car afford to do so because they live under a better political and economic system? Is America's status as a lone superpower a consequence of its un-Islamic ideas? Whether or not Muslims dare answer these questions honestly, the spectacle of America's comprehensive preeminence undermines the totalitarian goal of creating an Islamic empire.

So long as the splendors of America multiply—from vaccines and ubiquitous personal computers to moon landings and routine global air travel—so long as American advances in science and technology spur its galloping prosperity, honest men will resist the calls to surrender their minds to faith. Amid the omnipresent evidence of what man's rational mind can produce when left free to function, religionists face a considerable challenge to induce men to follow a creed of blind obedience to mystical authority.

And, implicitly if not explicitly, Islamic totalitarians recognize that. Qutb, like his intellectual heirs, acknowledged the obvious temptation of secular culture—and desperately sought to impugn the West. He contended that in "the most affluent and materially advanced" of Western societies such as America, people lead "the most miserable lives."[53]

> We must not be deluded by false appearances when we see that nations which do not believe or implement the Divine method are enjoying abundance and affluence. It is all a temporary prosperity which lasts until the natural laws have produced their effects, allowing the consequences of the miserable split between material excellence and spiritual fulfillment to appear in full.

Because Westerners "have lost touch with their souls," the West and the Westernizing Middle East were heading for disaster.[54] Misery and anxiety and suffering, Qutb claimed, would result from secular society. He prophesied rampant deaths from mental disease, suicide, and heart failure. Such diatribes painting secularism as the road to ruin eloquently betray that Islamists feel themselves on the defensive—that they feel obliged to explain away the allure of secular life.

Totalitarians denounce America as barbaric, because it is tremendously civilized. They denounce America as vicious, because it is in reality luminously virtuous: It is an exemplar of what men can accomplish when they are free to achieve their own happiness, earn unlimited wealth, and live by their own convictions. It is, to the holy warriors, an abomination that cannot be allowed to endure.

It must be brought down.

But these despicable killers—we often hear—are just a fringe group. What is more significant, they are supposedly bereft of ideological support among what they take to be their constituency, the global population of about one billion Muslims. Drawing on such premises, some people reach the soothing conclusion that the threat from Islamic totalitarians is much less formidable than it might appear to be.

Magnitude of the Threat

What is the constituency of the Islamic totalitarian movement? Who, if anyone, in the Muslim mainstream supports the movement's ideals and its actions? What is the opposition to it, and of what consequence are such opponents? Is there indeed a fundamental ideological gulf between the mainstream and the totalitarians?

Consider the beliefs and practice of the Muslim mainstream. How would most Muslims respond to Sayyid Qutb's statement that Islam is a "declaration that sovereignty is God's alone"?[55] The overwhelming majority would resoundingly agree. Every day, five times a day—from Morocco to the Sudan, Egypt to Bosnia, Afghanistan to Indonesia—millions of Muslims prostrate themselves in obedient prayer. Every year millions walk, sail, drive, and fly to reach Mecca to fulfill their duty of the *hajj*, or religious pilgrimage. Every day during the month of Ramadan, Muslims deny themselves food, drink, sex. In word and deed, mainstream Muslims attest that Islam is a supreme value in their lives.

Internecine hostilities—both sectarian and racial—divide Muslims, but one fundamental bond unites them. For Muslims, observes Bernard Lewis, "the basic division—the touchstone by which men are separated from one another, by which one distinguishes between brother and stranger—is that of faith, of membership in a religious community. . . . What is meant is. . . religion as a social and communal force, a measure of identity and a focus of group loyalty."[56] Belonging to the community of Allah's followers confers on the believer his self-worth—not his individual accomplishments and character. Their religion is a source of personal identity.

Even under Middle East regimes that are putatively secular, Islam is a sacred value. In Syria, under a Baathist regime (modeled on European fascism), impugning Islam is anathema. In 1967, a Syrian army magazine published an article condemning God and religion as "mummies which should be transferred to the museums of historical remains."[57] There ensued large demonstrations, reports one commentator, "in all the major Syrian cities . . ., leading to widescale strikes, the arrest of many religious leaders, and considerable violence."[58] The Syrian regime sentenced the writer and two editors to prison, in hopes of mollifying the agitated public. Devotion to Islam runs deep throughout the Middle East. Note that Khomeini's Islamic revolution in 1979 succeeded in what was at the time one of the Middle East's more Westernized nations.

Because mainstream Muslims take their religion seriously, pious subservience to authority is the norm. Muslims unthinkingly believe and comply with the say-so of authority. They unquestioningly swallow fantastical conspiracy theories,[59] and they willingly do as they are commanded to do. That dutiful obedience was on display in the so-called Danish cartoon crisis of 2006.

The crisis began after a Danish newspaper, *Jyllands-Posten*, published twelve cartoons pertaining to Islam and Muhammad, some of which were satirical. (The purpose was to test whether the fear of offending Muslims had created a climate of self-censorship in Europe.) Violence erupted across the Islamic world. Mobs invaded and torched Danish embassies in Lebanon, Libya, and Syria; elsewhere, mobs attacked other embassies using grenades and guns. Muslims called for the beheading of the cartoonists and offered bounties to whoever could execute the blasphemers. More than one hundred people died in riots across the world, with nearly 1,000 injured. All of this havoc came to pass, according to the standard account of the crisis, because Muslims had been outraged by the Danish cartoons of Muhammad. These alleged affronts to their prophet impelled Muslims to rush into the streets and demand blood.

But this ignores a crucial aspect of the Muslim reaction. Observe that *Jyllands-Posten* had published the images in September 2005. Those images, however, were far from self-evidently offensive to Muslim sensibilities. Just two months later in Egypt—the most populous Arab country—the newspaper *Al Fajr* republished six of the cartoons.[60] The Egyptian response? There was none. In Indonesia, the most populous Muslim country on earth, a Web site also published the cartoons—to indifferent yawns.[61] The riots in the Islamic world began only in January and peaked in February. Why the delay? Being subservient to authority, Muslims reached no conclusions of their own and had no reaction, until told what reaction to have.

Those orders soon came. The leaders of the world's fifty-seven Muslim nations had gathered for a summit in Mecca in December, and decided to stir up their people into a religious fervor over the cartoons.[62] When the masses were made to believe that a slight had been done to Islam, when they were handed Danish flags to burn, when they were ordered into the streets—they duly obeyed. They raged. Many rioters had not even seen the images; few newspapers published them in the Middle East. The mobs who ran amok were mindlessly obeying authority in the name of defending Islam. Were it not for the authorities that instigated the outrage, were it not for the mass of believers taking on faith the dictum of authority, there would have been no riots, no uproar, no death threats. Nothing.

Such obedience is consonant with the ideal of the totalitarians. They enjoin making Islam the all-embracing value in human life. This principle conditions what is to be regarded as a legitimate source of knowledge: the dicta of authority. It also conditions what kind of knowledge is to be regarded as worth pursuing: that which reinforces piety. On this point, a Taliban publication explained the movement's credo: "Any study besides that of the Quran is a distraction, except the Hadith (sayings of the Prophet) and jurisprudence in the religion. Knowledge is that He narrated to us, and anything other than that is the whispering of Satan."[63] Conforming with this notion means *not* asking questions, *not* challenging the received wisdom, *not* exploring nature, *not* investigating the world. Do mainstream Muslims in the Arab-Islamic world rebel against so preposterous a notion?

No. They evince a wholesale indifference to learning. A listing of twenty-seven countries ranked according to book sales—beginning with the United States and ending with Vietnam—does not include a single Muslim state. In 2002 the United Nations issued a report, prepared by a committee of Arab intellectuals, that stated: "The Arab world translates about 330 books annually, one-fifth of the number that Greece translates. The accumulative total of translated books since the Caliph Maa'moun's [sic] time [the ninth century] is about 100,000, almost the average that Spain translates in one year."[64]

Practically nonexistent in the Islamic world is the outlook of the scientist. Scientists must be willing to defy authority and tradition for the sake of truth. But a culture that prizes passive conformity with dogma militates against the individual who asserts himself cognitively in a systematic quest for knowledge. When, despite his culture, some budding scientist nevertheless emerges, his prospects of engaging in research might appear to be good. There is plenty of oil wealth available to underwrite scientific research. Yet in Saudi Arabia—one of the richest Muslim countries—there were just 1,915 active research scientists in 1987. (By comparison, at that time in the Western nation of Israel, whose population is about four times smaller than that of Saudi Arabia, there were 11,617 research scientists.) Scientific and technological advances emanating from the Islamic world are negligible.[65]

But in this culture one book is ever in demand and universally cherished: The Koran. Clerics are superstars whose sermons are sold on tape and air regularly on television. Piety is a virtue that the masses aspire to. Because the mainstream's commitment to Islam is so profound, there is considerable popular support for the totalitarians' ideal.

Jihadists are not vilified as reprobates or loathed for besmirching the peaceful reputation of Islam; they are widely lionized. Posters memorializing "martyred" young men bedeck street corners in Beirut, Gaza, and the West Bank; their horrific deeds are eulogized in fulsome obituaries posted on the Internet. Osama bin Laden and his deputies are celebrated as heroes. Stroll through downtown Sarajevo, and in bookstalls you can find on sale Saudi-sponsored books promoting absolute rule by sharia.[66] Hop into a taxi in Beirut, and instead of music from the radio you are as likely to hear speeches by Sheik Hassan Nasrallah, the religious leader of Hezbollah. "Lines from his speeches are popular ring tones on cellphones. His face is a common computer screensaver. Wall posters, key rings and even phone cards bear his image."[67]

The holy warriors fight for an Islamic regime, and an overwhelming mass of Muslims support and endorse them, because they regard that ideal as virtuous. This is why jihadists are able to broadcast their message, recruit fighters, run training camps, acquire weapons, and mount hugely expensive attacks that take years to orchestrate.

Untold numbers of Muslims do far more than condone the vile deeds of jihadists.

Consider the Muslim reaction to 9/11. While a spasm of mourning shook even stridently anti-American countries in Europe, in the Islamic world there was euphoria. In the southern Philippines, in Pakistan, in Bangladesh, in Saudi Arabia, in Nigeria, in Indonesia, and elsewhere, thousands of Muslims took to the streets in solidarity with bin Laden.[68] Palestinians handed out candy, set off firecrackers, and fired pistols into the air (as they typically do after suicide-bombings against Israel). That admiration persists. A journalist wandering through a McDonald's in Egypt, several years after the attacks, reports the reaction of some locals: One "eighteen year old university student volunteered . . . that she called up all her friends to share her joy after learning that thousands of Americans had died in Washington and New York. 'Everyone celebrated,' she said, dipping her French fries into ketchup, as her girlfriends giggled. 'People honked in the streets, cheering that finally America got what it truly deserved.' "[69]

Dissent from this prevalent sentiment was appallingly scarce. An Islamic scholar at the most prestigious Islamic university in Egypt, Al Azhar, publicly condemned the attacks; but he acknowledged that he was a lone voice.[70] There were no spontaneous mass rallies condemning the atrocities. Although some Muslims told pollsters that they considered the attacks to be acts of "terrorism," they maintained that these were acts of political defiance.

They may not embrace the means, in other words, but they nevertheless admire the cause.[71]

Critics of the totalitarian movement itself may be few, but they are not unheard of in the Islamic world. Abdul Rauf is the imam of the Herati Mosque, located in one of Kabul's most modern neighborhoods, and is reputed to be one of the few clerics in Afghanistan who dared oppose the Taliban when it was in power. "It is true," he told the *Washington Post*, "I criticized the Taliban because they were so harsh and tortured people." Considering the punishments inflicted on those who ignited the Taliban's wrath, such resistance seems impressive (perhaps even a sign of hope for the future of Afghanistan).

But in March 2006, when an "Afghan man was put on trial for converting to Christianity, Rauf led the emotional charge to demand his execution under Islamic law. The public would 'cut him [the convert] to pieces' if the authorities failed to act, Rauf said." This imam hardly fits the profile of a stern Talibanesque prig; he is described as "a cheerful man who rides his bicycle to his mosque each day," and who proudly showed the reporter an itinerary of a trip he had made to the United States, visiting mosques and churches. It is possible that Rauf rejects the totalitarian quest for a global caliphate, and it is possible that his criticism of the Taliban's methods was in earnest, but in explaining his campaign, he evinces a fundamental commitment to the ideal animating the totalitarians. He noted that "ours is the complete and final religion. If you leave it, that is like throwing God away. . . . [I]f you leave Islam, our law says you must be killed. If Abdul Rahman [the convert] stood before me right now, I would kill him myself."[72]

In the Arab-Islamic world, there is no countervailing *ideological* opposition. We do not hear advocates for reason and individualism in opposition to faith and submission. Absent is a counterpart to Thomas Jefferson bearding religious and royal authority—an intellectual force urging men to "Fix reason firmly in her seat, and call to her tribunal every fact, every opinion. Question with boldness even the existence of a God; because, if there be one, he must more approve of the homage of reason, than that of blindfolded fear."[73] There is no voice sonorously declaring that sovereignty belongs only to the individual, that each man exists not by permission, but by right, and ought to be free to pursue his own happiness.

Where the mainstream and critics diverge from the totalitarians is only over the question of means, not ends.

Nevertheless, some Western observers pin their hopes on "moderate" Muslims. The term does not mean "liberal or democratic but only anti-Islamist" Muslims (i.e., Muslims who are not totalitarians).[74] We cannot hear these voices of real opposition, because they lack the wherewithal to disseminate their ideas and are often suppressed. If only we gave them a chance, however, supposedly they could serve as credible proxies for the West in the effort to tamp down the influence of Islamic totalitarians. But such an enterprise is worse than futile.

The only intelligible meaning of "moderate" advocates of religion are those who try to combine devotion to faith with concessions to reason. They obey the dictates of Islam in some areas and not others, fencing off certain issues or areas of life from the purview of religion. Let us grant the premise that the West can find moderate Muslims and support them in a way that does not discredit them in Muslim eyes as saboteurs conspiring to undermine Islam. Could moderates really steer their culture away from the totalitarian movement?

The holy warriors hold that Islam must shape every last detail of man's life. The moderates accept the ideal of Islam but shy away from the vision of total state. Moderates might agree to allow sharia to govern schools, say, but not commerce; to dictate marriage laws, but not punishments for blasphemy, apostasy, or adultery. Yet in doing so, moderates ultimately advance the agenda of the totalitarians, since even delimited applications of Islam to government constitute an endorsement of it as the proper source of law.

The tension between moderates and the totalitarians is unsustainable. What happens when the totalitarians push for expanding the scope of sharia a bit more? If sharia can govern banking and trade, for example, why not other aspects of life? Why not also institute Islamic punishments, such as beheading apostates? Having accepted in principle the ideal of sharia, moderates have no grounds to reject further means to that end. They can offer no principled opposition to the slaughter of infidels who refuse to submit, or of apostates who claim the freedom to choose their own convictions. In the face of the incremental or rapid advance of the totalitarian goal, the moderates are in the long run impotent. If Islam is the ideal, why practice it in moderation?

Nor, unsurprisingly, is "moderation" the rallying cry that is rousing Muslims to action.

The cause galvanizing many Muslims is jihad. And the appeal of Islamic totalitarianism is not confined to nations that have Muslim majorities. Three of the four suicide-bombers in the 2005 attack on London were second-generation British citizens. Several of the terrorist plots foiled in the United States since 2001 involved American-born jihadists.[75] The killers are attracted by a moral ideal that they believe is worth dying for: the vision of righteously obliterating enemies of God and, on the ruins of the Western world, establishing a global Islamic regime. This vision appeals to Muslims from every walk of life, because it serves and is justified by their religious beliefs.

Because fidelity to Islam is entrenched and fundamentally unopposed in the culture, so too is support for the zealous killers aching to destroy America. That support is deep and wide; the recruitment pool, large and growing. With the passage of time, the enemy has grown fiercer, more confident of its eventual victory.

What will it take to defeat this enemy?

Defeating the Enemy

The trauma of 9/11 should have awakened our political leaders to a frightening truth. But they slept on.

Those heinous attacks constituted an act of war—and it was not even the opening salvo. Islamists had marched into battle decades ago (see chapter 1). Washington should have connected the dots—from 9/11 to the USS *Cole* to the embassy bombings in Africa to the Khobar Towers, all the way back to the Iranian hostage crisis of 1979—but our policymakers did no such thing. To the extent that this spiral of escalating attacks came to mind, it was regarded as a string of isolated crises—just one damn thing after another.

Consonant with that disintegrated, minutely concrete mindset, our leaders kept their minds firmly shut to another crucial fact. They failed to recognize that behind the wending trail of bloodshed there was a specific enemy—the Islamic totalitarian movement; and that all of its aggression served a specific ideal—the imposition of a global sharia regime. Absent from our foreign policy was the crucial recognition that Islamic totalitarians had launched a holy war against us. The catastrophe of 9/11 heightened the need to conceptualize the menace. But our intellectual and political leaders only clouded the issue further: they evasively latched on to pseudo-explanations of what actuates the jihadists.

All of this precludes any hope of taking effective action to defend ourselves. But when we properly define the enemy and its motivation, we arm ourselves with the necessary means of achieving victory. This knowledge enables us to determine the steps required to defeat the enemy. (We will return to this question in later chapters.)

The warriors, we have already seen, are committed idealists, though not the conventional sort who regard their ideal as good in theory but not in practice. It is precisely because they consistently unite their ideas and actions that they constitute such a deadly threat. They believe that their vision of enshrining Allah's dominion on earth is both just *and* achievable. The promise of earthly success gives their mystical ideal (a notion utterly divorced from facts) the semblance of reality—and the potent visceral rush that inspires men to give up their lives for an abstract vision.

We cannot uproot the threat merely by thwarting a few terrorists, here and there. Those who join the battle are endorsed and supported, cheered on and revered, by vast numbers of mainstream Muslims. What matters most is *why* the fighters fight—and why their abettors support them. The killers act on their convictions; capturing or killing Osama bin Laden is necessary but woefully inadequate. So long as the moral ideal remains viable in the minds of its adherents, some new leader will emerge, hydra-like, to perpetuate the struggle. Shut down a cluster of safe houses, or a major channel of arms trafficking, or a dozen training grounds—and new ones will open thanks to the undeterred abettors of jihad.

Victory requires breaking the enemy's will to fight. To render Islamic totalitarianism a nonthreat, we must obliterate the idea that their moral ideal is achievable. The enemy must suffer a punishing military onslaught, so that its ideal is demonstrated to be an unrealizable fantasy. The purpose of crushing the enemy's spirit is twofold: to end the present threat and to deter future aggression. When men have abandoned all hope of success, they lay down their arms and renounce the struggle. When men are convinced that whoever seeks to harm Americans will be ground to dust, they will be paralyzed by fear. To renew the struggle would be to assure their own destruction. Although some may continue to daydream of destroying "the Great Satan" and enforcing universal submission to Allah, few will join (or dare aid) their patently impossible quest. No ideal that is obviously futile attracts men who will fight and die for it.

Inseparable from the military aspect is the need to articulate our moral justification for fighting back. The precondition of marching into battle is knowing clearly what one is fighting for and knowing that it is morally good. That knowledge is the fount of moral confidence, the confidence that it is right to kill and to fight to the death for one's cause. Demonstrating our moral strength is crucial also for destroying the enemy's spirit. By broadcasting through our actions and in proud declarations that we know destroying the enemy is morally just, that we judge the enemy as thoroughly corrupt, and that we stand committed to our values—we can demoralize the enemy's forces and supporters.

To discredit the enemy's ideal, we must begin by targeting its inspiration and archpatron, Iran. Since the revolution of 1979, Iran has been the standard-bearer of Islamic totalitarianism. The revolution was the movement's first triumph. The Western world was left reeling in disbelief at the eruption of religious militancy; the Islamic world marveled at the spectacle and was galvanized. Far less powerful than the army or the police, the revolutionaries nevertheless overcame the Shah's "impious" regime. What made this all the more rousing to Muslims is that the toppled government had long enjoyed close ties with Washington.

Sparks from the Iranian revolution ignited fires in the souls of Muslims far and wide. Nationalism had dominated politics in the Middle East, but it was losing momentum, and after the revolution it was supplanted by Islam. Around that time, the Palestinian cause was almost routed, its moral ideal of nationalism practically discredited. But the revolution helped reinvigorate the Palestinian movement as a *religious* struggle. For one Palestinian activist who had soured on nationalism, Iran's revolution "demonstrated that even against an enemy as powerful as the Shah, a jihad of determined militants could overcome all obstacles." That young activist had written the widely-circulating book *Khomeini: The Islamic Alternative*; he was later a founder of Islamic Jihad, one of the most ferocious Palestinian groups.[76]

The fervor spread. Islamist activists from Southeast Asia, Western Europe, and some communist countries embarked on pilgrimages to Khomeini's regime. In Europe, some activists sought to foment Islamic militancy. A group of young Senegalese intellectuals visited post-revolution Iran, and on their return an Islamist passion rippled through Senegal. One of those intellectuals observed, "The face of the world is transformed, and mankind's very foundations have been shaken since the project of an Islamic society has emerged as a practical and viable alternative to all others."[77]

Tehran worked diligently to sustain this notion by sponsoring terrorists. It helped found, organize, train, proselytize, and direct Lebanese Hezbollah. For a time, senior Hezbollah leaders reported directly to Iran's government, while Iranian officials sat on the organization's governing council. Iran has often given Hezbollah more than $100 million a year. We saw in chapter 1 how the group functioned as a proxy force for Tehran's jihad against America (and the West). In April 1983, a suicide attack by Hezbollah on the U.S. Embassy in Beirut killed sixty-three, including seventeen Americans. Six months later, a massive suicide truck-bombing claimed the lives of 241 U.S. Marines. After that massacre, America withdrew from Lebanon.[78] That attack—like the terrorism that followed it—proved that Iran's jihadist militia could repel and coerce the world's most powerful nation.

Iran has come to symbolize the power that comes from comprehensively implementing Islam. Washington's decades of passive, appeasing responses to Iranian aggression has (correctly) taught Islamists that we are weak. This realization has emboldened their cause.

Many in the Islamic world have come to believe that Allah's faithful were able to rise to power in Iran, just as Iran's proxies succeeded in punishing the infidel Americans again and again, precisely *because of their fidelity to Islam*. It confirms a lesson of the Koran: "O Apostle! Rouse the believers to the fight. If there are twenty amongst you, patient and persevering, they will vanquish two hundred; if a hundred, they will vanquish a thousand of the unbelievers: For these are a people without understanding."[79] Iran makes the ideal actuating the jihadists appear righteous, potent, practical—and Washington's policy encouraged this belief.

Defining the nature of the enemy and crushing its standard-bearer—the jihadist regime in Tehran—are necessary steps toward defeating it.

(Further military action may be needed to snuff out whatever remains of the jihadist cause. In later chapters, we will explore what should be done to defeat the movement; see part 2 and chapter 7.)

———◆———

Common is the view that after 9/11 the Bush administration went to war to defend the United States and uphold our ideals. Many people now believe, however, that under Bush we tried the military option and it was shown to be futile, because it resulted in a fiasco. But in its conception and implementation, Bush's policy was a travesty of what a genuine war to uphold our values should look like. That policy (as the next three chapters argue) made a mockery of what it truly means to fight a war in self-defense.

PART 2

AMERICA'S SELF-CRIPPLED RESPONSE TO 9/11

Positioning itself as a contrast to decades of U.S. policy, the flag-waving, supposedly no-nonsense Bush administration appeared to many people to be an overdue tonic. The administration seemingly bucked conventional thinking in foreign policy: its response to 9/11 was apparently tough (think: "Either you are with us, or you are with the terrorists.") and expressed in morally-charged slogans ("axis of evil"). It fired up the nation. The public, in the early days, overwhelmingly backed Bush's policy. People expected to see America put an end to the enemy.

But Americans would be sorely disappointed. Bush's toughness was belied by an evasive non-identification of the enemy and by the actual goal of the Iraq and Afghanistan campaigns. The following three essays analyze fundamental aspects of Bush's policy and why its implementation proved to be so destructive of America's self-interest.

We begin with the centerpiece of the administration's policy, the crusade for democracy, and consider the underlying moral rationale for that strategy. Next we examine the self-crippling impact of Just War Theory on the conception and battlefield conduct of the war. Finally, we investigate the actual nature and goals of neoconservative foreign policy—a profound influence on Bush policy—and expose that outlook's subversive redefinition of the national interest.

CHAPTER THREE

The "Forward Strategy" for Failure

Yaron Brook and Elan Journo

A Strategy for Security?

The attacks of 9/11 exposed the magnitude of the threats we face, and, ever since then, one question has become a depressing fixture of our lives: Are we safe? Before long, many Americans came to believe that our salvation was imminent, for the means of achieving our security was at hand; no longer would we have to live in dread of further catastrophic attacks. These people were swept up in euphoric hope inspired by the Bush administration's new strategy in the Middle East. The strategy promised to deliver permanent security for our nation. It promised to eradicate the fundamental source of Islamic terrorism. It promised to make us safe.

The strategy's premise was simple: "[T]he security of our nation," President Bush explained, "depends on the advance of liberty in other nations";[1] we bring democracy to the Middle East, and thereby make ourselves safer. To many Americans, this sounded plausible: Western nations, such as ours, are peaceful, since they have no interest in waging war except in self-defense: their prosperity depends on trade, not on conquest or plunder; if there were more such nations in the world, the better off we would be. Informally, Bush called this idea the "forward strategy for freedom."[2]

By January 2005, an early milestone of this strategy was manifest to all. Seemingly every news outlet showed us the images of smiling Iraqis displaying their ink-stained fingers. They had just voted in the first elections in liberated Iraq. Those images, according to breathless pundits, symbolized a momentous development.

Commentators saw reason to believe Bush's grandiose prediction of 2003, when he declared: "Iraqi democracy will succeed—and that success will send forth the news, from Damascus to Tehran—that freedom can be the future of every nation. The establishment of a free Iraq at the heart of the Middle East will be a watershed event in the global democratic revolution."[3] At the summit of the Arab League in 2004, according to Reuters, Arab heads of state had "promised to promote democracy, expand popular participation in politics, and reinforce women's rights and civil society."[4] By the spring of 2005, several Arab regimes had announced plans to hold popular elections.

Even confirmed opponents of Bush applauded the strategy. An editorial in the New York Times in March 2005, for example, declared that the "long-frozen political order seems to be cracking all over the Middle East." The year so far had been full of "heartening surprises—each one remarkable in itself, and taken together truly astonishing [chief among them being Iraq's elections and the prospect of Egyptian parliamentary elections]. The Bush administration was entitled to claim a healthy share of the credit for many of these advances."[5] Senator Edward Kennedy (of all people) felt obliged to concede, albeit grudgingly, that "What's taken place in a number of those [Middle Eastern] countries is enormously constructive," adding that "It's a reflection the president has been involved."[6]

Washington pursued the forward strategy with messianic zeal. Iraq has had not just one, but several popular elections, as well as a referendum on a new constitution written by Iraqi leaders; with U.S. endorsement and prompting, the Palestinians held what international monitors declared were fair elections; and Egypt's authoritarian regime, under pressure from Washington, allowed the first contested parliamentary elections in more than a decade. There were elections as well in Lebanon (parliamentary) and Saudi Arabia (municipal). In sum, these developments seemed to indicate a salutary political awakening. The forward march toward "liberty in other nations" seemed irresistible and "the security of our nation," inevitable.

But has the democracy crusade moved us toward peace and freedom in the Middle East—and greater security at home?

Consider three elections and their implications for the region.

The elections in Iraq were touted as an outstanding success for America, but the new Iraqi government is far from friendly. It is dominated by a Shiite alliance led by the Islamic Dawa Party and the Supreme Council for Islamic Revolution in Iraq (SCIRI). The alliance has intimate ties with the first nation to undergo an Islamic revolution, Iran. Both Dawa and SCIRI were previously based in Iran, and SCIRI's leader has endorsed Lebanese Hezbollah, a terrorist proxy for Iran.[7] Tehran is thought to have a firm grip on the levers of power within Iraq's government, and it actively arms and funds anti-American insurgents. The fundamental principle of Iraq's new constitution—as of Iran's totalitarian regime—is Islam.

Instead of embracing pro-Western leaders, Iraqis have made a vicious Islamic warlord, Moktada al-Sadr, one of the most powerful men in Iraqi politics. While Sadr has not run for office, his bloc holds thirty seats in Iraq's assembly, controls two ministries, and wields a decisive swing vote: Iraq's current prime minister, Nuri al-Maliki, and his predecessor, Ibrahim al-Jaafari, both owe their jobs to Sadr's support. Sadr (who was wanted by Iraqi authorities for murder) is vociferously anti-American, favors Iranian-style theocratic rule, and has vowed to fight in defense of Iran.

Sadr has a private militia, the Mahdi Army, through which he has repeatedly attacked American forces. One of the fiercest encounters was in 2004 in Najaf. Confronted by U.S. forces, Sadr's militiamen entrenched themselves in a holy shrine. But the standoff ended when Grand Ayatollah Sistani, the leading Shiite cleric in Iraq, interceded on Sadr's behalf. Washington capitulated for fear of upsetting Shiites and let the militia go (officials no longer talk of arresting Sadr for murder). Since that standoff, the Mahdi Army has swollen nearly threefold to an estimated 15,000 men and, according to a Pentagon report, it has surpassed Al Qaeda in Iraq as "the most dangerous accelerant" of the sectarian violence.[8]

Emancipated from Saddam Hussein's tyranny, a large number of Iraqis embraced the opportunity to tyrannize each other by reprising sadistic feuds (both sectarian and ethnic)—and to lash out at their emancipators, the American forces. The insurgency, which has attracted warriors from outside Iraq, is serving as a kind of proving ground where jihadists can hone their skills. According to news reports, Lebanese Hezbollah has been training members of the Mahdi Army in Lebanon, while some Hezbollah operatives have helped with training on the ground in Iraq.[9] The new Iraq has become what the old one never was: a hotbed of Islamic terrorism. It is a worse threat to American interests than Saddam Hussein's regime ever was.

Consider the election results in the Palestinian territories. For years, Bush had asked Palestinians "to elect new leaders, . . . not compromised by terror."[10] And, finally, in the U.S.-endorsed elections of January 2006, the Palestinians *did* turn their backs on the cronies of Yasir Arafat; they rejected the incumbent leadership of Fatah—and elected the even more militant killers of Hamas: an Islamist group notorious for suicide bombings. Hamas won a landslide and now rules the Palestinian territories.

Refusing to recognize Israel's legitimacy, Hamas is committed to annihilating that state and establishing a totalitarian Islamic regime. In the previous year, Hezbollah took part in the U.S.-endorsed elections in Lebanon, formed part of that country's cabinet for the first time, and won control of two ministries.[11] In the summer of 2006, the Iranian-backed Hamas and Hezbollah killed and kidnapped Israeli soldiers—and precipitated a month-long war in the region. Since the cease-fire that ended the war, Hezbollah has continued to amass weapons and foment terrorism, emboldened by its popular electoral support.

Consider, as a final example of the trend, the 2005 parliamentary elections in Egypt, the Arab world's most populous country. The group that scored the most impressive gains was the Muslim Brotherhood—the intellectual origin of the Islamist movement, whose offshoots include Hamas and parts of Al Qaeda. The Brotherhood's founding credo is "Allah is our goal; the Qur'an is our constitution; the Prophet is our leader; struggle is our way; and death in the path of Allah is our highest aspiration."[12]

The Brotherhood's electoral success was staggering. Although the group is officially banned in Egypt, its candidates won eighty-eight seats—about 20 percent of all the seats—in Egypt's assembly, and became the largest opposition bloc the body has ever had.[13] This was all the more significant considering the regime's brutal attempts to protect its grip on power. During one round of voting, the *New York Times* reports, "police officers in riot gear and others in plainclothes and armed civilians working for the police began blocking polling stations, preventing supporters of the Brotherhood from casting their votes." Dozens were injured and several people died from gunshots to the head.[14] Some observers reckon that the Brotherhood could have won even more power, if it had not limited itself to running 125 candidates (it did so, presumably, to avoid an even tougher government crackdown).

The Muslim Brotherhood, Hamas, Lebanese Hezbollah, the Islamist regime in Iran, the Mahdi Army, Al Qaeda—these are all part of an ideological movement: Islamic totalitarianism. While differing on some details and in tactics, all of these groups share the movement's basic goal of enslaving the entire Middle East, and then the rest of the world, under a totalitarian regime ruled by Islamic law. The totalitarians will use any means to achieve their goal—terrorism, if it proves effective; all out war, if they can win; and politics, if it can bring them power over whole countries.

Bush's forward strategy has helped usher in a new era in the Middle East: By its promotion of elections, it has paved the road for Islamists to grab political power and to ease into office with the air of legitimacy and without the cost of bombs or bullets. Naturally, totalitarians across the region are encouraged. They exhibit a renewed sense of confidence. The Iran-Hamas-Hezbollah war against Israel in 2006 is one major symptom of that confidence; another is Iran's naked belligerence through insurgent proxies in Iraq, and its righteously defiant pursuit of nuclear technology.

The situation in the Middle East is worse for America today than it was in the wake of 9/11. Iraq is a bloody fiasco. The chaos in Iraq makes it a haven for anti-American terrorists. Iran's influence in Iraq and in the region is growing. Saudi Arabia, along with five other Arab states, announced its intention to pursue nuclear technology. In Lebanon, thousands of people have taken part in massive street demonstrations demanding greater power for Hezbollah in the government. The Hamas regime, though starved of Western aid, remains in power, and Palestinians continue to fire rockets at Israeli towns.

A further effect of the elections in the region has been the invigoration of Islamists in Afghanistan. Legions of undefeated Taliban and Al Qaeda warriors in that country have regrouped and renewed their jihad. Flush with money, amassing recruits, and armed with guns, rockets, and explosives, they are fighting to regain power. They have mounted a string of massive suicide bombings and rocket attacks against American and NATO forces; more U.S. troops have died in Afghanistan during 2005 and 2006 than during the peak of the war.[15] With astounding boldness, the Taliban have assassinated clerics and judges deemed friendly to the new government, and fired rockets at schools for using "un-Islamic" books. The Taliban have effectively taken over certain regions of the country.[16]

Jihadists continue to carry out and plot mass-casualty atrocities against the West. In 2004 they bombed commuter trains during rush hour in Madrid. The next summer, suicide bombers blew themselves up on London's underground. In August 2006, British police foiled a plot to set off a wave of bombings on trans-Atlantic airliners. British authorities recently disclosed that they were tracking 200 cells involving more than 1,600 individuals who were "actively engaged in plotting or facilitating terrorist acts here and overseas."[17] The question now is not *if* there will be another catastrophic attack, but only *when*.

By any objective assessment, the forward strategy was a dismal failure. What went wrong?

Some commentators, particularly so-called "realists" in foreign policy, condemned the strategy as intrinsically unworkable. In January 2007, Dimitri Simes, publisher of the *National Interest*, argued: "The debacle that is Iraq reaffirms the lesson that there is no such thing as a good crusade. This was true a thousand years ago when European Christian knights tried to impose their faith and way of life on the Holy Land, . . . and it is equally true today. Divine missions and sensible foreign policy just don't mix." Inspiring the

Bush administration's crusade is the (purported) "true calling of spreading liberty throughout the world, even at the barrel of a gun."[18] Bush's strategy was driven by an ideal—spreading democracy—and that idealism is what made it impractical. This complaint was also voiced early on in the war. About six months before Iraq's first elections were held, amid continuing insurgent attacks, Anthony Cordesman, a defense analyst writing in the *New York Times*, bluntly summed up this line of thinking: "What we need now is pragmatism, not ideology."[19]

The "realist" critique flows from a rejection of "the assumption that state behavior is a fit subject for moral judgment" (as diplomat George Kennan once noted of this outlook).[20] The ideology and character of a regime are irrelevant to how we should act toward it; there is no point in distinguishing between friends and foes. Practicality (i.e., achieving U.S. security) requires amoral diplomatic deals. This implies that we should talk and make deals with any regime, however monstrous or hostile.

"Realists" urge action divorced from moral principles, but history demonstrates that such a policy is suicidal. Recall that, in compliance with "realism," Washington backed jihadists forces, despite their perverse ideals, in the fight against the Soviets in Afghanistan—jihadists who, in keeping with their ideology, later turned their sights on the United States. The same amoralism animated the British in the 1930s. Britain disregarded Hitler's stated ambition and his vicious ideology (set out in *Mein Kampf* and broadcast at mass rallies throughout Germany), and agreed to a "land for peace" deal. Given Hitler's goals, the deal predictably encouraged his belligerence, and so the Nazi war machine proceeded to enslave and exterminate millions of human beings.

The disasters of "realism" underscore the need for moral ideals in foreign policy, and the "realist" explanation for the failure of Bush's strategy is false.

Consider another, increasingly prevalent, explanation for what went wrong—the idea that Bush's strategy was a good idea that was poorly implemented. Proponents of this view believed that the problem was not Bush's goal of spreading democracy, which they regarded as a noble ideal worth pursuing, but rather the administration's failure to pursue this goal properly. For example, Michael Rubin of the American Enterprise Institute laments that "Instead of securing Iraq's borders, the Bush administration accepted Syrian and Iranian pledges of non-interference."[21] Max Boot, a columnist for the *Los Angeles Times* and a fellow at the Council on Foreign Relations, was a supporter of Bush's strategy, but acknowledged numerous ways in which the mission was botched, including: "the lack of pre-invasion diplomacy, the lack of post-invasion planning, the lack of ground troops, the lack of intelligence, the lack of coordination and oversight, the lack of armor, the lack of electricity."[22]

The concrete means were supposedly inadequate or badly implemented. The strategy could be made to work, if we could shrewdly tinker with troop levels, border security, the training of Iraqi police, and so forth, and if we could install a competent secretary of defense to see to it that the strategy was implemented properly.

But none of these adjustments, nor any others, would have averted the disaster wrought by the forward strategy. The problem did not lie with a shortage of resources or blunders in executing the strategy. The problem lay with the strategy's basic goal, whose legitimacy critics failed to challenge.

The strategy failed to make us safer because making us safer was never its real goal. That goal was mandated by the corrupt moral ideal driving the strategy.

What, then, was the actual goal of the strategy?

A Forward Strategy for . . . What End?

Let us begin by considering what the strategy's putative goal would have required.

Suppose that on September 12, 2001, Bush's strategists had asked themselves the following: What steps are necessary to make American lives safe, given the lethal threat of Islamic terrorism?

The rational answer: We must defeat the enemy.

When foreign aggressors are diligently working to slaughter Americans, our government is obligated to use retaliatory force to eliminate the threat permanently. This is what it must do to completely restore the protection of the individual rights of Americans. Defeating the enemy is necessary to bring about a return to normal life—life in which Americans are free to produce and thrive without the perpetual dread of terrorist atrocities.

Making the enemy permanently non-threatening is the objective measure of success in war. Recall, for example, our last indisputably successful war—World War II. By 1945, the air attacks ended, ground combat ended, naval battles ended; the war was over—because the Allied powers defeated Nazi Germany and Imperial Japan. The threat was over. People in the West rejoiced and began returning to their normal lives.

The Allied powers achieved victory because they committed themselves to crushing the enemy. They understood that the enemy was Nazism and Japanese imperialism and that the political manifestations of these ideologies had to be stopped. They also understood, in some terms, that merely assassinating

Hitler or Japan's emperor Hirohito would not be enough, because the people of Germany and Japan supported the goals of their regime (after all, Hitler was democratically elected and Hirohito was a venerated ruler). Victory required a punishing military onslaught not only to stop the enemy's war machine, but also to demoralize its supporters.

The Allies inflicted the pain of war so intensely that the enemy laid down its arms and abandoned its cause—permanently. They flattened German cities, pulverized factories and railroads, devastated the country's infrastructure. The campaign against Japan likewise sought to break the enemy's will to fight. On one day of extremely fierce combat, for example, U.S. bombers dropped 500-pound incendiary clusters every fifty feet. "Within thirty minutes," one historian writes,

> a 28-mile-per-hour ground wind sent the flames roaring out of control. Temperatures approached 1,800 degrees Fahrenheit. . . . [General Curtis LeMay] wished to destroy completely the material and psychological capital of the Japanese people, on the brutal theory that once civilians had tasted what their soldiers had done to others, only then might their murderous armies crack. Advocacy for a savage militarism from the rear, he thought, might dissipate when one's house was in flames. People would not show up to work to fabricate artillery shells that killed Americans when there was no work to show up to. . . . The planes returned with their undercarriages seared and the smell of human flesh among the crews. Over 80,000 Japanese died outright; 40,918 were injured; 267,171 buildings were destroyed. One million Japanese were homeless.

The fire in Tokyo, the empire's center, burned for four days; the glow of the inferno could be seen from 150 miles away.[23]

To defeat Japan thoroughly, however, required even more: To cut short the war and save untold thousands of American lives, the U.S. dropped atomic bombs on Hiroshima and Nagasaki. The bombs laid waste to vast tracts of land, killed thousands of Japanese—and demonstrated that if Japan continued to threaten America, thousands more Japanese would suffer and die.

That overwhelming and ruthless use of force achieved its intended purpose. It ended the threat to the lives of Americans and returned them to safety—by demonstrating to the Germans and the Japanese that any attempt to implement their vicious ideologies would bring them only destruction. Defeated materially and broken in spirit, these enemies gave up. Since then Nazism and Japanese imperialism have essentially withered as ideological forces.

Today, American self-defense requires the same kind of military action.

We are not in some "new kind of conflict" that must drag on for genera-tions. As in World War II, the enemy we must defeat is an ideological move-ment: Islamic totalitarianism. Just as the Nazis sought to dominate Europe and then the world, so the Islamists dream of imposing a global caliphate. To them, Western secularism—and America in particular—constitutes an obstacle to the expansion of Islam's dominion and must be extirpated by force. The attacks of 9/11 were the culmination, so far, of a long succession of deadly strikes against us. The supposedly "faceless, stateless" terrorists are part of the totalitarian movement. They are motivated to fight and able to kill—because they are inspired and armed by regimes that back the move-ment and embody its ideal of Islamic domination. Chief among them are Iran and Saudi Arabia. Without Iran's support, for example, legions of Hamas and Hezbollah jihadists would be untrained, unarmed, unmotivated, impo-tent (see chapters 1, 2, and 7).

Victory today requires destroying regimes that provide logistical and moral support for Islamic totalitarianism. An overwhelming show of force against Iran—and the promise to repeat it against other hostile regimes—would do much to end support for the Islamist movement. For it would snuff out the movement's beacon of inspiration. Nearly thirty years after its Islamic revolu-tion, Iran is brazenly chasing nuclear weapons and threatening the world's most powerful nation. To many Muslims, Iran symbolizes the power of totali-tarian Islam to overcome irreligious regimes (such as that of the Shah) and to reshape the geopolitical landscape.

A war against Islamic totalitarians would target not just the leadership of a hostile regime; it must demoralize the movement and its many supporters, so that they, too, abandon their cause as futile. The holy warriors are able to train, buy arms, hide their explosives, plan and carry out their attacks, only because vast numbers of Muslims agree with their goals. These support-ers of jihad against the West who cheer when Americans die; who protect, support, and encourage the terrorists lusting to kill us; who are accomplices to mass murder; who urge their children to become "martyrs" in the path of Allah—they must experience a surfeit of the pain that their jihad has visited upon us. We must demonstrate to them that any attempt to perpetuate their cause will bring them personal destruction; they must be made to see that their cause is manifestly unachievable, hopelessly lost.[24]

Thus the Japanese were forced to renounce their cause. Having been abjectly humiliated, they did not rampage in the streets nor launch an insur-gency; by crushing them, we did not create new enemies. An observation by General Douglas MacArthur, the commander in charge of occupied Japan, points to the reason why. At the end of the war, the Japanese suddenly felt the concentrated shock of total defeat; their whole world crumbled. It was not merely the overthrow of their military might—it was the collapse of a faith, it was the disintegration of everything they had believed in and lived by and fought for. It left a complete vacuum, morally, mentally, and physically.

That collapse, disintegration, and vacuum is essentially what we need to effect among the myriad supporters of Islamic totalitarianism in the Middle East. (Notice that the vacuum left by Japan's defeat cleared the way for the country to embrace rational values and build a new, peaceful regime. The Japanese, observes one writer, were "in a mood to question everything to which they had been loyal," while "everything the Americans did was food for thought.")[25]

There are many tactical options in prosecuting such a war, but such a war is necessary to defeat Islamic totalitarianism and end the threat it presents to American lives.

But the forward strategy of freedom called for something completely different. At no point—not even in the wake of 9/11—did Bush declare his willingness to inflict serious damage on our enemies in the Middle East (whom Washington evasively calls "terrorists"). At every opportunity he took pains to assuage the grumbling of the "Arab Street" and the international community by affirming that our quarrel was only with the (allegedly) tiny minority of "radicals," not with the vast majority of Muslims who (supposedly) reject the jihadists. Instead of aiming to defeat our enemies, the strategy's fanciful goal was to replace the Taliban and Saddam Hussein with democratic regimes. Explaining his strategy, President Bush stated:

> [W]e're advancing our security at home by advancing the cause of freedom across the world, because, in the long run, the only way to defeat the terrorists is to defeat their dark vision of hatred and fear by offering the hopeful alternative of human freedom. . . . the security of our nation depends on the advance of liberty in other nations.[26]

Pared to its essentials, the strategy's rationale came to this. We had just two options: Either we brought elections to them (and somehow become safer)—or they annihilated us.

Imagine that this strategy had guided America in World War II. Suppose that after the attack on Pearl Harbor, Americans were told that security would come, not by fighting the enemy until its unconditional surrender, but by deposing Hitler and Hirohito, and then setting up elections for their formerly enslaved people. What do you think would have happened? Would there have been any reason to believe that the Germans would not have elected another Nazi, or the Japanese another imperialist?

Precisely because this approach was not taken, and precisely because the Allied forces waged a vigorously assertive war to destroy the enemy, World War II was won decisively within four years of Pearl Harbor. Yet more than five years after 9/11, against a far weaker enemy, our soldiers still die every day in Iraq. And now the Islamists confidently believe that their ideal is more viable than ever, partly because we have helped them gain political power.

Of course, Bush's hope was that elections would bring to power pro-democracy, pro-American leaders; that establishing a democracy in Iraq would set off a chain reaction in which the entire Middle East would be transformed politically. Elected new regimes would allegedly have the effect of drying out the metaphorical swamps wherein a "dark vision of hatred and fear" apparently infects Muslims and impels them to slaughter Westerners. The desire for liberty, Bush assured us, was universal ("I believe that God has planted in every human heart the desire to live in freedom");[27] therefore, if only we could break the chains that oppress the peoples of the Middle East, they would gratefully befriend and emulate the West, rather than loathe and war against it. If we were to topple Saddam Hussein and deliver ballot boxes, Iraqis would be exposed to liberty and (just like any freedom-loving people) seek to realize this innate, though long-suppressed, ideal. By implication, an all-out war to defeat the enemy was unnecessary, because U.S.-engineered elections would bring us long-term security.

Was Bush's hope about who would win, shared by commentators and other politicians, honestly mistaken? Could genuinely pro-Western leaders be elected in the culture of the Middle East? Any objective assessment of the region would dispel that hope.

The region's culture is and has been dominated by primitive tribalism, by mysticism, by resentment toward any ideas that challenge Islam. Popular reactions to real or imagined slights to the religion express the widespread hostility to freedom. In 1989, *The Satanic Verses*, a novel by Salman Rushdie that allegedly insults Islam, was met with a brutal response. Few if any Muslims bothered to read the book, judge it firsthand, and reach an independent assessment of it—but they fervidly demanded that Rushdie be executed. Muslim reaction to the publication of Danish cartoons of Muhammad in 2006 again underscored, in blood, the animus to freedom of speech. Muslim rioters, who attacked Western embassies in the Middle East, demanded the beheading of the cartoonists whose drawings were deemed unholy. And observe that censorship is routine not only in highly religious regimes such as

Saudi Arabia, but also in ostensibly "moderate" ones such as Egypt, where the public sometimes clamors for it.

This opposition to freedom is not an accidental feature of particular regimes. Its source is a cultural antipathy to the values on which freedom depends. Political freedom in America is the product of the eighteenth-century Enlightenment, an epoch that venerated the individual and the sovereignty of his rational mind. And freedom can arise only in a culture that recognizes the irreplaceable value of a man's life and that grasps the life-sustaining value of worldly, scientific learning. But the Arab-Islamic world today rejects the values necessary for freedom to take root (let alone flourish).

The endemic contempt for the individual is apparent in the deep-seated worship of family and clan. The individual is seen as possessing neither sovereignty over his own life nor independent value; he is regarded as merely a subordinate cell in a larger organism, which can and does demand his sacrifice. The group's members kill to preserve family "honor"; brothers butcher sisters merely suspected of "disgracing" the family name. Yoked to the unchosen bonds of whatever tribe claims him, man must bow to its authority over his life regardless of what he believes to be true or good. Hence the custom of arranged marriages and the shunning of those who dare find a mate outside the tribe.

While a Muslim who renounces material goods and memorizes the Koran is esteemed for his devotion, an individual who values progress and pursues secular knowledge is resented as disloyal to religious tradition. Accordingly, the modern Islamic world has given rise to only a minuscule number of scientists or innovators, who have produced nothing of significance. Intellectual giants (such as Newton and Einstein), innovators (such as Thomas Edison), and entrepreneurs (such as Bill Gates) are nonexistent in the Middle East. Such men cannot develop in a culture that denigrates worldly knowledge, isolates itself from the books of the West, and wallows in self-righteous irrationality. A culture that deems self-assertion—whether in pursuit of scientific enlightenment, untraditional values, or individual happiness—an offense against tradition and the tribe, has no reason to embrace the rights of the individual. Individual rights are precisely the principles defining and protecting man's freedom to act on his own goals according to his own judgment.

Most Muslims in the Middle East are not the people that Bush would like us to believe they are: They do not have a repressed love of freedom; they are not lovers of prosperity and individual fulfillment; they are not our friends. Vast numbers of them are rabidly anti-American. To believe otherwise is to evade the jubilant Palestinians, Egyptians, and Iraqis celebrating the attacks of 9/11; the street demonstrations across the Islamic world lionizing Osama bin Laden; the popular glorification of "martyrs" on posters and in videos; the dedicated support for totalitarian organizations such as the Muslim Brotherhood and Lebanese Hezbollah. What so many Muslims harbor is not hopeful aspiration for, but savage hostility toward, rational ideals.

The relevant facts about the region are universally available and incontestable. Given an opportunity to choose their leaders, it is clear whom Muslims in the region would bring to power. Yet the Bush administration wished to believe that Iraqis craved freedom and prosperity, that they were just like Americans (except for the misfortune of living under a dictator); it wished to believe in this notion so much, that the administration embraced it in flagrant defiance of reality.

Through various elections, however, the voices of the people in the region have been heard. The people have demanded rule by Hamas in the Palestinian territories, rule by the Muslim Brotherhood in Egypt, rule by Hezbollah in Lebanon, rule by SCIRI and Dawa in Iraq. Such results have exposed the forward strategy for the sheer fantasy it is and always was.

Bush's strategy was concocted and advocated dishonestly: It was a product of evasion. The facts were plain, but Bush refused to accept them. Bush's plan was not some sophisticated alternative *means* of achieving victory—a means that somehow sidesteps a self-assertive war; victory was never its purpose. Rather, his plan was a rejection of the very *goal* of defeating the enemy. If not victory, what was the ultimate goal of the forward strategy?

The Crusade for Democracy

Although Bush's strategy was called the "forward strategy for *freedom*," this designation is a vicious fraud. The strategy had nothing to do with political freedom. An accurate title would have been the "forward strategy for *democracy*"—for unlimited majority rule—which is what it actually endorsed. There is a profound—and revealing—difference between advocating for freedom and advocating for democracy.

In today's intellectual chaos, these two terms are regarded as equivalents; in fact, however, they are antithetical. Freedom is fundamentally incompatible with democracy. Political freedom means the absence of physical coercion. Freedom is premised on the idea of individualism: the principle that every man is an independent, sovereign being; that he is not an interchangeable fragment of the tribe; that his life, liberty, and possessions are his by moral right, not by the permission of any group. It is a profound value, because in order to produce food, cultivate land, earn a living, build cars, perform surgery—in order to live—man must think and act on the judgment of his own rational mind. To do that, man must be left alone, left free from the initiation of physical force by the government and by other men.

Since freedom is necessary for man to live, a proper government is one that protects the freedom of individuals. It does that by recognizing and protecting their rights to life, liberty, property, and the pursuit of happiness. It must seek out and punish those—whether domestic criminals or foreign aggressors—who violate the rights of its citizens. Above all, the government's own power must be strictly and precisely delimited, so that neither the government nor any mob seeking to wield the state's power can abrogate the freedom of citizens. This kind of government renders the individual's freedom untouchable, by putting it off-limits to the mob or would-be power-lusters. A man's life remains his own, and he is left free to pursue it (while reciprocally respecting the freedom of others to do the same). This is the system that the Founding Fathers created in America: It is a republic delimited by the Constitution of the United States and the Bill of Rights. It is not a democracy.

The Founders recognized that a democracy—a system that confers unlimited power on the majority—is antithetical to freedom. Democracy rests on the primacy of the group. The system's supreme principle is that the will—the desires—of the collective is the proper standard regarding political matters; thus, the majority can arrogate to itself the power to exploit and tyrannize others. If your gang is large enough, you can get away with whatever you want. James Madison observed that in a system of unlimited majority rule

> there is nothing to check the inducements to sacrifice the weaker party or an obnoxious individual. Hence it is that such democracies have ever been spectacles of turbulence and contention; have ever been found incompatible with personal security or the rights of property; and have in general been as short in their lives as they have been violent in their deaths.[28]

Democracy is tyranny by the mob.

Accordingly, the constitutional framework of the United States prohibits the majority from voting away the rights of anyone. It is intended to prevent the mob from voting to execute a Socrates, who taught unconventional ideas. It is intended to prevent the majority from democratically electing a dictator such as Hitler or Robert Mugabe, who expropriates and oppresses a minority (e.g., Jews in Germany, white farmers in Zimbabwe) and devastates the lives of all. By delimiting the power that government is permitted to exercise, even if a majority demands that it exercise that power, the U.S. Constitution serves to safeguard the freedom of individuals.

The original American system is the system of political freedom—and it is incompatible with democracy. What Bush's strategy advocated for globally, however, was democracy.

Granted, the political system that Washington wished to spread in the Middle East differed from the original direct democracy of ancient Athens in form, and it had some of the trappings of American political institutions; but it nevertheless enshrined the will of the majority. In Iraq, it put the whims of Iraqi mobs first. Iraqis drafting the country's new constitution were unconcerned with safeguarding the rights of the individual; instead we bore witness to the ugly spectacle of rival pressure groups, representing ethnic and sectarian factions, wrangling to assert themselves as the voice of the collective will. Recall the protracted and histrionic clashes among those factions while they divvied up ministries in Iraq's government and selected a prime minister. And Washington's commitment to this perverse system was unambiguous.

Given the invasion of Iraq, if self-defense were part of the goal of the forward strategy, then one would logically expect that, for the sake of protecting American lives, Washington would have at least insisted on ensuring that the new regime be non-threatening, so that we did not have to face a resurgent threat. But Bush proclaimed all along that America would never determine the precise character of Iraq's (or Afghanistan's) new regime. The Iraqis were left to contrive their own constitution. Whatever the Iraqis chose, whomever they elected—Washington promised to endorse. The decision was entirely theirs. When asked whether the U.S. would acquiesce to an Iranian-style militant regime in the new Iraq, Bush said yes. Why should America help create a new hostile regime, a worse threat to our security than Saddam Hussein was? Because, Bush explained, "democracy is democracy. . . . If that's what the people choose, that's what the people choose."[29]

To appreciate just how serious Washington was about putting the will of Iraqi mobs above the rights of Americans, consider how it conducted the war.

From the outset, Washington committed us to a war of liberation. Just as we toppled the Taliban, to liberate the Afghans—so we toppled Saddam Hussein, to liberate the Iraqis. The campaign in Iraq, after all, was called Operation Iraqi Freedom, not Operation American Defense. "Shock and awe"—the supposedly merciless bombing of Baghdad—never materialized. The reason was that Washington's goal precluded devastating Iraq's infrastructure and crushing whatever threat the Hussein regime posed to us; its goal was to provide welfare services and hasten the arrival of elections.

Bush had promised that America will "stand ready to help the citizens of a liberated Iraq. We will deliver medicine to the sick, and we are now moving into place nearly three million emergency rations to feed the hungry."[30] And, indeed, the fighting had hardly begun when Washington launched the so-called reconstruction. Our military was ordered to commit troops and re- sources (which were needed to defend our personnel) to the tasks of reopen- ing schools, printing textbooks, fixing up hospitals, repairing dams. This was a Peace Corps, not an Army corps, mission. Washington doled out food and medicine and aid to Iraqis, but it tied the hands of our military.

The U.S. military was ordered to tiptoe around Iraq. "We have a very, very deliberate process for targeting," explained Brigadier General Vincent Brooks, deputy director of operations for the United States Central Com- mand, at a briefing in 2003. "It's unlike any other targeting process in the world. . . . [W]e do everything physically and scientifically possible to be pre- cise in our targeting and also to minimize secondary effects, whether it's on people or on structures."[31] So our forces refrained from bombing high-priority targets such as power plants, or in some cases even military targets located in historic sites. Troops were coached in all manner of cultural-sensitivity training, lest they offend Muslim sensibilities, and ordered to avoid treading in holy shrines or firing at mosques (where insurgents hide). The welfare of Iraqis was placed above the lives of our soldiers, who were thrust into the line of fire but prevented from using all necessary force to win the war or, tragi- cally, even to defend themselves. (No wonder an insurgency has flourished, emboldened by Washington's self-crippling policies.) Treating the lives of our military personnel as expendable, Washington wantonly spills their blood for the sake of democracy-building.[32]

In the run-up to the war, Bush promised that "The first to benefit from a free Iraq would be the Iraqi people themselves. . . . [T]hey live in scarcity and fear, under a dictator who has brought them nothing but war, and misery, and torture. Their lives and their freedom matter little to Saddam Hussein—but Iraqi lives and freedom matter greatly to us."[33]

Their lives did matter greatly to Washington—regardless of the cost to the lives or security of Americans.

The forward strategy dictated that we shower Iraqis with food, medicine, textbooks, billions in aid, a vast reconstruction, so that they could hold elec- tions. We had to do this even if it meant the deaths of thousands of U.S. troops and a new Iraqi regime that was more hostile than the one it replaced.

This policy, and the calamity it has produced, was too much for (most) Americans to stomach. But such was the zealous commitment of Bush and others to the spread of democracy, that they conceived of Iraq as merely the beginning. Leaving aside whether they thought it was politically feasible, their goal was a far larger campaign.

In his State of the Union address in 2006, Bush proclaimed that America is "committed to an historic long-term goal: To secure the peace of the world, we seek the end of tyranny in our world."[34] To carry out this global crusade for democracy is supposedly to fulfill our nation's "destiny," our moral duty as a noble people. On another occasion, Bush asserted that "the advance of freedom is the calling of our time."[35] This mission, he claimed in another speech, was conferred upon us by God: "[H]istory has an author who fills time and eternity with his purpose. . . . We did not ask for this mission, yet there is honor in history's call."[36]

Picture what such an undertaking would entail, in practical terms, given the nightmare that Iraq has become. About 140,000 troops are stuck in the quagmire there today. At the peak of the fighting, as many as 300,000 of our military were involved. According to one estimate, Operation Iraqi Freedom has cost about $318 billion.[37] So far in Iraq more than 3,000 Americans have died. About 22,000 have come home missing arms, limping, burned, blinded, deafened, psychologically scarred, brain damaged. Although the casualties of the war may be largely unseen, the carnage is all too real. What the advocates of a wider democracy crusade were calling for was morally obscene: not just one hellish ordeal like Iraq (which is horrendous in itself), but dozens of new campaigns that grind up American troops and flush away our nation's lifeblood, campaigns that drag on indefinitely as we fulfill the open-ended "calling of our time."

There was no conceivable reason to believe that a strategy so contemptuous of American lives was at all concerned with our self-defense. When its deceptions and lies were peeled away, what remained was a pernicious strategy that puts nothing above the goal of spreading democracy. Such dedication was mandated by the fundamental premise that serves as the strategy's justification.

Observe what the dogged advocates of the strategy reject as illegitimate: a self-assertive war to defend America. It was unimaginable to them that America should fight a war against Islamic totalitarianism with the intensity and righteousness that we did in World War II; that the U.S. should seek to demoralize the enemy; that we should, as Winston Churchill put it, "create conditions intolerable to the mass of the [enemy] population;"[38] that the U.S. should seek victory, for its own self-defense. All of this was off the table. But sending young American men to die in order to bring Iraqis the vote was deemed virtuous, a noble imperative.

Advocates of the forward strategy were fervently committed to spreading democracy, because they were guided by a moral ideal. The principle shaping their thinking was the idea that pursuing values for your own benefit is evil, but selfless service to others is good. Virtue, on this morality, is self-sacrifice.

This ethical ideal dominates our culture. We are told by secular and religious authorities, left and right, that to be moral is to give up our values selflessly. We are bombarded with a seemingly endless variety of slogans that inculcate this same droning message: Put other people first; renounce your goals for the sake of others; don't be selfish. As Bush put it: "Serve in a cause larger than your wants, larger than yourself"; "our duty is fulfilled in service to one another."[39]

In the religious variant of this moral code, the ideal is personified in Jesus. He suffered the agonies of crucifixion and perished on the cross—for the sake of all mankind. It is the self-abnegation of Jesus that Christian moralists enjoin their followers to emulate, and accordingly, over the centuries, Christian saints have been extolled for their asceticism and self-effacement. Though religion is the main propagator of this moral standard, it has also been propounded in various secularized forms.

The morality of self-sacrifice is today almost universally equated with morality per se. It is the standard of right and wrong that people accept unquestioningly, as if it were a fact of nature. Observe that even non-religious people regard Mother Theresa as a moral hero, because she devoted her life to ministering to the sick and hungry. Conversely, the achievements of a productive businessman like Bill Gates are deemed to have (at best) no moral significance. On this view, whoever pursues profits is plainly looking out for himself; he is being "selfish." This creed teaches men to damn profit-seeking and, more widely, to suspect any self-assertion toward one's goals. It teaches that only acting for the sake of others is virtuous.

The injunction to selfless service is addressed to the "haves"—those who have earned a value and have something to give up—because on this moral code they have no right to keep their wealth, to enjoy their freedom, to pursue justice, to protect themselves. Whom must they serve? Whoever has failed or never bothered to achieve a value: the "have-nots." Their lack of a value, regardless of its cause, is taken as a moral claim on the productive and able. Because America is a "have"—strong, wealthy, prosperous—it has no right to prosecute a war to destroy Islamic totalitarianism. It must instead renounce the pursuit of justice. Which is what the Christian version of this morality counsels the innocent victim to do: "[R]esist not evil: but whosoever shall smite thee on thy right cheek, turn to him the other also," and "Love your enemies, bless them that curse you, do good to them that hate you, and pray for them which despitefully use you, and persecute you."[40]

But the oppressed, impoverished, primitive Iraqis are definitely "have-nots." They have no food, no electricity, no freedom. It is they, not we, who have a moral claim to our time and money and lives, because they have not earned those values. The deep-pocketed America must therefore jettison the goal of its security and engage in selfless missions to bring succor to these destitute people. This comports perfectly both with Christian precepts and with the dogmas of secular moralists on the left (and the right) who demand that America embark on global "humanitarian" adventures rather than unleash its powerful military and defend itself.

The principle of self-sacrifice implies that the desires of Iraqis, however irrational and destructive, must be accorded moral legitimacy. Instead of prevailing upon them to adopt a new, secular regime that will be non-threatening to America, we must efface that goal and respect the whims of tribal hordes. It is their moral right to pen a constitution enshrining Islam as the supreme law of the land and to elect Islamists to lead their nation. They are the suffering and "needy," we the prosperous and wealthy; on the ethics of self-sacrifice, the productive must be sacrificed to the unproductive.

But, as we have seen, carrying out the injunctions of this ideal contradicts the needs of U.S. security. It is self-destructive—and that is why it is regarded as noble. As Bush stated approvingly, we Americans know how to "sacrifice for the liberty of strangers."[41]

A sacrifice is the surrender of a value for the sake of a lesser value or a non-value; it entails a net loss. Giving up something trivial for the sake of a big reward at the end, for instance, scrimping and saving today in order to buy a car next year, is not a sacrifice. But giving up your savings to a random stranger, is. It is no sacrifice to enlist in the military and risk your life in order to defend your cherished freedom. It is a sacrifice to send American soldiers to Iraq not to defend their own liberty and ours, but to ensure that Iraqis have functioning sewers. The ideal of self-sacrifice constitutes a fundamental rejection of man's right to exist for his own sake.

The forward strategy was a faithful application of this moral code. America is the innocent victim of Islamist aggression, but on this code we have no right to exist or to defend our freedom. To mount a military campaign against the enemy in defense of our lives would be self-interested. Our duty, on this morality, was to renounce our self-interest. Ultimately, the goal of the crusade for democracy was not to destroy the threats arrayed against us; the goal was for America to sacrifice itself.

What, then, are we to make of the Bush administration's contradictory rhetoric? It claimed, seemingly in earnest, to be seeking America's security. We were told for instance that "any nation that continues to harbor or support terrorism will be regarded by the United States as a hostile regime";[42] and that "We will not waver; we will not tire; we will not falter; and we will not fail" in the face of the enemy.[43] At the same time, we were deluged with maudlin, though sincere, talk about sacrificing in order to lift the Middle East out of misery, poverty, and suffering. And what were we to make of the claims about the strategy's chances of making us safer—in defiance of all facts to the contrary?

The rhetoric is not solely or primarily aimed at winning over the American public. The rhetoric serves as rationalization for a profoundly irrational moral ideal.

Our leaders recognized that we faced a mortal threat, but they shrank from the kind of action necessary for our self-defense. We can see that in the initial reaction to 9/11. For a brief period after the attacks, the American public and its leaders did feel a genuine and profound outrage—and their (healthy) response was to demand retaliation. The nation was primed to unleash its full military might to annihilate the threat. Symbolizing that righteous indignation was the name chosen for the military campaign against the Taliban regime in Afghanistan: Operation Infinite Justice. The prevailing mood conveyed a clear message: America was entitled to defend itself. But this reaction was evanescent.

Even before the reality of the attacks faded, the flush of indignation subsided—as did the willingness to fight for our self-defense. In deference to the feelings of Muslims, Operation Infinite Justice was renamed Operation Enduring Freedom. After drawing a line in the sand separating regimes that are with us from those that are with our enemies, Washington hastened to erase that line by inviting various sponsors of terrorism, including Iran and Syria, to join a coalition against terrorism. The initial confidence that our leaders felt, the sense that they had right on their side, petered out.

They recoiled from that goal of self-defense when they considered it in the light of their deeply held moral premises. Their moral ideal told them that acting to defend America would be "selfish" and thus immoral. They could not endorse or pursue such a course of action. But their ideal further told them that to act selflessly is virtuous: the forward strategy, therefore, is obviously a moral and noble strategy, because its aim is self-sacrificial ministration to the needs of the meek and destitute. This was a policy that the Bush administration could endorse and act on.

The claims about ensuring the well-being of Iraqis reflected the strategy's fundamental moral impetus. The claims about defending America were necessary for the advocates of the strategy to delude themselves and the American public. They needed to make themselves believe that they could pursue a self-sacrificial policy *and* America's security—that they could pursue both and need not choose between the two.

In essentials, what our leaders wanted to believe was that their self-destructive policy was actually in our self-interest, that somehow it *is* a self-sacrifice (hence noble and moral) and yet *not* a self-sacrifice (hence achieves American security). This is why the administration insisted that "Helping the people of Iraq is the morally right thing to do—America does not abandon its friends in the face of adversity. *Helping the people of Iraq, however, is also in our own national interest.*"[44] This delusion involved two intertwined self-deceptions: that the forward strategy would occasion benefits in practice (i.e., security to America); and that a self-assertive war on the model of World War II, though apparently a practical way to make us safe, was ultimately suicidal.

Portraying Iraqis, and others in the Muslim Middle East, as our "friends in the face of adversity" was key to this delusion. They were characterized as latent friends who, when unshackled, would freely express their goodwill, and form regimes that would become our allies. Proponents of the strategy had to tell themselves, and the public, that the vast majority of Muslims just want a better life, "moderate" leaders, and peace—not totalitarian rule by Islamists (as in fact so many do). If one pretended that the Iraqis were pining for liberty, it came to seem that they would welcome our troops with flowers and candy, and that the mission would be a cakewalk. If one evaded the truth and insisted on the self-deception that we would effectively be lending a hand to allies who share our values, then it came to seem vaguely plausible that the loss of American lives on this mission was not actually a loss because major benefits redounded back to America: By selflessly liberating Iraqis (and Afghans) we would, incidentally, be attaining the eventual security of our nation.

Bound up with that self-deception was another one. Its purpose was to discredit assertive war (such as we waged in World War II) as counterproductive and therefore impractical. Evading logic and the lessons of history, advocates of the forward strategy wished to believe that a war driven by self-interest (hence ignoble and immoral) would, after all, undermine our self-interest (by making us more, not less, vulnerable). This kind of war, the rhetoric would have us believe, was not an option worth entertaining. The delusion relied, again, on the rosy portrayal of the lovable peoples of the Middle East. The killers were said to be a scattered group lurking in shadows and operating across borders. For targeting the dispersed jihadists, the methods of past wars, such as carpet-bombing, were far too coarse and would fail to kill off the scattered enemy. Further, if we were to use such means to flatten the Iraqi city of Falluja to quell the insurgency, for instance, or to topple Iran's totalitarian regime, we would thereby ignite the fury of Muslims caught up in the bombing. And that would turn the entire region against us.

Part of the alleged impracticality of a self-assertive war is that it would profoundly and adversely alter the ideological landscape in the region. Bush and other advocates of the forward strategy claimed (preposterously) that all human beings are endowed with an "innate" love of liberty, that the multitude of Muslims in the region are "moderates" who passionately long for political freedom, and that if we nourished their longing for freedom, they would cease to hate or threaten us. But, we are told, if America were to deploy overwhelming military force against their hostile regimes and demoralize large numbers of Muslims, we would thereby deliver the masses to the hands of bin Laden and other Islamic totalitarians. Demoralizing them would somehow overturn their purportedly "innate" desire for freedom and make them long to be enslaved under a sharia regime. By acting on our self-interest, so the rationalization went, we would create new enemies and undermine our self-interest.

But there is no reason to believe that a devastating war—such as the one we waged against Japan—could fail to achieve its purpose: to destroy the enemy. We need to inflict widespread suffering and death because the enemy's supporters and facilitators are many and widespread. We need to demoralize them because (as noted earlier) people demoralized in this fashion are motivated to doubt the beliefs and leaders that inspired their belligerence, promised them triumph, yet brought them a shattering defeat. Demoralizing Muslims who endorse and perpetuate the jihad would indeed overturn their ideas—their chosen allegiance to the vicious ideology of totalitarian Islam. Seeing that their cause is hopeless, they would be driven to abandon, not to intensify or renew, their fight. Scenarios predicting our doom if we dare assert ourselves are factually groundless and incoherent.

The rhetoric emanating from the Bush administration and its supporters was unavoidably contradictory. Our leaders needed to make themselves, and us, believe that the inherently self-destructive forward strategy was the only way to proceed. It was (on their terms) the only moral path, but it must also have been made to seem practical, that is, to our advantage.

The forward strategy was like umpteen other policies and doctrines that, in various ways, portray self-sacrifice as beneficial to the victim. The moral injunction to selflessness would hardly have the power that it does, were it not for the (empty) promise of some kind of eventual reward. For example, during certain periods Christianity (and Islam) stressed the everlasting rewards that a believer can hope to attain in Heaven, if he dutifully serves God's will, effaces his desire for wealth and sexual pleasure, and selflessly ministers to the suffering. Heaven on earth—a workers' paradise of limitless leisure and fulfillment—was Communism's promise to the proletariat who renounced personal gain and labored selflessly for the sake of the collective ("from each according to his ability, to each according to his needs").

The forward strategy belongs in the same category as another contemporary scheme, which commands near-universal support: foreign aid. Both liberal and conservative advocates of foreign aid claim that by (selflessly) doling out billions of dollars in aid, America will somehow find itself better off. When no such gains ever materialize, we are rebuked for having been too stingy—and commanded to give more, much more, to give till it hurts, since doing so is allegedly in our interest. For example, in the wake of the 2005 suicide bombings in London, Bush and the British Prime Minister Tony Blair claimed that we must give away $50 billion to feed Africans impoverished by their tribal wars and anticapitalist ideas and to prop up the anti-Western terrorist regime in the Palestinian Territories. Why? Presumably, the suicide bombings were proof that we simply had not given enough, and, as Blair claimed (speaking for Bush and other supporters of aid) more aid would help us triumph over terrorism, someday.[45] The forward strategy can be viewed as a perverse continuation of foreign aid: Since money alone was insufficient, we should selflessly bring elections to the world's oppressed and sink billions into vast reconstruction projects for their sake.

Just as bribes in the form of foreign aid will supposedly make us safer but have not and cannot—so too sacrificing U.S. lives to spread democracy in the Middle East, and ultimately across the globe, will supposedly make us safer but has not and cannot. The actual effects are unmistakable.

The forward strategy was an immoral policy, and so its consequences are necessarily self-destructive. You cannot sacrifice your military strength *and* defend yourself in the face of threats.

The contradiction becomes harder to evade as more Americans die in Iraq and as more Islamist terror plots are uncovered. While the evidence mounted, however, the Bush administration remained undeterred, responding only with further evasions. Despite the unequivocal results of elections in the region that empowered Islamists; despite the overwhelming Muslim celebration of the war initiated by the Iran-Hamas-Hezbollah axis against Israel; despite the violent return of the Taliban in Afghanistan; despite the raging civil war in Iraq; despite the wholesale refutation of Bush's predictions and hopes to date, he claimed in January 2007: "From Afghanistan to Lebanon to the Palestinian Territories, millions of ordinary people are sick of the violence, and want a future of peace and opportunity for their children." Despite the reality that no Iraqis to speak of have made a choice for freedom, and while an overwhelming number of them remain openly hostile both to America and to freedom, Bush promises to stand with "the Iraqis who have made the choice for freedom." Iraq's fledgling democracy has yet to flower, he claimed, because it was being impeded by a lack of security. "So

America will *change our strategy* to help the Iraqis carry out their campaign to put down sectarian violence and bring security to the people of Baghdad." [Emphasis added.] Bush vowed to deploy a "surge" of some 20,000 additional U.S. troops in Iraq.[46]

Although characterized as a change in strategy, this was just a change in means, not ends. Spreading democracy remained the unquestioned, self-delusional end, for which more troops and a push for security were the means. Before the war, Saddam Hussein's regime was the obstacle that had to be removed so that Iraqis could have democracy. Then, it was the utter chaos of insurgency and civil war that obstructed the realization of an Iraqi democracy. In both cases, American men and women in uniform lay down their own lives for the sake of Iraqis. Amid the inevitable results of a democracy's mob rule and the predictable sectarian war, the Bush administration looked on with purposefully unseeing eyes and rededicated America to a "surge" of senseless sacrifices. The multiplying evasions enable Bush and other advocates of the strategy to fool themselves, and any remaining Americans who still believe in the strategy.

But no amount of self-delusion can erase the facts.

After five years of war, America now faces a threat that we helped to make stronger. This is precisely the result to which the forward strategy had to lead, given its moral premises and the evasions of its proponents. The strategy entails sacrificing American lives, not merely for the sake of indifferent strangers, but for the sake of our enemy.

We have galvanized the undefeated enemy. The forward strategy has taught jihadists everywhere a profoundly heartening lesson: that America fights so that Muslims can assert their desire for Islamist leadership; that America does not destroy those who threaten the lives of its citizens; that America renounces its self-interest on principle, because we do not believe we have a right to defend ourselves. A "paper tiger" is how Osama bin Laden characterized America prior to 9/11, and he thereby inspired many Muslims to join the jihad. Nothing that we have done since 9/11 has contradicted the jihadists' view; the forward strategy and America's other policies have confirmed it. Note Tehran's glee at the grotesque spectacle of America's suicidal policy. To say that Iran in particular feels invulnerable or that jihadists in general are encouraged is to understate matters.

Meanwhile, Bush's strategy has drained not only the material strength of the United States, but also our will to fight. The nation is in retreat. Sickened and demoralized by the debacle in Iraq, many Americans dismiss the possibility of success. This ethos is typified by the Iraq Study Group, whose purpose was to offer forward-looking remedies for the deteriorating situation in Iraq and the region. In December 2006, the group issued a report specifying seventy-nine recommendations, but these options boil down to a maddeningly limited range: Stick with the failed idealistic strategy (i.e., send more troops to engage in democracy-building); or abandon it (pull out the troops); and, either way, concede the "realist" claim that moral principles are a hindrance to foreign policy (and, of course, appease the hostile regimes in Syria and Iran). Ruled out from consideration was a self-assertive war to defeat the enemy because, tragically, many misconstrued the forward strategy as epitomizing, and thus discrediting, that option.

Consequently, the amoralists, seemingly vindicated by the Iraq Study Group, are winning a larger audience. They advise us to check our principles at the door, pull up a seat at the negotiating table, and hash out a deal: "It's not appeasement to talk to your enemies," James Baker reassures us, referring to the prospect of diplomatic talks with North Korea (Baker is co-chairman of the Iraq Study Group). Nicholas Kristof, a columnist for the *New York Times*, joins the chorus: "We sometimes do better talking to monsters than trying to slay them."[47]

But the correct lesson to draw is that we must reject neither idealism nor war, but the particular moral ideal that drove the forward strategy. A campaign guided by the ideal of self-sacrifice and renunciation cannot bring us victory. We need a different ideal.

An Unknown Ideal

Our leaders insisted that the forward strategy was indispensable to victory. They claimed that only this strategy was noble, because it was self-sacrificial, and that only it was practical because it would somehow protect our lives. We are asked to believe that in slitting our own throats, we will do ourselves no real harm, that this is actually the cure to our affliction. What the strategy's advocates would like us to believe is that there is no alternative to the ideal of selflessness.

But we are confronted by a choice—and the alternatives are mutually exclusive. The choice is between self-sacrifice—and self-interest. There is no middle ground. There is no way to unite these alternatives. We must choose one or the other. If we are to make our lives safe, we must embrace the ideal of America's self-interest.

Though largely unknown and misconceived, this moral principle is necessary to the achievement of America's national security. Let us briefly consider what it stands for and what it would mean in practice.[48]

If we are to pursue America's self-interest, we must above all be passionate advocates for rational moral ideals. We need to recognize that embracing the right ideals is indispensable to achieving our long-term, practical goal of national security. Key to upholding our national self-interest is championing the ideal of political freedom—not crusading for democracy.

Freedom, as noted earlier, is a product of certain values and moral premises. Fundamentally, it depends on the moral code of rational egoism. Whereas the morality of self-sacrifice punishes the able and innocent, by commanding them to renounce their values; egoism, as defined in the philosophy of Ayn Rand, holds that the highest moral purpose of man's life is achieving his own happiness. Egoism holds that each individual has an unconditional moral right to his own life, that no man should sacrifice himself, that each must be left free from physical coercion by other men and the government. Politically, this entails a government that recognizes the individual as a sovereign being and upholds his inviolable right to his life and possessions. This is the implicit moral basis of the Founders' original system of government as the protector of the rights of individuals.

If we take the ideal of freedom seriously, then we must staunchly defend ourselves from foreign aggression. The liberty of Americans cannot endure, unless our government takes the military steps necessary to protect our right to live in freedom. As a necessary first step, we should proclaim our commitment to this ideal, and promote it as a universal value for mankind. By demonstrating that we hold our own ideals as objectively right, as standards for all to live up to, we evince confidence in our values. The knowledge that America upholds its own ideals and will defend them to the death is a powerful deterrent in the minds of actual and would-be enemies.

A derivative benefit is that we can encourage the best among men, wherever they may be, to embrace the ideal of political freedom. To free nations, to nations moving toward freedom, and to genuine freedom fighters, we should give our moral endorsement, which is a considerable, if often underappreciated, value. For example, we should endorse the Taiwanese who are resisting the claims of authoritarian China to rule the island state. We should declare that a rights-respecting system of government is morally right and that an authoritarian one is morally wrong.

Although America should be an *intellectual* advocate for freedom, this precludes devoting material resources to "spread freedom." It is only proper for our government to provide such resources to help a true ally, and only when doing so is necessary for the protection of the rights of Americans. It is never moral for America to send its troops for the sole purpose of liberating a people and then pile sacrifice upon sacrifice for the sake of nation-building. It is never moral to send our troops on selfless missions or to fight wars in which America's security is not directly at stake. Such wars—and the forward strategy itself—violate the rights of our troops and of all other American citizens by imperiling their freedom and security.

In order to protect the freedom of Americans, we must be able to distinguish friends from foes; we must, in other words, judge other regimes and treat them accordingly. The criterion for evaluating other regimes is the principle that government is properly established to uphold: freedom. A country that does respect the individual rights of its citizens has a valid claim to sovereignty. By befriending such a country, we stand to gain a potential trading partner and ally. Because tyrannies violate, instead of protect, the rights of their citizens, such regimes are illegitimate and have no right to exist whatsoever. Tyrannies are by their nature potential threats to America (and any free nation). History has repeatedly shown that a regime that enslaves its own citizens will not feel shy about plundering and murdering beyond its borders. Rather than treating tyrannies as peace-partners whom we can tame with the right mix of bribes, we should shun and denounce them loudly—and, when necessary, defend ourselves militarily against their aggression.

Determining which course of action, strategy, or foreign policy actually serves America's self-interest requires rational deliberation and reference to valid principles. It cannot be achieved by wishful thinking (e.g., by pretending that our self-immolation can lead to our future benefit), nor by whatever our leaders pray will be expedient for the range of the moment (e.g., by "talking with monsters" and appeasing enemies). Instead, the goal of securing the enduring freedom of Americans, which includes security from foreign threats, requires figuring out rationally what constitutes a present threat; what is the most efficient means of permanently eliminating a given threat; which regimes are our allies and which are enemies (among other issues). What is required, in short, is a commitment to the full awareness of the relevant facts. That necessitates following the facts wherever they lead—and not being led by the corrupt delusions that the morality of self-sacrifice entails.

Today, the facts tell us that Islamic totalitarianism is waging war on America. This movement commands wide support and is nourished principally by Iran and Saudi Arabia. The moral ideal of rational egoism counsels an unequivocal response: Defend the lives of Americans. That goal requires, as argued earlier, an overwhelming military campaign to destroy the enemy, leaving it permanently non-threatening. We need to wage as ruthless, unrelenting, and righteous a war as we waged sixty years ago against Germany and Japan. Only that kind of war can make us safe and enshrine our freedom. It is the only moral response and therefore the only practical one.

As to what America should do once it has defeated this enemy, again, the guiding moral principle should be that of our national self-interest.

It might be in our interest to install a free political system in a Middle Eastern country that we have defeated—if we have good reason to believe that we can create a permanently non-threatening regime and do so without sacrificing U.S. wealth or lives. And if we were to choose such a course, the precise character of the new regime would have to be decided by America. For instance, in contrast to Bush's selfless approach to the constitutions of Iraq and Afghanistan, in postwar Japan the United States did not give the Japanese people a free hand to draw up whatever constitution they wished, nor to bring to power whomever they liked. We set the terms and guided the creation of the new state, and in part because this is how Japan was reborn, it became an important friend to America. (Observe that the Japanese were receptive to new political ideals only after they were thoroughly defeated in war; Iraqis were never defeated and, on the contrary, were encouraged to believe that their tribalism and devotion to Islam were legitimate foundations for a new government.)

But we have no moral duty to embroil ourselves in selfless nation-building. In a war of retaliation against a present threat, we are morally entitled to crush an enemy regime because we are innocent victims defending our unconditional right to be free. Our government's obligation is to protect the lives of Americans, not the welfare of people in the Middle East. The responsibility for the suffering or death of people in a defeated regime belongs to those who initiated force against us. If it proves to be in our national self-interest to withdraw immediately after victory, leaving the defeated inhabitants to sift through the rubble and rebuild on their own, then we should do exactly that. In doing so, we must instill in them the definite knowledge that, whatever new regime they adopt, it too will face devastation if it threatens America.

If Islamic totalitarians and their many followers know without a doubt that the consequence of threatening us is their own demise, the world will be a peaceful place for Americans. And that, ultimately, is the end for which our government and its policies are the means: to defend our freedom so that we can live and prosper.

The struggle to defend our freedom depends fundamentally on an ideological battle. The clash is one that our leaders persist in evading and obscuring, but which cannot be escaped. At issue is the moral principle that shapes America's foreign policy. The conflict comes down to this: *Do Americans have a duty to sacrifice themselves for strangers—or do we have a moral right to exist and pursue our individual happiness?* This is the battle that we must fight and win in America, if we are to triumph over Islamic totalitarianism.

CHAPTER FOUR

"Just War Theory" vs. American Self-Defense

Yaron Brook and Alex Epstein

On September 11, and in the weeks after, we all felt the same things. We felt grief, that we had lost so many who had been so good. We felt anger, at whoever could commit or support such an evil act. We felt disbelief, that the world's only superpower could let this happen. And we felt fear, from the newfound realization that such evil could rain on any of us. But above all, we felt the desire for *overwhelming retaliation* against whomever was responsible for these atrocities, directly or indirectly, so that no one would dare launch or support such an attack on America ever again.

To conjure up the emotions we felt on 9/11, many intellectuals claim, is dangerous, because it promotes the "simplistic" desire for revenge and casts aside the "complexity" of the factors that led to the 9/11 attacks. But, in fact, the desire for overwhelming retaliation most Americans felt after 9/11—and feel rarely, if ever, now—was the result of an *objective conviction*: that a truly monstrous evil had been perpetrated, and that if the enemies responsible for the 9/11 attacks were not dealt with decisively, we would suffer the same fate (or worse) again.

After 9/11, our leaders—seemingly sharing our conviction in the necessity of decisive retaliation—promised to do everything possible to make America safe from terrorist attack. In an almost universally applauded speech, President Bush pledged to eradicate the enemy by waging a war that was to begin with Al Qaeda and the Taliban but that would "not end until every terrorist group of global reach has been . . . defeated." In the same speech, Bush vowed: "I will not yield; I will not rest; I will not relent in waging this struggle for freedom and security for the American people."[1]

To fulfill the promise to defeat the terrorist enemy that struck on 9/11, our leaders would first have to identify who exactly that enemy is and then be willing to do whatever is necessary to defeat him. Let us examine what this would entail, and compare it with the actions that our leaders actually took.

Who is the enemy that attacked on 9/11? It is not "terrorism"—just as our enemy in World War II was not kamikaze strikes or U-boat attacks. Terrorism is a tactic employed by a certain group for a certain cause. That group and, above all, the cause they fight for are our enemy.

The group that threatens us with terrorism—the group of which Al Qaeda is but one terrorist faction—is a militant, religious, ideological movement best designated as "Islamic totalitarianism." The Islamic totalitarian movement, which enjoys widespread and growing support throughout the Arab-Islamic world, encompasses those who believe that all must live in total subjugation to the dogmas of Islam and who conclude that jihad ("holy war") must be waged against those who refuse to do so. Islamic totalitarians regard the freedom, prosperity, and pursuit of worldly happiness animating the West (and especially America and Israel) as the height of depravity. They seek to eradicate Western culture, first in the Middle East and then in the West itself, with the ultimate aim of bringing about the worldwide triumph of Islam. This goal is achievable, adherents of the movement believe, because the West is a "paper tiger" that can be brought to its knees by sufficiently devoted Islamic warriors.

Given that the enemy that attacked on 9/11 is primarily ideological, what, if anything, can our government's guns do to defeat it? Our government cannot directly attack the deepest, philosophical roots of Islamic totalitarianism; however, to defeat Islamic totalitarianism as a *physical threat*, it does not need to do so. Why? Because an indispensable precondition of an active, threatening Islamic totalitarian movement—one for which individuals are willing to take up arms—is its active support by Arab and Islamic states that assist, embody, and implement it. Without this state support, Islamic totalitarianism, and thus Islamic terrorism, could not exist as a major threat.

We can see how the end of state support for a movement can destroy the threat it poses in the cases of Communism and Nazism, two militant movements with world-conquering, totalitarian ambitions. As Angelo M. Codevilla, Professor of International Relations at Boston University, writes:

> Recall for a moment the Communist movement's breadth and depth. The Communist Party was just the tip of the iceberg. Every political party, every labor union, every newspaper, every school, every profession, every social organization had sympathizers with Communism who played a significant role in

its life. . . . Where now are all those people, young and old, who would argue and demonstrate, and scheme and spy and kill and betray for the grand cause of Communism? They were no more when the Soviet Union was no more, just as sunflowers would cease to exist were there no sun. As for those ferocious Nazis . . . only the name remains, as a hackneyed insult. Human causes are embodied by human institutions. With them they flourish, without them they die. Communists and Nazis everywhere ceased to be a problem when the regimes that inspired them died.[2]

For Islamic totalitarianism, the "sun" (the equivalent of Communism's Soviet Union) is Iran. Iran was founded on the principles of Islamic totalitarianism, implements the ideals of the movement in a full-fledged militant Islamic theocracy, and thus embodies its cause—providing the movement with a model as well as indispensable spiritual hope and fuel. Iran is also a leading supporter of the terrorist groups Hamas, Islamic Jihad, and Hezbollah. (Compared with Iran, the Taliban in Afghanistan was a bit player.) The second leading state supporter of Islamic totalitarianism is Saudi Arabia, which has spent more than *seventy-five billion dollars* on the Wahhabi sect of Islam that inspires legions of Islamic totalitarians, including Osama bin Laden.

Without physical and spiritual support by these states, the Islamic totalitarian cause would be a hopeless, discredited one, with few if any willing to kill in its name. Thus, the first order of business in a proper response to 9/11 would have been to end state support of Islamic totalitarianism—including ending the Iranian regime that is its fatherland. As a secondary priority, a proper fight against the enemy that attacked on 9/11 would have involved ending state sponsorship of terrorism by Arab states derivatively connected to Islamic totalitarianism—states such as Syria (and, before it was ended, Saddam Hussein's Iraq). These regimes are active supporters of Arab-Islamic terrorism and mouth support for the Islamic totalitarian cause, but are not ideologically committed to it; these regimes support this cause out of political expediency. Supporting Islamic totalitarianism gains power for them; by supporting anti-Western causes and jihadists, Arab states direct the misery of their people toward America and Israel and away from their own brutal rule. Supporting Islamic totalitarianism also gains money for Arab states; for example, the leaders of Syria, a stagnant nation with no oil wealth, are wealthy because oil-rich Iran pays them for providing assistance to terrorist organizations such as Hezbollah. Dealing effectively with these accessories to Islamic totalitarianism would require, first and foremost, getting rid of the primary supporters of the movement. The next step would be, where necessary, making clear to these derivative regimes that any cooperation with that movement or its aims is not expedient, but a guarantee of their destruction.

What specific military actions would have been required post-9/11 to end state support of Islamic totalitarianism is a question for specialists in military strategy, but even a cursory look at history can tell us one thing for sure: It would have required the willingness to take *devastating military action against enemy regimes*—to oust their leaders and prominent supporters, to make examples of certain regimes or cities in order to win the surrender of others, and to inflict suffering on complicit civilian populations, who enable terrorist-supporting regimes to remain in power.

Observe what it took for the United States and the Allies to defeat Germany and Japan and thus win World War II. Before the Germans and Japanese surrendered, the Allies had firebombed every major Japanese city and bombed most German cities—killing hundreds of thousands. Explaining the rationale for the German bombings, Churchill wrote, "the severe, the ruthless bombing of Germany on an ever-increasing scale will not only cripple her war effort . . . but will create conditions intolerable to the mass of the German population." And as we well know, what ended the war—and the Nazi and Japanese imperialist threat to this day—was America's dropping of two atomic bombs on Japan.

The Civil War provides another stark example of what can be required to win a war. In 1864, as the war was dragging on in endless, bloody battle, the Northern general William Tecumseh Sherman helped end it with a devastating campaign against Georgia's civilian population. After burning the city of Atlanta, Sherman's army ravaged much of the rest of Georgia by burning estates; taking food and livestock; and destroying warehouses, crops, and railway lines. These actions had the effect not only of disrupting the supply of provisions to Lee's army in Virginia, but also (and more importantly) of making the war real to the civilian population that was supporting it from the rear. This, in turn, broke the spirit of the men on the front lines, who were now worried and demoralized by what was happening to their homes and families.

In both World War II and the Civil War, once massive defeats were handed to the enemy, the causes that drove the military threats were thoroughly defeated as political forces. There are no threatening Nazis or Japanese imperialists today, nor was there any significant political force agitating for the reemergence of the slave South after the Civil War.

To have decisively defeated Islamic totalitarianism post-9/11, America would have had to both correctly identify the enemy and show the same unmitigated willingness to defeat its identified enemies as it had in past wars. In the weeks after 9/11, the American people, for their part, seemed willing to do whatever was necessary to prevent another 9/11. And throughout the

Arab and Muslim world, many feared that they would be made to pay for the aggression of their nations. An expert on the Middle East reports that although 9/11 was greeted by much celebration by civilians in the Muslim world, many feared "that an angry America might crush them. . . . Palestinian warlords referred to the events as Al Nakhba—'the disaster'—and from Gaza to Baghdad the order spread that victory parties must be out of sight of cameras and that any inflammatory footage must be seized."[3] But the fear of our enemies in the Middle East quickly disappeared once it became clear that few, if any, of them would pay for the atrocities of 9/11.

Observe that nearly five years after the terrorist attacks of 9/11—longer than it took to defeat the far more powerful Japanese after Pearl Harbor—the two leading supporters of Islamic totalitarianism and the majority of their accessories remain intact and visibly operative. Iran is aggressively pursuing nuclear weapons, led by a president who declares that our ally Israel must be "wiped off the map," and by mullahs who lead the nation in weekly chants of "Death to America." Abroad, Iran's terrorist agents kill American troops in Iraq, while its propagandists attempt to push Iraq into an Islamic theocracy. Saudi Arabia continues to fund schools and institutions around the world that preach hatred of America and advocate Islamic totalitarianism. Syria remains the headquarters of numerous terrorist organizations and an active supporter of the Iraqi insurgency that is killing American troops. The Palestinian Authority continues a terrorist jihad initiated by Yasir Arafat—a jihad that can be expected only to escalate under the entity's new leadership by the Islamic totalitarian group Hamas. Throughout the Arab-Islamic world, "spiritual leaders" and state-owned presses ceaselessly incite attacks against the West without fear of reprisal.

America has done nothing to end the threat posed by Iran and Saudi Arabia, nor by Syria and the Palestinian Authority. In the rare cases that it has taken any action toward these regimes, its action has been some form of appeasement: extending them invitations to join an "anti-terrorism" coalition (while excluding Israel); responding to the Palestinians' jihad with a promised Palestinian state; declaring "eternal friendship" with Saudi Arabia and inviting its leaders to vacation with our president; responding to Iran's active pursuit of nuclear weapons with the "threat" of possible, eventual, inspections by the U.N.

Of course, America has done something militarily in response to 9/11; it has taken military action against two regimes: the Taliban in Afghanistan and Saddam Hussein's Iraq. But in addition to these not having been the two most important regimes to target, our military campaigns in each case have drastically departed from the successful wars of the past in their logic, aims, methods—and in their results. In Afghanistan, we gave the Taliban advance notice of military action, refused to bomb many top leaders out of their hideouts for fear of civilian casualties, and allowed many key leaders to escape in the Battle of Tora Bora. And in Iraq, we have done far worse. While we have taken Saddam Hussein out of power, we have neither eradicated the remnants of his Baathist regime, nor defeated the insurgency that has arisen, nor taken any serious precaution against the rise of a Shiite theocracy that would be a far more effective abettor of Islamic totalitarianism than Saddam Hussein ever was.

In terms of ending the (limited) threat posed to America by the respective countries, the "war" in Afghanistan was a partial failure, and the "war" in Iraq is a total failure. Our leadership, however, evaluates these endeavors not primarily in terms of whether they end threats and dissuade other hostile regimes from continuing aggression, but in terms of whether they bestow the "good life" on the Middle Eastern peoples by ridding them of unpopular dictators and allowing them to vote in whatever government they choose (no matter how anti-American). This objective is presently consuming endless resources and thousands of American lives in Iraq, where we are sustaining a hostile Iraqi population until they can independently run their new nation—in which Islam is constitutionally the basic law of the land.

How is all of this supposed to fulfill our leaders' pledge to defend America? The democratically elected Iraqi government, we are told, will somehow lead to a renaissance of "freedom" in the Middle East, which will somehow stop terrorism in some distant future. In the meantime, we are told, we should show "resolve," take off our shoes at the airport, and pay attention to the color-coded terror alerts so we can know how likely we are to be slaughtered.

Empty talk of "complete victory" notwithstanding, our official foreign policy regarding America's security against Islamic terrorism is: accepted defeat. We have not been willing to take military action against the most important threats against us, and the type of military action we have been willing to take has not succeeded in making us safer. And most disturbing of all, despite our travesty of a foreign policy, the vast majority of once-enraged Americans has not demanded anything better. Most Americans acknowledge that Iraq is a debacle, that we will not be safe anytime soon, and that we have no plans to deal effectively with threats such as Iran's nuclear weapons program—yet there is widespread resignation that this is the best we can do. *This*—in response to a threat caused by pip-squeak nations, against the most powerful military in history.

Why? What explains the defeatism of the leaders and citizens of the most powerful nation on earth?

One crucial factor is the failure of our intellectual and political leadership to clearly identify the nature of our enemy, to recognize that terrorism stems from a religious ideological movement that seeks our destruction and that that movement is widely supported by Muslim peoples and states.

One intellectual motivation for this evasion is the doctrine of multiculturalism, which holds that all cultures are equal, and thus that it is immoral for Western culture to declare itself superior to any other. Having swallowed this doctrine, most of our intellectuals and politicians are reluctant to identify a clearly evil, militant ideological movement as an aspect of Arab-Islamic culture or to acknowledge its widespread support in that culture.

An even more significant motivation is the religiosity of many Americans (especially conservatives). While the militant methods of Islamic totalitarianism are anathema to religious Americans, the ethical prescriptions of the movement—a life of faith, material renunciation, and sacrifice for a "higher" cause—are consistent with everything religious Americans hold as ideal. These Americans are thus reluctant to indict such ideas as the cause of a massive evil and, instead, are drawn to the theory that our enemy is confined to isolated individuals such as Osama bin Laden, Saddam Hussein, and a few crazy followers. Our leaders go even further; not only are they reluctant to indict Islamic ideas, they bend over backward to claim that no truly Islamic movement can be responsible for terrorism because "Islam is peace." Islamic terrorists, they claim, have "hijacked a great religion."

America's intellectual failure to identify the nature of the enemy is a major cause of its defeatism—but this failure, and its responsibility for our policies, only goes so far. For example, none of our politicians identify our enemy as "Islamic totalitarianism"; however, they all know and admit that Iran and Syria are active sponsors of terrorism, that Iran is developing missiles and a nuclear weapon, that Saudi Arabia turns out legions of wannabe terrorists, and many other facts pointing to the conclusion that if we are to be safe, these states must be stopped. Shortly after 9/11, President Bush demonstrated some understanding of the role of state support of terrorism when he declared: "From this day forward, any nation that continues to harbor or support terrorism will be regarded by the United States as a hostile regime." Despite his misgivings about indicting any variant of any religion, he has condemned "Islamic Radicalism" as a major source of the terrorist threat.

If America were to take military action to end the threats we face, even based on our leaders' limited understanding of these threats, it would be far more significant and effective than what we have done so far. Why, then, haven't our leaders taken such actions?

The reason is that, despite their claims that they will do whatever is necessary to defend America, our leaders believe that it would be wrong—*morally wrong*—to do so. They believe this because they consistently accept a certain moral theory of war—one that has come to be universally taught in our universities and war colleges. This theory is accepted, at least implicitly, not only by intellectuals, but by our politicians, the leadership of our military, and the media. And while the American people are not explicitly familiar with this theory, they regard the precepts on which it is based and the policies to which it leads as morally uncontroversial. The theory is called Just War Theory. To understand today's disastrous policies, and to reverse them, it is essential to understand what this theory holds.

"Just War Theory"

Consider the following passages from the book *Just and Unjust Wars* by Michael Walzer:

> A soldier must take careful aim *at* his military target and *away from* nonmilitary targets. He can only shoot if he has a reasonably clear shot; he can only attack if a direct attack is possible . . . he cannot kill civilians simply because he finds them between himself and his enemies.[4]

> Simply not to intend the deaths of civilians is too easy. . . . What we look for . . . is some sign of a positive commitment to save civilian lives. . . . if saving civilian lives means risking soldiers' lives the risk must be accepted.[5]

Walzer's prescriptions are not the idle musings of an ivory tower philosopher; they are exactly the sort of "rules of engagement" under which U.S. soldiers are fighting—and dying—overseas. When our Marines in Baghdad do not shoot back when fired upon from a mosque, or when our helicopter pilots are shot down while flying too low in an attempt to avoid civilian casualties while in pursuit of their targets, they are following the dictum that we should show a "positive commitment to save civilian lives" even if this entails "risking soldiers' lives."

Just and Unjust Wars serves as the major textbook in the ethics classes taught at West Point and dozens of others colleges and military schools. More broadly, Just War Theory—for which *Just and Unjust Wars* is the most popular modern text—is the sole moral theory of war taught today.

Just War Theory is conventionally advocated in contrast to two other views of the morality of war: pacifism and "realism." Pacifism holds that the use of military force is never moral. Just War theorists correctly criticize this view on the grounds that evil aggressors exist who seek to kill and dominate the innocent, and that force is often the only effective way to stop them. War, they hold, is therefore sometimes morally necessary.

"Realism" is the view that war has no moral limitations. Just War Theory rejects this theory as well, holding that war, when necessary, must be conducted in accordance with strict moral principles. Since "realism" renounces morality, Just War theorists observe, its advocates cannot in principle oppose wars or acts of war in which the guilty unjustly kill the innocent. More broadly, Just War theorists argue, "realism" is deficient because it denies the need to think carefully about the moral issues raised by war. Given that, in wartime, thousands or millions of lives hang in the balance—given that war is a major undertaking with the potential to do massive good or massive evil—we are obligated to consider the important, and non-obvious, moral questions that war raises. These questions include: Under what circumstances should a nation go to war? And: What should a nation's policies be toward the soldiers and civilians of enemy nations?

These questions, Just War theorists argue, must be thought about systematically, in advance of any particular war, so that we can do the right thing when the circumstances arise. These are not questions to be answered by the seat of our president's pants, in response to the international or domestic whim of the moment. To act in such a way, they say, would be an injustice to all those who are sent to war, and especially to those whose lives are ended because of it.

All of these arguments against pacifism and "realism"—and for systematic analysis of the morality of war—are valid. They lend credence to the claim that Just War Theory is a practical and moral theory of war. But an investigation of Just War Theory—and its consistent practice in our so-called "war on terror"—demonstrates that it is neither practical nor moral. To the extent that Just War Theory is followed, it is a prescription for suicide for innocent nations, and thus a profoundly unjust code.

All forms of Just War Theory provide guidelines that fall into two categories: justice in entering a war, and justice in waging a war. (These two categories are known as *jus ad bellum*, and *jus in bello*, respectively.) Broadly speaking, Just War Theory holds that a nation can go to war only in response to the impetus of a "just cause," with force as a "last resort," after all other non-military options have been considered and tried—with its decision to go to war motivated by "good intentions," with the aim of bringing about a "good outcome." And it holds that a nation must wage war only by means that are "proportional" to the ends it seeks, and while practicing "discrimination" between combatants and non-combatants. Finally, in a requirement that applies to both categories, Just War Theory holds that the decision-making power for when, why, and how to wage war—including the declaration of war—must rest with a "legitimate authority."

By themselves, these guidelines—"good intentions," "just cause," "last resort," "proportionality," "discrimination," and "legitimate authority"—are highly ambiguous. Their meaning and interpretation depend on the view of the "just," the "good," and the "legitimate" presupposed by Just War Theory—that is, the theory's *basic view of morality*. Although advocates of Just War Theory differ on many specifics about the nature of morality, they all hold one fundamental idea in common. To zero in on this idea, let us turn to the origins of Just War Theory: the writings of the Christian theologian Saint Augustine on the proper use of violence by individuals.

In his work, Augustine asked whether a Christian can ever justify killing another, given the Biblical imperative to "turn the other cheek." Augustine's answer was this: One can use force, not to protect oneself, but to protect one's neighbor. As the scholar Jean Elshtain, author of the highly regarded book *Just War Against Terror*, explains:

> For early Christians like Augustine, killing to defend oneself alone was not enjoined: It is better to suffer harm than to inflict it. But the obligation of charity obliges one to move in another direction: To save the lives of others, it may be necessary to imperil and even take the lives of their tormenters.[6]

Thus, according to Augustine, if only *you* are attacked, you are obligated to turn the other cheek and die, because personal self-defense is immoral; only if someone attacks your neighbor's cheek are you permitted to retaliate.

Augustine's theory is not about justice in the sense of the innocent defending their lives against the guilty. In Augustine's view, the guiding purpose and standard for the just use of force by individuals—trumping guilt or innocence—is that it must be an act of selfless service to others.

All of which boils down to this: One's life is not an end in itself, to be defended righteously for its own sake—but a means to some "higher" end, to be sacrificed or preserved as is required by one's moral duty to serve others. This is a perfectly consistent expression of the present-day morality of *altruism*.

"Altruism" literally means "other-ism"; it holds that one should live one's life in selfless service to the needs of others, with sacrifice for their sake as the highest virtue. To act for one's own sake, according to altruism, is immoral (or, at best, amoral). The morality of altruism is descended from Christianity but is accepted today in various forms by both the religious and the non-religious. While consistent adherence to altruism is widely recognized as impractical, altruism is nevertheless almost universally upheld as the moral ideal, and almost never challenged. Observe that while few seek to live a Mother Theresa-like life, no one questions that her life was a moral archetype.

Augustine did not write systematically about the application to war of his altruistic, Christian views on the use of violence, though he did apply these views to strongly endorse the practice of fighting wars to relieve suffering and spread Christianity to other nations. After Augustine, other Christian theologians greatly expanded Just War Theory (as it later came to be known). Eventually, it was developed by both religious and secular philosophers, and adopted in various forms by groups as disparate as Christians and atheists, by self-proclaimed "hawks" and borderline pacifists, by moral absolutists and moral relativists. The most significant development in Just War Theory since Augustine's time is that the theory has come to include an endorsement of what it calls a "right to self-defense." But because Just War Theory has maintained its Augustinian, altruistic roots, its alleged "right" to self-defense turns out to be no such thing.

Let us explore in detail the meaning and consequences of the guidelines of Just War Theory, focusing on their employment in America's "war on terror." Consider first the requirement that a nation go to war only in response to a "just cause." What constitutes a "just cause" for war? The classic "just cause" that led Augustine to sanction war, and that Just War theorists have endorsed ever since, is a "humanitarian crisis": a situation in which a foreign people is suffering from aggression or oppression or genocide. Walzer goes so far as to say that "the chief dilemma of international politics is whether people in danger should be rescued by military forces from outside."[7] Many Just War theorists hold that the sacrifice of American soldiers and American wealth for "peacekeeping" and "humanitarian" missions (where no threat to the U.S. is at stake)—such as in Sudan, Kosovo, Bosnia, Rwanda, and Somalia—is *morally mandatory.*

Where in such "just causes" is the justice for the innocent, hardworking individuals who are forced to fund this "humanitarianism," let alone for those who *die* in such missions? The "justice" is to be found in Just War Theory's *standard of justice*: the altruistic notion that justice means selfless service to the needs of others. In practice this means that the world's "haves" (the productive, the virtuous, the happy) are to sacrifice for the sake of the world's "have-nots." American soldiers, in this view, should not fight for themselves and their freedom; they should fight to serve anyone who needs them.

Given that Just War Theory regards individuals, not as ends in themselves, but as means to the ends of others, what is its view of the right to *self*-defense, that is, the right of a people to defend its own lives and freedom, not for the sake of a "humanitarian" cause, but for its *own* sake?

While in name Just War Theory claims to uphold a right to self-defense, in substance it denies this right. Self-defense, the theory holds, is a "just cause" for war. This means that if the people of a nation are suffering aggression, oppression, or genocide, and are themselves capable of stopping it, they are morally entitled to respond militarily. But—and this is the crucial part—only under strict conditions. Aggression from another nation is a "just cause," according to Just War Theory, but only as a "last resort"—and only if the decision to go to war is motivated by "good intentions." (These qualifications apply to "humanitarian" "just causes" as well, but we will focus on their application to alleged wars of self-defense).

Let us first examine the requirement that war must be a "last resort." This restriction is often portrayed as a sensible policy that simply entails taking the act of going to war seriously, rather than going to war willy-nilly. But, in fact, war as a "last resort" goes far beyond forbidding wars of whim or aggression; it means that a nation cannot go to war immediately even when there is an objective threat—that is, when another nation has shown the willingness to initiate aggression against it. Because the use of military force involves the harming of others, Just War Theory holds, every other conceivable avenue short of using military force must be tried: appeasement, U.N. resolutions, being persuaded by the crocodile tears of enemy leaders, and anything else that pacifists (or U.N. ambassadors) can muster.

What is an innocent nation to do when it knows of a threat that, if left unaddressed, could result in a catastrophic attack on it at some point in the future—such as the knowledge possessed by the U.S. of Iran, a nation that sponsors terrorism, spreads Islamic totalitarianism, develops nuclear weapons, has attacked U.S. interests in the past, and promises the eventual destruction of America? Such projections are dismissed by Just War theorists as merely hypothetical ("How can we know what the future will hold?"). Projections of future attacks, they hold, are tainted by self-serving motives—that is, too much concern for one's own life and liberty, too little concern with the consequences of war on others (such as the Iranians)—and thus morally out of the question as a cause for action. For example, in 2002, Walzer told the New York Times: "we don't have to wait to be attacked; that's true. But you do have to wait until you are about to be attacked."[8]

The requirement that war be a "last resort" is inimical to the requirements of self-defense, which demand that serious threats be stopped as soon as possible. Observe that evil nations and movements do not commit major atrocities out of the blue; they need time to build their forces, gain converts, extract concessions, and win small victories; they need to convince themselves and their followers that they have a chance of success. The earlier their intended victims retaliate, the less damage the thugs can do, and the easier it is to dispose of them.

Consider Germany in the 1930s. Hitler, who had stated publicly his intentions for domination of Europe and the world, was an objective threat to his neighbors. He was a threat as soon as he came to power, and then increasingly so as he built up a military, explicitly rejecting existing treaties with England and France. Yet these nations took no military action against his regime. Then Germany annexed Austria, and was met with no military response. When Nazi troops occupied the Rhineland (a disputed area on the border with France), they were given a pass. When Hitler asked the European leaders to hand him the free state of Czechoslovakia, they did. It took the invasion of Poland to prompt the European nations to take military action against the Nazis. They practiced war as a "last resort"; and we know the result.

Or consider the rise of Islamic totalitarianism. In 1979, a new Iranian regime founded on Islamic totalitarian principles held fifty-two Americans hostage for 444 days, while America helplessly begged for their return and Iranian leaders had a world stage to proclaim their superiority to the nation they call the "Great Satan." Not one American died during the hostage-taking—but, with America on her knees, the burgeoning anti-American movement achieved a crucial victory.

What would Just War Theory say about whether this situation warranted a military response? Did it rise to the level of a direct attack sufficient to place us at the point of "last resort" with Iran and other nations that sponsor Islamic terrorism? Not according to Jimmy Carter. What about after 241 Marines were killed in Lebanon in 1983? Not according to Ronald Reagan. Or after Khomeini's fatwa offered terrorists a bounty to destroy writer Salman Rushdie and his American publisher for expressing an "un-Islamic" viewpoint in 1989? Not according to George H. W. Bush. Or after the first World Trade Center bombing in 1993? Not according to Bill Clinton. The pattern is telling.

Since there is no definable threshold at which to declare something a "last resort," the threshold tends to default to some kind of a range-of-the-moment, perceptual-level event, such as a massive, direct attack by an enemy nation (e.g., 9/11). Until then, Just War theorists and their pacifist spiritual brothers can always concoct new schemes for appeasement, or new fantasies that the enemy has reformed, or new rationalizations that their aggression is our fault—and thus claim that to wage war would be immoral. By the time war becomes a "last resort," an innocent nation has endured far more risk, fear, and destruction than was necessary—and will have to endure far more in order to defeat a long-appeased and thus more powerful enemy. "Self-defense" as a "last resort" is not self-defense.

Further undermining the self-defense of an innocent nation is the requirement of Just War Theory that the decision to go to war be motivated by "good intentions"—that is, seeking a "good outcome." This requirement, by naming the motive and purpose of war, goes to the heart of what Just War Theory means and demands.

What does "good" mean here? It means "altruistic."

According to Just War Theory, it is wrong for a nation to be exclusively concerned with its own well-being in deciding whether to go to war; it must demonstrate concern for the well-being of the world as a whole—including the well-being of the nation it is attacking. Only such a concern will yield a "good outcome"—that is, an altruistic outcome.

Insofar as it constitutes "good intentions" for any part of a mission to be devoted to a nation's own defense, it is justified as altruistic: by the "sacrifices" that leaders and especially soldiers make to "serve their country"—a country that is defended as an altruistic one. For example, when President Bush discussed why America is a country worth defending, he emphasized our charity, our service to other nations, the religiosity of many Americans, and so on. He did not emphasize the fact that we devote our lives to making money and pursuing happiness.

In implementing Just War Theory, the less a nation is concerned with the well-being of its own citizens, and the more it is concerned with that of others, the more it proves its "good intentions." The more it seems to be going to war for the sake of its own citizens, the more suspect its motives. Observe this at work in the two wars our government has entered since 9/11: the wars in Afghanistan and Iraq.

The impetus for both wars, especially in Afghanistan, was clearly the events of September 11 and the realization of the extent of the terrorist threat to America. But observe that while President Bush said that America has a right to defend itself, he did not consider the elimination of the threat posed by these countries to be a sufficient justification for war in either case. In both wars, he defended his actions, not just as a response to the threat of terrorists to America, but as a response to their threat to the "world." Bush supplemented the alleged self-defense portions of each mission with massive campaigns to relieve Afghan and Iraqi suffering—suffering that constituted uncontroversially "just causes." And in the case of the war in Iraq, he made a crucial component of his justification the goal of preserving the "integrity" of the U.N. (an organization whose myriad dictators are committed opponents of American interests), whose resolutions Saddam had violated.

In the buildup to the war in Iraq, President Bush was especially concerned with giving the mission an altruistic purpose. He sought to justify the self-defense aspect of the war on the grounds of preemption, an idea controversial among commentators, politicians, and Just War theorists. Thus, President Bush made sure to focus, above all, on the goal of freeing the Iraqi people of a tyrant and showering them with food, collectively owned oil, and "democracy." The name of the war, "Operation Iraqi Freedom," perfectly reflects Bush's moral priorities.

As an expert who is sympathetic to Just War Theory wrote in the *Claremont Review of Books*:

> In the run-up to Operation Iraqi Freedom, to have listened to President Bush, or to his principal civilian and military advisors, was to learn how profoundly just-war thinking has influenced the leadership of the world's most powerful nation. One may of course disagree with their conclusions, but one has to be impressed by the evident care they took to provide moral justification for their actions. Measured by any objective standard, Operation Iraqi Freedom plausibly met all the criteria for just war.[9]

Whenever President Bush wanted to defend the morality of the wars we have fought, he insisted that we fight for reasons "larger than our nation's defense." When Bush referred to our "good intentions" in Iraq, as he frequently did, he spoke not of our intention to defend ourselves, but of the intentions of American citizens to pay and of American soldiers to die so that Iraqis can hold a mob vote.

An injunction to go to war with altruistic intentions, seeking an altruistic outcome, is in direct contradiction to the requirements of self-defense; it forbids the very essence of self-defense in the context of war: identifying and defeating enemy nations.

To identify a nation as an enemy is to recognize it as a committed initiator of force that threatens one's own life, that forfeits its right to exist, and that in justice deserves whatever is necessary to end the threat it poses. By Just War Theory's moral standards, however, *there is no such thing as an enemy nation*. Even when a nation initiates aggression, it is not regarded as the proper object of retaliation, but as a haven of "others" to be served. (This notion is, unsurprisingly, rooted in Augustine's religion, Christianity, which countenances us to love everyone—especially, as proof of extreme virtue, to "love thine enemy.")

Observe that America has not gone to war with one *nation* since September 11. In each war, President Bush has made clear that we are in Afghanistan or Iraq to aid the "Afghan people" or the "Iraqi people," and that we oppose only their current leaders. In the case of Iraq, he has made the well-being of the Iraqis, including the satisfaction of their religious and political desires, the overriding purpose of the war.

Given that the purpose of war, according to Just War Theory, is the well-being of others (including those who are, in fact, one's enemies), it is logical that Just War Theory also precludes a nation from waging war in a manner that will destroy its enemies. It is imperative, according to Just War Theory, that war be fought by unselfish, sacrificial means, in which great value is accorded to the citizens of enemy nations. This is the meaning of the requirements of "proportionality" and "discrimination." *Proportionality* is the idea that the value gained by the ends a war seeks must be "proportional" to the damage incurred during the war. To advocate that ends and damage be "proportional" presupposes a standard of value by which these are to be weighed. What is the relative weight, for example, that the U.S. government should accord an American civilian and an Iraqi civilian? Since Just War Theory holds that a government's intentions are "good" to the extent that it places value on other peoples, including enemies, by its standard of value a government of an innocent nation should place equal value on the lives of its citizens and those of enemy nations. On this view, in America's "war on terror," we have to "balance" the lives of American soldiers and civilians with the lives of the enemy nation's soldiers and civilians. According to Walzer, "In our judgments of the fighting, we abstract from all consideration of the justice of the cause. We do this because the moral status of individual soldiers on both sides is very much the same. . . . [T]hey face one another as moral equals."[9]

This is what our present and future military leaders are learning at West Point. They are being taught that no matter the cause of war, they are risking their lives to fight and kill their moral equals—that they must regard protecting the life of a fellow soldier as morally equivalent with saving the life of the enemy.

———◆———

The requirement of "proportionality" is one reason why we did not do any damage to the infrastructure of Iraq or Afghanistan, so as not to inflict "disproportionate" suffering on the people. And it is probably the reason that the promised "shock and awe" bombing of Iraq never materialized. Proportionality means that in fighting a war we cannot conduct ourselves in a way that hastens victory or that minimizes our casualties.

The requirement of "proportionality," as bad as it is, is made even worse by the requirement of "discrimination," which is a clarification on the value a government is to accord various types of people under "proportionality." The requirement of "discrimination" holds that a nation defending itself must differentiate between combatants and noncombatants, valuing noncombatants more highly by providing them with "immunity." Just War Theory regards all noncombatants as "innocents" with "rights" to be respected. We must, on this view, make every effort to avoid killing noncombatants—a category Elshtain defines as "women, children, the aged and infirm, all unarmed persons going about daily lives, and prisoners of war."[10] To those who would reject such imperatives in order to defend one's own people, Elshtain replies: "The demands of proportionality and discrimination are strenuous and cannot be alternatively satisfied or ignored, depending on whether they serve one's war aims."[11]

Observe the inversion of justice here. Benevolent, individualistic, life-loving Americans, and death-worshipping, collectivist, nihilistic Arabs—such as the dancing Arabs who celebrated 9/11—are regarded as equally worthy of protection by the American military. The exception is if the American is a soldier and the Arab is a civilian, in which case the Arab's life is of *greater* value.

The requirements of "proportionality" and "discrimination" are deadly to the nation that takes them seriously. A nation fully committed to defending itself must value the lives of its citizens more than the lives of its enemy's citizens; it must be morally confident in its goodness, in its right to exist, and of the rightness of killing whomever in enemy nations it must to preserve the lives and liberty of its citizens. Self-defense may well require killing more of the enemy's citizens than the enemy has killed of ours. It is commonly necessary in war to break the spirit of a foreign people whose nation has initiated aggression in which they are complicit. This often requires killing civilians, and in some cases even targeting them, as America did in World War II. These actions were regarded as just by leaders who viewed civilians of enemy nations as part of the national war machine and rarely truly innocent—and who viewed any deaths of actual innocents, including children, as wholly the moral responsibility of the nation that initiated war.

Just War Theory forbids such tactics. A nation with "good intentions," practicing "proportionality" and "discrimination," cannot possibly raze a city as Sherman did. This is why, although Sherman's actions helped to end the Civil War, he is a reviled figure among Just War theorists: His goal was to preserve his side by inflicting unbearable misery on its enemy's civilian population—the opposite of "good intentions." Many Just War theorists hold—as by their standard they are obliged to hold—that the dropping of atomic bombs on Hiroshima and Nagasaki in 1945 was immoral. America, they claim, should have valued Japanese civilians over the hundreds of thousands of GIs who would have died invading Japan.

In Afghanistan and Iraq, we see the consequences of not being led by a Sherman-like policy. Our policy of dropping food packages in Afghanistan gained us the scorn of our enemy, who was often the beneficiary of these gifts. Our declared purpose of helping the Afghan people provided security for Osama bin Laden, his deputies, and his Taliban supporters; they knew that we would be reluctant to bomb them out of their hideouts for fear of killing the Afghans we were there to serve.

In Iraq, since our declared purpose is the well-being and happiness of Iraqi citizens, the countless hostile Iraqis feel free to condemn our troops, to incite violence against them, and to provide refuge to insurgents. President Bush has stressed that we did not go to war *against* Iraq (only against Saddam), but *for* the Iraqi people. Thus, we did not make it a priority to defeat them. Almost daily in Iraq, our troops risk their lives because of rules of engagement that place the lives of Iraqi civilians above their own. This was evident in our withdrawal from Falluja in 2004 when we feared civilian casualties, and in the fact that when we returned to Falluja in 2005 we allowed tens of thousands of people, including thousands of insurgents, to leave the town before the battle began. Indeed, from the first bombing, the war has been conducted in a way so as to minimize Iraqi casualties, and at almost any cost. Is it any wonder that an insurgency arose? Is it any wonder that leaders and citizens of other terrorist nations feel no real pressure to stop threatening America?

In the "war on terror," the U.S. is following the pronouncements of Just War Theory in regard to civilians with incredible dedication, and has received much acclaim among Just War theorists for doing so. In Elshtain's evaluation of the war in Afghanistan, she writes:

> The United States must do everything to minimize civilian deaths—and it is doing so. . . . The United States must investigate every incident in which civilians are killed—and it is doing so. The United States must make some sort of recompense for unintended civilian casualties, and it may be making plans to do so—an unusual, even unheard of, act in wartime.[12]

She adds:

> It is fair to say that in Afghanistan the U.S. military is doing its best to respond proportionately. If it were not, the infrastructure of civilian life in that country would have been devastated completely, and it is not. Instead, schools are opening, women are returning to work, movie theaters are filled to capacity, and people can once again listen to music and dance at weddings.[13]

What she does not mention—but what must never be forgotten—is the price that has been paid for such supposedly "just" conduct. That price is the hundreds of heroic American men and women who have been killed so that Afghans and Iraqis may live and their mosques may stand (to say nothing of whatever unknown price the rest of us will pay when the undefeated enemy next attacks America).

The final Just War requirement that we will discuss is the mandate that the decision-maker who chooses both when and how to go to war must be a "legitimate authority." Historically, this has been a minor restriction, meaning simply that a government (not a private militia or gang) should declare war. In recent decades, however, it has become a major restriction, because Just War theorists regard a "legitimate" authority as one who will ensure that force is used with "good intentions," that is, unselfishly. For example, many Just War theorists have come to hold that a war is invalid unless authorized and supervised by the U.N. And even those who do not regard U.N. approval as strictly necessary, such as President Bush, value the approval of other nations as evidence of lack of selfishness. Observe Bush's frantic desire to make an Iraq mission that was suitable to the U.N. and then, failing that, to assemble any and every insignificant nation into a "coalition of the willing."

Self-defense requires that a nation assess, independently and objectively, by the standard of the lives of its own citizens, what to do. To subordinate that to a coalition or to Kofi Annan—for the reason that they are not concerned with our interests—is unjust and suicidal.

In the "war on terror," America has taken self-destructive action after self-destructive action in the name of winning over the U.N. and "coalition partners." America's missions in Afghanistan and Iraq were stymied by the vetoes of such so-called allies as the Saudis (who denied us use of aircraft landing strips) and of other nations (who urged us to limit the number of ground troops in Afghanistan), forcing us to rely on duplicitous warlords who connived in the escape of Al Qaeda and the Taliban. As a result of Bush's submission to "legitimate authorities," we have sacrificed victory.

All of the requirements of Just War Theory help to explain why the Bush administration had felt justified in going to war only in Afghanistan and Iraq—and only then with major "humanitarian" purposes in each mission, which failed to eliminate the threats posed by the nations.

Just War Theory has also had a major influence in determining the wars our government does *not* think it is justified to fight. President Bush had taken no military action whatsoever against Iran, none against Saudi Arabia, none against Syria. President Bush was not ignorant of these threats—he was well aware of the fact that these countries sponsor terrorism; in the case of Iran and Syria, he had said so repeatedly. But he had done nothing militarily to stop the threats these countries posed, nor was there any indication he would do so. Instead, he continued to engage in "diplomatic" bribery, nudging the U.N., inviting terrorist nations into "anti-terrorism" coalitions, and other completely ineffective—indeed, self-destructive—moves.

As discussed earlier, our improper identification of the enemy, motivated by multiculturalism and religion, has played a major part in our misselection of targets. Additionally, the altruistic war in Iraq has so discredited the idea of military action, by fatally engaging our troops for no clear purpose and with no clear standard of victory, that few Americans want to go to war again. But another major reason why we are reluctant to target our major enemies today—and why we did not target them from the outset—is that they do not meet Just War Theory's qualifications for military action.

Of course, from a self-defense standpoint, Iran was and is the most important regime to defeat—much more so than Iraq. But under Just War criteria, the case for war with Iran would be almost impossible to make, whereas the case for war with Iraq was relatively simple. Iran was not ruled by a universally accepted "monster"; Iraq was. The "will of the Iranian people" had not been obviously thwarted; the "will of the Iraqis" had been. Iran had not violated nearly two dozen U.N. resolutions; Iraq had. The Iranian people had not been subject to mass slaughter; the Iraqis had. These considerations, while nearly irrelevant in terms of self-defense, are decisive by the criteria of Just War Theory.

What about the fact that Iran is the spiritual fatherland of the ideology driving Islamic terrorists? Or the fact that the "will of the Iranian people" largely supports the deadly ideology that seeks the extermination of the West? Or the fact that Iran is developing a nuclear arsenal? Or the fact that Iran has sponsored terrorist attacks on Americans abroad on numerous occasions in the past? According to Just War Theory, so long as Iran has not yet unleashed a devastating, direct attack against us, and so long as there is no altruistic emergency, these facts do not justify military action or the threat of military action; at most, they are justification for endless "diplomacy" or a request for a U.N. resolution. In an interview in 2004, Bush said: "We'll continue pressing [Iran] diplomatically. . . . Diplomacy failed for 11 years in Iraq . . . and this new diplomatic effort [in Iran started] barely a year ago."[14] Could anything be more encouraging for the nations and groups seeking to wage a long-term battle against the West?

In the case of our refusal to take or threaten military action against the leading sponsors of Islamic terrorism, we see the true meaning of the restrictions of Just War Theory regarding when a nation can go to war, and how it must fight. A nation that will go to war only as a "last resort," in response to a "just cause," with "good intentions"—and once it goes, employ "proportionality" and "discrimination"—is a nation that will endure unnecessary risks and even mass death before going to war. And even if it goes to war, it will fight with both hands tied behind its back.

Just War Theory, to summarize, is the application of the morality of altruism to war. It holds that the citizens of an innocent nation are not ends in themselves, but means to some "higher" end. In today's version, it claims that the citizens of an innocent nation can "defend" themselves—as a means to realizing the goal of sacrificing themselves to the needs of others (including those who are in fact their enemies). This is not a right to self-defense, but a "duty" to practice altruism.

To the extent that Just War Theory is practiced, it leads to unnecessary fear, suffering, and death visited on innocent nations—and to the rise of evil movements and regimes—all while it claims to be virtuous and practical.

Because it purports to support self-defense while actually forbidding its preconditions, Just War Theory is uniquely dangerous. Unlike pacifism, it is eminently plausible to today's Americans. Americans will not accept *en masse* a theory that explicitly forbids them self-defense against their evil enemies. But they will accept a theory that claims to endorse both self-defense and the altruistic morality that they have grown up believing is the ideal. They do not realize that it is either-or.

What, in fact, happens to policies that could potentially lead to self-defense, such as giving every state sponsor of Islamic terrorism an ultimatum to cease and desist, or else? The altruism underlying Just War Theory makes our leaders morally rule out such policies without consideration. And then, whatever course of action they do consider and pursue, they portray as in America's self-defense and self-interest.

The ultimate embodiment of Just War Theory and its embrace of self-destructive policies under the partial cloak of self-defense was the overall foreign policy of President Bush: the "Forward Strategy of Freedom." This strategy was the Bush administration's policy of spreading "democracy" throughout the Middle East and other backward areas. The first major step of this strategy is the establishment of a "free Iraq," which allegedly will be an inspirational "beacon of freedom" for the rest of the Middle East and inspire them toward "democratic reform."

These are goals that Just War Theory would applaud; they embody "good intentions" (i.e., altruistic intentions) in our foreign policy and in our choice of wars. True to the popular advocacy of Just War Theory, however, President

Bush did not frame the Forward Strategy of Freedom as good only on altruistic grounds; if he did, the American people would not tolerate it (nor would he). He argued that this strategy was the one that will best serve America, that by encouraging the "liberation" of oppressed nations we promote our own security. For example, in his State of the Union Address in 2005, Bush proclaimed: "The survival of liberty in our land increasingly depends on the success of liberty in other lands. The best hope for peace in our world is the expansion of freedom in all the world."

Why is the Forward Strategy of Freedom our "best hope"? Because, as Bush and others pointed out, free nations do not initiate aggression (including terrorism), whereas unfree ones do. So a "free," "democratic" Middle East promotes our self-defense.

In analyzing whether this policy is in fact in America's self-defense, let us leave aside for a moment its massive evasions about what freedom is and requires—the fact that *freedom* (i.e., individual liberty) and *democracy* (i.e., unlimited majority rule over the individual) are entirely different and incompatible things, the second being an enemy of the first. Even assuming that our leaders had any idea what freedom is, and how to most efficiently establish it, would this be a policy in America's self-defense?

Absolutely not. The one half-truth in the argument for the Forward Strategy of Freedom is that truly free nations do not initiate aggression against other nations. But so what? There are dozens of statist nations that do not threaten America, either, because they fear us or have no ideological interest in fighting us.

The question of what is in America's self-defense comes down to: What is the best way to make other nations *non-threatening* as quickly as possible? To consider this question objectively, one must be willing to consider *all* our options, including: quickly deposing terrorist and especially Islamic totalitarian regimes, threatening the inhabitants with retribution if they threaten America again, and then moving on to ending support of terrorism by other regimes. Given the options available to us, it is inconceivable that the best strategy is to spend endless military resources to set up a "democracy" in Iraq, and then pray that every terrorist nation decides to adopt a free, constitutional government. To make the Middle East even semi-free would cost a tremendous amount of time, money, and American lives. Given the options available to us, the Forward Strategy of Freedom is entirely self-sacrificial. But because the Bush administration had morally ruled out a true strategy of self-defense, it could delude itself into believing that, as its members repeatedly told us, it was doing "everything possible" to protect us.

Because Just War Theory removes from the table the possibility of forthrightly defeating our enemies, its advocates must concoct bizarrely indirect means of stopping them (*bizarre* is the only adjective that does justice to a policy of hinging American security on the similarities between today's Iraqis and Jefferson-era Americans). Observe that in Bush's policy the "liberation" of Iraq was not seen as part of defeating that country, but as *replacing* the necessity of defeating it. And the magical inspiration it is supposed to provide to Iran, Syria, Saudi Arabia, and so on, will allegedly replace the necessity of militarily confronting those nations. Since Bush felt morally unwilling to defeat our enemies, he regarded it as necessary to delegate that task to their subservient and sympathetic populations. Instead of making us more secure, this policy has inspired the Iraqi insurgency, made Iran and Saudi Arabia feel more confident than ever, and may well allow the Iraqi people to eventually vote their country into an Islamic dictatorship akin to Iran. (Given the big victories by religious Shiite politicians in Iraqi elections so far, they are well on their way.) And because our failure to defeat our enemies only contributes to the success of Islamic totalitarianism, our support for elections in the Middle East foretells that Islamic totalitarians will "democratically" be given greater influence; we have already seen increases in the political influence of even more committed supporters of Islamic totalitarians in Saudi Arabia, of Hezbollah in Lebanon, of the Muslim Brotherhood in Egypt, and of Hamas in the Palestinian Authority.

To call this a policy of American self-interest or American self-defense is to invert the meaning of these concepts. This is a policy of American self-destruction, and it is made possible by a theory that morally rules out self-defense while claiming to support it.

The president's version of Just War Theory is not the only one; there are many different varieties of the theory, and their various advocates emphasize and interpret the rules differently. Some, such as the Pope, are borderline pacifists and emphasize the "last resort" rule. Others, under the influence of multiculturalism, believe that most "peacekeeping" missions are wrong, not because they are sacrificial, but because one should not "impose" one's definition of a better life on a foreign people.

But such disagreements are ultimately insignificant as far as America's self-defense is concerned, because none challenges the theory's basic altruist premises. Observe that the media, Democrats, and intellectuals did not criticize the Bush administration for its failure to smash the insurgency in Iraq or for doing nothing to fight the threat posed by Iran. Most criticisms of Bush amounted to him not being altruistic enough. They accused him of "rushing" to war despite the desires of other nations; they tallied civilian casualties; they fixated on humiliated prisoners of war; they treated any deficiency in Afghan or Iraqi standards of living as a moral travesty on the part of America. Thus, the competing proponents of Just War Theory differ with the Bush administration not on *whether* America's security should be sacrificed for the sake of others, but only on *how*.

Just War Theory, in the final analysis, is anti-self-defense and anti-justice. By preaching self-sacrifice to the needs of others, Just War Theory has led to the sacrifice of the civilized for the sake of the barbarous, the sacrifice of victims of aggression for the sake of its perpetrators, the sacrifice of noble Americans for the sake of ignoble Iraqis—the sacrifice of the greatest nation in history for the sake of the worst nations today.

The Morality of Victory

In terms of fundamentals, Just War Theory is completely unopposed by any other theory of war today.

For those concerned about self-defense, the alleged alternative to Just War Theory is "realism": the idea that there is no connection between morality and war. "Realists" hold that war should be entered into and fought according to strictly "practical" considerations. But this position is not a viable alternative to Just War Theory. First, as Just War theorists rightly point out, "realism" evades the fact that war is an act of monumental moral significance, and by treating it otherwise one sanctions truly horrific things, such as wars of aggression. Second, the dictum that one must evaluate war according to simply "practical" considerations is intellectually empty, since *there is no such thing as practicality detached from morality*.

Any claim that a course of action is "practical" presupposes some basic end that the course of action achieves. For example, any claim that "diplomacy" with Iran is practical, or that an ultimatum against Iran is practical, or that sending a nuclear warhead to Iran is practical, presupposes some basic goal that it will achieve—whether that goal be the approval of others, or the "stability" of the Middle East, or winning "hearts and minds," or eliminating the Iranian threat. The question of what basic ends one should pursue in war is inescapable to the issue of practicality—and it is a *moral* question.

Because "realism" rejects the need for moral evaluation, and because the need for moral evaluation cannot be escaped, its advocates necessarily take certain goals for granted as "obviously" practical. Which goals? Those widely seen as valid—that is, the goals of altruism.

Consider the case of former secretary of state Colin Powell, a prominent "realist." Does he call for America's unequivocal, uncompromising self-defense using its full military might, since that would be eminently practical in achieving America's self-interest? No. Instead, when he ran the State Department, he sought to avoid war, to appease any and every enemy, to court "world opinion," to build coalitions, to avoid civilian casualties—while at the same time somehow to protect America. In other words, he did everything that pacifism and Just War Theory would have him do.[15] While Powell and his ilk may say that they eschew moral analysis in matters of foreign policy and war, altruism nevertheless shapes what they think and seek to do.

"Realism," therefore, is no antidote to Just War Theory. It is not even a theory of war but an intellectual parasite that camouflages the destructive nature of altruism with a professed concern for "practicality." To bury the moral issues involved in war for the sake of "practicality" does not erase them; rather, it serves to entrench the status quo, by offering covert altruism as the only alternative to overt altruism.

There is no escape from morality, and no reconciling self-defense with the morality of altruism. To escape from the destructiveness of Just War Theory, therefore, we must embrace a moral approach to war that rejects altruism and fully upholds self-defense, thus providing the moral foundation for free, innocent nations to secure the lives and liberty of their citizens in the face of aggression.

Such a moral foundation exists in the morality of rational self-interest (also known as rational egoism or rational selfishness), the code of ethics originated by philosopher Ayn Rand.

Rational self-interest holds that every individual ought to live his own life for his own sake, by his own independent effort—without sacrificing himself to others or others to himself. It holds that the individual's self-interest is achieved, not by doing whatever he feels like doing, and not by placing his goals in opposition to his neighbors' freedom, but by living a life of reason, productivity, and trade.

According to rational egoism, the greatest threat a rational man faces to the achievement of his goals—and the greatest threat to a harmonious, prosperous, free society—is the initiation of physical force by others. In justice, when someone initiates force against an innocent man—whether by violence, theft, or fraud—the initiator of force deserves to be met with retaliatory force.

In the egoistic approach, the need for individuals to be free from the initiation of force necessitates the existence of governments—and the option of war. A proper government places the retaliatory use of force under principled, objective control. A proper government is founded on the principle of individual rights—the rights to life, liberty, property, and the pursuit of happiness. These rights sanction the individual's freedom of action; they recognize the right of every individual to pursue his own goals by his own judgment: to produce, trade, speak, write, love, and live as he chooses, free of the threat of force. A proper government is the agent and servant of its citizens. It exists only to protect their rights by forbidding the initiation of force and by retaliating against those who initiate it—whether the aggressor is a criminal at home or a nation abroad.

Like an innocent individual, an innocent nation does not seek to exist at the expense of other nations, by force. But once force is initiated against it and its citizens, it must respond righteously with force; anything else is an injustice toward its citizens and an abdication of its moral purpose: to protect their rights.

Once the basic egoist view of morality and government is understood, the egoist view of war follows readily: The sole moral purpose of war is the same as the sole moral purpose of any other action by a proper government—that is, to protect the individual rights of its citizens. Every moral issue pertaining to war must be judged by this standard—and *only* by this standard.

Achieving the purpose of "self-defense" means the *complete restoration of the protection of individual rights* and thus the complete return to normal life, achieved by the permanent elimination of the threat. This is the only proper meaning of "complete victory." Defeat in the war with Islamic totalitarianism does not simply mean that America becomes an Islamic theocracy or that our soldiers fight battles in the streets of Atlanta; these prospects are, fortunately, extremely unlikely. Defeat means any enduring negative change to the American way of life as the result of an active enemy, such as the colored alerts, or the provisions of the Patriot Act that allow virtually anyone to be investigated as a terrorist subject, or the random airport searches suffered by innocent travelers.

The "self" in "self-defense" includes not just a nation's civilians, but also its soldiers. Contrary to the policies of the Bush administration, American soldiers are not sacrificial animals, but full citizens of the United States. Rational soldiers are motivated by their own values, by their own desire to live free of the threat of violence against themselves and their loved ones. The fact that a soldier chooses a risky profession does not make him any less entitled to every protection his government can provide. To send soldiers into battle, as we have done in Iraq, with rules of engagement that place the lives of Iraqis above their own, is a moral crime.

By the standard of individual rights, a nation can morally go to war *only* for the purpose of self-defense, and can morally do in war only what is necessary for that purpose. Both wars of self-sacrifice ("humanitarian" wars) and wars of aggression—and acts of self-sacrifice or aggression within war—violate the rights of citizens, especially of soldiers. Both entail forcibly sacrificing the lives and money of individuals for the sake of some "higher" cause—whether relieving the suffering of the Somalis or satisfying the power-lust of a president.

The necessity of war in self-defense arises when a nation is attacked or threatened by a foreign aggressor. In some cases it might be possible to stop such an aggressor through lesser coercive means, such as sanctions or ultimatums. Once it becomes clear that the enemy is undeterred, however, military force is not a "last resort," but the *only* resort.

In response to the Iranian hostage-taking of 1979, for example, America was morally obligated to inflict massive retribution on the Iranian regime immediately. As Ayn Rand said at the time, the proper response to the assault was to "march with force the first or second day after the hostages were taken."[16] For America to do anything less in such a situation is to capitulate to the aggressors and to abdicate its moral responsibility to its citizens. America did something less and is still paying the price.

All aggression, including terrorism, is fueled by hope—the hope of success in achieving some irrational goal or furthering some irrational cause. For a nation like the United States to be secure from threats for the long term, its enemies must know that initiating force against it will bring nothing but their own destruction. Supporters of any cause that seeks the destruction of the U.S. must be made to realize that that cause is doomed.

Acts of aggression left unpunished can lead only to further acts of aggression. Appeasing the initiators of force, as we have seen throughout history, leads to more and greater violence. Thus a proper, rights-respecting government does not appease its force-wielding enemies; it acts to eliminate them. Such action, when executed consistently in self-defense, will not only destroy the particular initiator of force; it will also deter other such threats. Indeed, it is America's reputation for appeasement, for being a "paper tiger," that fuels the belief of Islamic totalitarians that they can bring down America.

It is important to note that a proper morality does not require that one be directly attacked in order to retaliate. We need not sit idly by as Iran builds nuclear weapons and missile launchers; we need not wait to respond until they have destroyed an American city. A preemptive strike is justified if the nation involved is an objective threat—that is, if it has shown, in action or in official statements, its willingness to initiate or advocate force against us. For America to identify a nation as an objective threat does not mean to identify exactly when or how that threat will materialize (that is impossible); rather, it means to identify that a nation or regime has the will and means to attack or support an attack against the United States. A nation that threatens innocent nations thereby forfeits its right to exist and deserves whatever consequences innocent nations visit on it. There is an analogy here to domestic criminals. When a government establishes that a man is making death threats against his wife, or has hatched a plot to kill her, it properly throws him in jail—it does not wait until her corpse is found, on the grounds that he might change his mind and not carry out the threat.

To fight and win a proper war of self-defense requires two basic courses of action: (1) objectively identify the nature of the threat and (2) do whatever is necessary to destroy the threat and return to normal life, with minimum loss of life and liberty on the part of the citizens of the defending nation.

The specific identity of any given threat and what is necessary to destroy it is not the province of morality; it requires specialized cultural and military knowledge (whereas morality applies only to the basic principles governing human life). But the morality of rational self-interest provides crucial, principled guidance in identifying and then destroying a threat. It holds that the identification of a threat, just like any identification, can be achieved only by means of a scrupulously rational process—unclouded by considerations such as an unwarranted affinity for religion, or the desire to be liked by foreign leaders, or the dogma that all cultures are equal. As for what to do about any given threat, egoism gives the crucial sanction, in enemy territory, to kill and destroy *whomever and whatever* needs to be killed and destroyed in order to end the threat to the victim country. Such a policy, contrary to Just War Theory, upholds both the principle of justice and the principle of individual rights. Depending on the circumstances, legitimate targets can include the leaders, soldiers, *and civilians* of the enemy nation.

There is a popular notion, held by nearly every advocate of Just War Theory, that only a handful of crazed dictators and bomb-toting terrorists are our enemies; all other residents of the unfortunate, backward states are "innocent" civilians, tragically trapped among these few killers. Accordingly, we must wage war, not against a nation, but against the few evildoers within it, treating the rest of the population with the same respect we accord American citizens. This notion is false and deadly.

As Churchill and General Sherman understood, civilians play a crucial role in sustaining the military aggression of an enemy country, and directly targeting them can save the lives of one's own soldiers and civilians. During the Civil War, the civilian population of the South provided motivation and encouragement for its soldiers, greatly prolonging their willingness to wage war against the North. So long as the civilians were exempted from the direct consequences of their actions, they continued to fuel the war effort of the South, which in turn took thousands upon thousands of northern lives. By directly targeting the civilian population, Sherman was performing an act of moral heroism: fully living up to his responsibility of protecting the citizens of the North.

Now take the case of Islamic terrorism, a threat in which civilians are also a crucial source of spiritual support. Many civilians across the Arab world give terrorists encouragement by worshipping them as heroes. Newspapers in many Arab countries spread anti-Americanism and glorify the martyrdom of the terrorists. Clerics promise terrorists a glorious afterlife. *Madrassas* indoctrinate students with Islamic totalitarianism. Even civilians who do not entirely support the methods of Islamic terrorists are often sympathetic to and encouraging of their goal of Islamic world domination. Enemy civilians are also a crucial source of material support for terrorists; these civilians frequently provide terrorists with hideouts, money, and weapons. Rich statesmen pay large bounties to the families of suicide bombers.

Most civilians of oppressive regimes do nothing to oppose or resist or change their governments. This passivity does not render them innocent; it renders them accomplices to the evils of their regimes. This passivity is one of the major factors enabling these regimes to commit atrocities against innocents at home and abroad. Unless oppressed civilians take active steps to object to the evil ways of their government, or to go underground, they are morally responsible for the actions of their government. (The positive or negative consequences of the actions one's government performs in one's name is one reason why being active in regard to politics, especially intellectually active in this realm, is a selfish obligation.)

"Individual citizens in a country that goes to war," Ayn Rand once said in response to a question on this topic,

> are responsible for that war. This is why they should be interested in politics and careful about not having the wrong kind of government. If in this context one could make a distinction between the actions of a government and the actions of individual citizens, why would we need politics at all? All governments would be on one side, doing something among themselves, while we private citizens would go along in happy, idyllic tribalism. But that picture is false. We are responsible for the government we have, and that is why it is important to take the science of politics very seriously. If we become a dictatorship, and a freer country attacks us, it would be their right.[17]

To summarize: The civilian population of an aggressor nation is not some separate entity unrelated to its government. An act of war is the act of a *nation*—an interconnected political, cultural, economic, and geographical unity. Whenever a nation initiates aggression against us, including by supporting anti-American terrorist groups and militant causes, it has forfeited its right to exist, and we have a right to do whatever is necessary to end the threat it poses.

Given that a nation's civilian population is a crucial, physically and spiritually indispensable part of its initiation of force—of its violation of the rights of a victim nation—it is a morally legitimate target of the retaliation of a victim nation. Any alleged imperative to spare noncombatants *as such* is unjust and deadly.

That said, if it is possible to isolate innocent individuals—such as dissidents, freedom fighters, and children—without military cost, they should not be killed; it is unjust and against one's rational self-interest to senselessly kill the innocent; it is good to have more rational, pro-America people in the world. Rational, selfish soldiers do not desire mindless destruction of anyone, let alone innocents; they are willing to kill only because they desire freedom and realize that it requires using force against those who initiate force. Insofar as the innocents cannot be isolated in the achievement of our military objectives, however, sparing their lives means sacrificing our own; and although the loss of their lives is unfortunate, we should kill them without hesitation.

Any true freedom fighter caught in America's fire understands the nature of the situation his nation has put us in, supports our cause, hopes for the best, and blames his government and fellow citizens for the danger he is placed in. He recognizes the principle that any innocent deaths in war are the sole moral responsibility of the aggressor nation.

Doing whatever is necessary in war means doing *whatever* is necessary. Once the facts are rationally evaluated, if it is found that using tactical nuclear weapons against Iran's nuclear facilities or flattening Falluja to end the Iraqi insurgency will save American lives, then these actions are morally mandatory, and to refrain from taking them is morally evil.

To close our discussion of a self-interested, truly just approach to war, let us apply it to two issues that have been extremely prominent in the ongoing war in Iraq: the proper treatment of POWs, and when and how we should occupy a foreign people, including the issue of whether we should establish a free or semi-free society in an occupied country.

Let us begin with POWs. How should POWs be treated? Given the purpose of war, the answer must be: in a way that protects the individual rights of one's citizens. It is often the case that it is in one's interest to treat POWs well, because this will encourage enemy soldiers to surrender rather than fight to the death. If more enemy troops surrender, fewer of one's own troops will die. In a situation where POWs are no threat, treating them well is in one's self-interest—and treating them badly or killing them is sadistic and self-destructive. However, treating prisoners well does not make sense if, for example, they are hampering one's efforts to win, or if they are refusing to divulge vital information that could save the lives of one's own troops. If humiliation or torture is an effective method of extracting information that would save American lives, we should humiliate or torture prisoners as necessary.

Of course, if a POW is truly innocent—that is, a genuine opponent of his regime who was forced to fight for it—he will eagerly provide the victim nation with all the information to which he is privy; no torture will be necessary. Thus, torture is potentially necessary only for the guilty. Those who wish to hide information that could protect the lives and rights of Americans in the name of fidelity to the triumph of Islam have forfeited all rights and deserve any form of abuse that can possibly be used to extract information.

Whether and under what conditions torture is practical is a specialized military question. The moral point is: If and to the extent torture is an effective technique to save American lives, and it is used on those who are initiating force against us, then it is morally obligatory. The idea, prevalent in Washington and in the halls of academia, that it is wrong and inhumane to torture Al Qaeda operatives scheming to kill Americans is suicidal. To not do whatever is necessary to extract information from the inhuman monsters that plan the mass murder of Americans is a horrific violation of the moral purpose of government, which is to protect the lives of its citizens.

Terrorists caught on the battlefield are not innocent until proven guilty; they are by that fact proven guilty of pursuing the deaths of Americans. Just as it is legitimate to kill them in the battlefield, so it is legitimate to use whatever force is necessary on them in an effort to achieve victory once they are caught.

The question of occupation—when one should occupy a country, and what one's goal should be in occupying it—properly arises only *after* the nation in question has been defeated. If a nation has not been defeated, it cannot be successfully occupied.

Once an aggressor country is defeated, there is a legitimate question of what the victor should do. There are numerous options, ranging from letting the most powerful domestic faction take over (with the knowledge that any aggression against America will lead to the same fate as the predecessor), to handing over the reins to a friendly strongman or tribe, to making a serious effort to establish a proper, free society.

There is only one standard by which to properly evaluate the situation and choose between these options: What is the least expensive, most effective way to ensure America's long-term security—that is, to protect the individual rights of Americans? Again, much of this depends on specialized questions of military strategy and the cultural-political conditions of the defeated country. But such a strategy can be properly formulated only if the strategists recognize that the freedom of an enemy country is *at most* a means to an end for the innocent nation, *never* an end in itself.

In the event that the establishment of a proper government is in America's self-defense, every aspect of setting up that government must be governed by that purpose. If we are risking American lives and spending billions of dollars, we must do everything possible to ensure that the new government is non-threatening, if not a staunch ally.

The egoist approach to war—that is, the *genuinely* just war theory—is completely at odds with Bush's Forward Strategy of Freedom, which, aside from rejecting the need to defeat our enemies, lets hostile Middle East mobs choose whatever government they wish. When Bush was asked whether he would accept an Iran-style Islamic Republic in Iraq—after some 2,000 American lives had been lost and some 200 billion dollars spent—he said he would, because "democracy is democracy."[18] Democracy *is* democracy—that is, democracy is mob rule, which is precisely why it must be rejected in any proper occupation. (When a population has proven itself to be non-threatening to America, it should be given the power to vote, but only in the selection of leaders, not the content of the constitution.) Note that in Japan, General Douglas MacArthur did not ask the Japanese to write a constitution but forced a constitution written by Americans onto the Japanese. Both America and Japan have benefited from this for sixty years.

If, during the course of an occupation, a major insurgency arises against the occupier, then a state of war has resumed—and the insurgency should then be crushed by any means necessary, just like the government that preceded it. But if a war has been fought properly, with the enemy seeing the futility of his ways and offering his unconditional surrender, such an insurgency is very unlikely. The insurgency in Iraq is made possible by President Bush's failure to actually defeat that nation. If we had fought the war properly from the outset, the thought of an insurgency would be terrifying both to today's insurgents and to the many civilians that support and protect them. Contrast the fiasco in Iraq today to the occupation of Japan after World War II—in which zero Americans were killed by insurgents.

Conclusion

When Ayn Rand wrote about the moral code she originated, the code of rational self-interest, she stressed that morality is a matter of life and death. The right ethics, she held, lead to individual (and societal) survival, prosperity, happiness; the wrong ethics leads to misery, poverty, death.

This is true in every field but is especially true in the realm of war, as the present struggle has made clear. We are losing the war on Islamic totalitarianism because our leadership, political and military, is crippled by the morality of altruism, embodied in the tenets of Just War Theory. The moral code inherent in Just War Theory defines rules that undercut, inhibit, and subvert any hope of success in war, because it demands that one regard one's own life as the sacrificial object of others. The moral code of rational self-interest, by contrast, defines principles to attain the values that one's life and happiness require—including success in war and national self-defense. Altruism is the morality of defeat, and rational self-interest is the morality of victory.

America faces a choice between two irreconcilable foes: self-defense or altruism—which are but forms of the basic choice we all face: life or death. Let us choose life.[19]

CHAPTER FIVE

Neoconservative Foreign Policy: An Autopsy

Yaron Brook and Alex Epstein

The Rise and Fall of the Neoconservative Foreign Policy

When asked during the 2000 presidential campaign about his foreign policy convictions, George W. Bush said that a president's "guiding question" should be: "What's in the best interests of the United States? What's in the best interests of our people?"[1]

A president focused on American interests, he made clear, would not risk troops' lives in "nation-building" missions overseas:

> I don't think our troops ought to be used for what's called nation-building. I think our troops ought to be used to fight and win war. I think our troops ought to be used to help overthrow the dictator when it's in our best interests. But in [Somalia] it was a nation-building exercise, and same with Haiti. I wouldn't have supported either.[2]

In denouncing "nation-building" Bush was in line with a long-standing animus of Americans against using our military to try to fix the endless problems of other nations. But at the same time, he was going against a major contingent of conservatives, the *neoconservatives*, who had long been arguing for more, not less, nation-building.

By 2003, though, George W. Bush had adopted the neoconservatives' position. He sent the American military to war in Iraq, not simply to "overthrow the dictator," but to build the primitive, tribal nation of Iraq into a "democratic," peaceful, and prosperous one. This "Operation Iraqi Freedom," he explained, was only the first step of a larger "forward strategy of freedom" whose ultimate goal was "the end of tyranny in our world"[3]—a prescription for *worldwide* nation-building. All of this, he stressed, was necessary for America's "national interest."

President Bush's profound shift in foreign policy views reflected the profound impact that 9/11 had on him and on the American public at large.

Before 9/11, Americans were basically satisfied with the existing foreign policy. They had little desire to make any significant changes, and certainly not in the direction of more nation-building. The status quo seemed to be working; Americans seemed basically safe. The Soviet Union had fallen, and America was the world's lone superpower. To be sure, we faced occasional aggression, including Islamic terrorist attacks against Americans overseas—but these were not large enough or close enough for most to lose sleep over, let alone demand fundamental changes in foreign policy.

Everything changed on that Tuesday morning when nineteen members of a terrorist network centered in Afghanistan slaughtered thousands of Americans in the name of an Islamic totalitarian movement supported by states throughout the Arab-Islamic world. What once seemed like a safe world was now obviously fraught with danger. And what once seemed like an appropriate foreign policy toward terrorism and its state supporters was now obviously incapable of protecting America. Prior to 9/11, terrorism was treated primarily as a problem of isolated gangs roaming the earth, to be combated by police investigations of the particular participants in any given attack; our leaders turned a blind eye to the ideology driving the terrorists and to the indispensable role of state support for international terrorist groups. State sponsors of terrorism were treated as respected members of the "international community," and, to the extent their aggression was acknowledged, it was dealt with via "diplomacy," a euphemism for inaction and appeasement. Diplomacy had been the dominant response in 1979, when a new Islamist Iranian regime supported a 444-day hostage-taking of fifty Americans—as part of an Islamic totalitarian movement openly committed to achieving Islamic world domination, including the destruction of Israel and America. Diplomacy had been the response when the terrorist agents of Arab-Islamic regimes killed Marines in Lebanon in 1983—and bombed a TWA flight in 1986—and bombed the World Trade Center in 1993—and bombed the Khobar towers in 1996—and bombed the U.S. embassies in Kenya and Tanzania in 1998—and bombed the USS *Cole* in 2000. Diplomacy had also been the response when Iran issued a death decree on a British author for "un-Islamic" writings, threatening American bookstores and publishers associated with him, and thus denying Americans their sacred right to free speech. Throughout all of this, Americans had accepted that our leaders knew what they were doing with regard to protecting America from terrorism and other threats. On 9/11, Americans saw with brutal clarity that our actions had been somewhere between shortsighted and blind. The country and its president were ripe for a dramatic departure from the policies that had guided and failed America pre-9/11.

The only prominent group of intellectuals that offered a seemingly compelling alternative claiming to protect America in the modern, dangerous world (a standard by which neither pacifists nor Buchananite xenophobes qualify) were *neoconservatives*.

Neoconservatives had long been critics of America's pre-9/11 foreign policy, the technical name for which is "realism." "Realism" holds that all nations are, in one form or another, "rational" actors that pursue common interests such as money, power, and prestige. Given such common goals among nations, "realists" hold, no matter what another nation's statements or actions toward the United States, there is always a chance for a diplomatic deal in which both sides make concessions; any other nation will be "rational" and realize that an all-out military conflict with superpower America is not in its interest. Thus, America's pursuing its "national interest" means a constant diplomatic game of toothless resolutions, amorphous "pressure," and dressed-up bribery to keep the world's assorted threatening nations in line. The only time "realists" are willing to abandon this game in favor of using genuine military force against threatening regimes is in the face of some catastrophic attack. Otherwise, they regard it as not in our "national interest" to deal with other nations by military means. Why take such a drastic step when a successful deal may be just around the corner?

In the 1980s and 1990s, as "realism" dominated foreign policy, neoconservatives criticized it for having a false view of regimes, and a "narrow," shortsighted view of the "national interest" in which only tangible, immediate threats to American security warranted military action. They rightly pointed out that "realism" was a shortsighted prescription for long-range disaster—a policy of inaction and appeasement in the face of very real threats, and thus a guarantor that those threats would grow bolder and stronger. A neoconservative essay published in 2000 expresses this viewpoint:

> The United States, both at the level of elite opinion and popular sentiment, appears to have become the Alfred E. Newman of superpowers—its national motto: "What, me worry?" . . . [T]here is today a "present danger." It has no name. It is not to be found in any single strategic adversary. . . . Our present danger is one of declining military strength, flagging will and confusion about our role in the world. It is a danger, to be sure, of our own devising. Yet, if neglected, it is likely to yield very real external dangers, as threatening in their way as the Soviet Union was a quarter century ago.[4]

In place of "realism," neoconservatives advocated a policy often called "interventionism," one component of which calls for America to work assertively to overthrow threatening regimes and to replace them with peaceful "democracies." Bad regimes, they asserted vaguely, were responsible for threats like terrorism; such threats could never emerge from "democracies." "Interventionism," they said, took a "broad" and ultimately more realistic view of America's "national interest," by dealing with threats before they metastasized into catastrophes and by actively replacing threatening governments with "democracies" that would become our allies. In place of a series of "realist" responses to the crisis of the moment, they claimed, they were offering a long-range *foreign policy* to protect America now and in the future.

After 9/11, the neoconservatives felt intellectually vindicated, and they argued for "interventionism" with regard to state sponsors of terrorism. An editorial in the leading neoconservative publication, the *Weekly Standard*, called for a "war to replace the government of each nation on earth that allows terrorists to live and operate within its borders."[5] The replacement governments would be "democracies" that would allegedly ensure that new threatening regimes would not take the place of old ones.

These ideas exerted a major influence on President Bush immediately after 9/11, an influence that grew over the years. On September 20, 2001, influenced by neoconservative colleagues and speechwriters, he proclaimed a desire to end state sponsorship of terrorism:

> Every nation, in every region, now has a decision to make: either you are with us, or you are with the terrorists. . . . From this day forward, any nation that continues to harbor or support terrorism will be regarded by the United States as a hostile regime.[6]

His neoconservative deputy secretary of defense, Paul Wolfowitz, publicly called for "ending states who sponsor terrorism"[7] (though the "realists" in the State Department caused the administration to partially recant).

Soon thereafter, President Bush made clear that he wanted to replace the state sponsors of terrorism with "democracies," beginning with Afghanistan. When he dropped bombs on that country, he supplemented them with food packages and a tripling of foreign aid; he declared the Afghan people America's "friend" and said that we would "liberate" them and help them establish a "democracy" to replace the terrorist-sponsoring Taliban.

The full influence of neoconservatism was evident by the time of the Iraq War. Prior to 9/11, the idea of democratic "regime change" in Iraq with the ultimate aim of "spreading democracy" throughout the Arab-Islamic world was unpopular outside neoconservative circles—dismissed as a "nation-building" boondoggle waiting to happen. After 9/11, George W. Bush became convinced—and convinced Americans—that such a quest was utterly necessary in today's dangerous world, and that it could and would succeed. "Iraqi democracy will succeed," he said in 2003, "and that success will send forth the news, from Damascus to Tehran—that freedom can be the future of every nation. The establishment of a free Iraq at the heart of the Middle East will be a watershed event in the global democratic revolution."[8]

Thus, the neoconservative foreign policy of "regime change" and "spreading democracy" had become the American foreign policy—and the hope of Americans for protecting the nation.

As neoconservative columnist Charles Krauthammer wrote in 2005:

> What neoconservatives have long been advocating is now being articulated and practiced at the highest levels of government by a war cabinet composed of individuals who, coming from a very different place, have joined . . . the neoconservative camp and are carrying the neoconservative idea throughout the world.[9]

At first, Operation Iraqi Freedom—and thus our new neoconservative foreign policy—seemed to most observers to be a success. The basic expectation of the war's architects had been that by ousting a tyrant, "liberating" Iraqis, and allowing them to set up a "democracy" in Iraq, we would at once be deterring future threats from Iran and Syria, setting up a friendly, allied regime in Iraq, and empowering pro-American influences throughout the Middle East. And when the American military easily took Baghdad, when we witnessed Kodak moments of grateful Iraqis hugging American soldiers or razing a statue of Saddam Hussein, when President Bush declared "major combat operations in Iraq have ended,"[10] neoconservatives in particular thought that everything was working. Their feeling of triumph was captured on the back page of the *Weekly Standard* on April 21, 2003, in which the magazine parodied prominent Iraq War critics by printing a fake apology admitting that their opposition to Operation Iraqi Freedom reflected stupidity and ignorance. "We're Idiots. We Admit It," the parody read. "We, the Undersigned, Agree that We Got this Whole War in Iraq Business Spectacularly Wrong. We didn't see that it was a war of liberation, not a war of colonization. . . . We thought the Iraqi people would resent American troops. We thought the war would drag on and on. . . . We wanted to preserve the status quo."[11] Future cover stories of the *Weekly Standard* featured inspiring titles such as "Victory: The Restoration of American Awe and the Opening of the Arab Mind" and "The Commander: How Tommy Franks Won the Iraq War."[12]

But the luster of the Iraq War quickly wore off as American troops faced an insurgency that the Bush team had not anticipated; it turned out that many of the lovable, freedom-loving Iraqis we had heard about prewar were in fact recalcitrant, dictatorship-seeking Iraqis. Still, even through 2005, many viewed the Iraq War as a partial success due to the capture of Saddam Hussein and such alleged milestones as a "transfer of power" in 2004, an election and the passage of a constitution in January 2005, and a ratified constitution in December 2005—events that were heralded even by many of the president's most dependable critics, such as the *New York Times*.

But, by mid-2007, the Iraq War was rightly regarded by most as a disaster that utterly failed to live up to its promise. The Bush-neoconservative vision of deterred enemies, a friendly Iraq, and the inspiration of potential allies around the world has not materialized. Instead, for the price of more than 3,200 American soldiers, and counting, we have gotten an Iraq in a state of civil war whose government (to the extent it has one) follows a constitution avowedly ruled by Islamic law and is allied with Iran; more-confident, less-deterred regimes in Iran and Syria; and the increasing power and prestige of Islamic totalitarians around the world: in Egypt, in the Palestinian territories, in Saudi Arabia, in Lebanon. And all of this from a policy that was supposed to provide us with a clear-eyed, farsighted view of our "national interest"—as against the blindness and short-range mentality of our former "realist" policies.

How have we managed to fail so spectacularly to secure our interests in the perfect neoconservative war? The state of affairs it has brought about is so bad, so much worse than anticipated, that it cannot be explained by particular personalities (such as Bush or Rumsfeld) or particular strategic decisions (such as insufficient troop levels). Such a failure can be explained only by *fundamental* flaws in the policy.

On this count, most of the president's critics and critics of neoconservatism heartily agree; however, their identification of neoconservatism's fundamental problems has been abysmal. The criticism is dominated by the formerly discredited "realists," who argue that the Iraq War demonstrates that "war is not the answer" to our problems—that the United States was too "unilateralist," "arrogant," "militaristic"—and that we must revert to more "diplomacy" to deal with today's threats. Thus, in response to Iran's ongoing support of terrorism and pursuit of nuclear weapons, to North Korea's nuclear tests, to Saudi Arabia's ongoing financing of Islamic totalitarianism—they counsel more "diplomacy," "negotiations," and "multilateralism." In other words, we should attempt to appease the aggressors who threaten us with bribes that reward their aggression, and we should allow our foreign policy to be dictated by the anti-Americans at the United Nations. These are the exact same policies that did absolutely nothing to prevent 9/11 or to thwart the many threats we face today.

If these are the lessons we draw from the failure of neoconservatism, we will be no better off without that policy than with it. It is imperative, then, that we gain a genuine understanding of neoconservatism's failure to protect American interests. Providing this understanding is the purpose of this essay. In our view, the basic reason for neoconservatism's failure to protect America is that neoconservatism, despite its claims, is fundamentally opposed to America's true national interest.

What Is the "National Interest"?

When most Americans hear the term "national interest" in foreign policy discussions, they think of our government protecting our lives, liberty, and property from foreign aggressors, today and in the future. Thus, when neoconservatives use the term "national interest," most Americans assume that they mean the protection of American lives and rights. But this assumption is wrong. To neoconservatives, the "national interest" means something entirely different than the protection of American individual rights. To understand what, we must look to the intellectual origins of the neoconservative movement.

The movement of "neoconservatives" (a term initially used by one of its critics) began as a group of disillusioned leftist-socialist intellectuals. Among them were Irving Kristol, the widely-acknowledged "godfather" of neoconservatism and founder of the influential journals *The Public Interest* and *The National Interest*; Norman Podhoretz, long-time editor of *Commentary*; Nathan Glazer, a Harvard professor of sociology; and Daniel Bell, another Harvard sociologist.

The cause of the original neoconservatives' disillusionment was the massive failure of socialism worldwide, which had become undeniable by the 1960s, combined with their leftist brethren's response to it.

In the early twentieth century, American leftists were professed idealists. They were true believers in the philosophy of *collectivism*: the idea that the *group* (collective) has supremacy over the individual, both metaphysically and morally—and therefore that the individual must live in service to the collective, sacrificing for "its" sake. Collectivism is the social-political application of the morality of altruism: the idea that individuals have a duty to live a life of selfless service to others. The variety of collectivism that leftists subscribed to was socialism (as against fascism). They sought to convert America into a socialist state in which "scientific" social planners would coercively direct individuals and "redistribute" their property for the "greater good" of the collective. Many leftists believed, in line with socialist theory, that this system would lead to a level of prosperity, harmony, and happiness that the "atomistic," "unplanned" system of capitalism could never approach.

The Left's vision of the flourishing socialist Utopia collapsed as socialist experiment after socialist experiment produced the exact opposite results. Enslaving individuals and seizing their production led to destruction wherever and to whatever extent it was implemented, from the Communist socialism of Soviet Russia and Red China, to the National Socialism (Nazism) of Germany, to the disastrous socialist economics of Great Britain. At this point, as pro-capitalist philosopher Ayn Rand has observed, the Left faced a choice: Either renounce socialism and promote capitalism—or maintain allegiance to socialism, knowing full well what type of consequences it must lead to.

Most leftists chose the second. Knowing that they could no longer promise prosperity and happiness, they embraced an anti-wealth, anti-American, nihilist agenda. Whereas the Old Left had at least ostensibly stood for intellectualism, pro-Americanism, and prosperity-seeking, the New Left exhibited mindless hippiedom, anti-industrialism, environmentalism, naked egalitarianism, and unvarnished hatred of America's military. Despite incontrovertible evidence of the continuous atrocities committed by the Union of Soviet Socialist Republics, American leftists continued to support that regime while denouncing all things American.

The soon-to-be neoconservatives were among the members of the Old Left who opposed the New Left. Irving Kristol and his comrades felt increasingly alienated from their former allies—and from the socialist policies they had once championed. They had come to believe that some variant of a free economy, not a command-and-control socialist state, was necessary for human well-being. And they recognized, by the 1960s, that the Soviet Union was an evil aggressor that threatened civilization and must be fought, at least intellectually if not militarily.

But this "neoconservative" transformation went only so far. Kristol and company's essential criticism of socialism pertained to its *practicality as a political program*; they came to oppose such socialist fixtures as state economic planning, social engineering of individuals into collectivist drones, and totalitarian government. Crucially, though, they did not renounce socialism's *collectivist moral ideal*. They still believed that the individual should be subjugated for the "greater good" of "society" and the state. They just decided that the ideal was best approximated *through* the American political system rather than by overthrowing it.

One might ask how America's form of government can be viewed as conducive to the ideals of thoroughgoing collectivists—given that it was founded on the *individual's* right to life, liberty, and the pursuit of happiness. The answer is that the America neoconservatives embraced was not the individualistic America of the Founding Fathers; it was the collectivist and statist post-New Deal America. This modern American government—which violated individual rights with its social security and welfare programs and its massive regulation of business all in the name of group "rights" and had done so increasingly for decades—was seen by the neoconservatives as a basically good thing that just needed some tweaking in order to achieve the government's moral purpose: "the national interest" (i.e., the alleged good of the collective at the expense of the individual). The neoconservatives saw in modern, welfare-state America the opportunity to achieve collectivist goals without the obvious and bloody failures of avowedly socialist systems.

There was a time in American history when the individualism upon which America was founded was advocated, albeit highly inconsistently, by American conservatives—many of whom called for something of a return to the original American system. (Individualism is the view that in social issues, including politics, the *individual*, not the group, is the important unit.) The best representative of individualism in conservatism in the past fifty years was Barry Goldwater, who wrote: "The legitimate functions of government are actually conducive to freedom. Maintaining internal order, keeping foreign foes at bay, administering justice, removing obstacles to the free interchange of goods—the exercise of these powers makes it possible for men to follow their chosen pursuits with maximum freedom."[13]

The neoconservatives, however, openly regarded an individualistic government as immoral. The "socialist ideal," writes Irving Kristol, is a "*necessary* ideal, offering elements that were wanting in capitalist society—elements indispensable for the preservation, not to say perfection, of our humanity." Socialism, he says, is properly "community-oriented" instead of "individual-oriented"; it encourages individuals to transcend the "vulgar, materialistic, and divisive acquisitiveness that characterized the capitalist type of individual."[14] Criticizing the original American system, Kristol writes: "A society founded solely on 'individual rights' was a society that ultimately deprived men of those virtues which could only exist in a *political community* which is something other than a 'society.'" Such a society, he says, lacked "a sense of distributive justice, a fund of shared moral values, and a common vision of the good life sufficiently attractive and powerful to transcend the knowledge that each individual's life ends only in death."[15]

Translation: Individuals' lives are only truly meaningful if they sacrifice for some collective, "higher" purpose that "transcends" their unimportant, finite selves. That "higher" purpose—not individuals' lives, liberty, and property—is the "national interest."

For traditional socialists, that purpose was the material well-being of the proletariat. But as Kristol's comments demeaning "materialism" indicate, the "higher" purpose of the neoconservatives is more concerned with the alleged moral and spiritual well-being of a nation. (One reason for this difference is that the neoconservatives are strongly influenced by the philosophy of Plato.) In this sense, neoconservatism is more a *nationalist* or *fascist* form of collectivism than socialist.

Ayn Rand highlights this difference between fascism and socialism in her essay "The Fascist New Frontier":

> The basic moral-political principle running through [fascism and socialism] is clear: the subordination and sacrifice of the individual to the collective.
>
> That principle (derived from the ethics of altruism) is the ideological root of all statist systems, in any variation, from welfare statism to a totalitarian dictatorship. . . .
>
> The socialist-communist axis keeps promising to achieve abundance, material comfort and security for its victims, in some indeterminate future. The fascist-Nazi axis scorns material comfort and security, and keeps extolling some undefined sort of spiritual duty, service and conquest. The socialist-communist axis offers its victims an alleged social ideal. The fascist-Nazi axis offers nothing but loose talk about some unspecified form of *racial* or *national* "greatness."[16]

For neoconservatives, such *nationalistic* pursuit of "national greatness" *is* the "national interest"—the interest, not of an individualistic nation whose purpose is to protect the rights of individual citizens, but of an *organic* nation whose "greatness" is found in the subjugation of the individuals it comprises.

Fittingly, during the late 1990s, "national greatness" became the rallying cry of top neoconservatives. In an influential 1997 *Wall Street Journal* op-ed, neoconservatives William Kristol (son of Irving Kristol) and David Brooks called directly for "national greatness conservatism." They criticized "the antigovernment, 'leave us alone' sentiment that was crucial to the Republican victory of 1994. . . . Wishing to be left alone isn't a governing doctrine." (Actually, it was exactly the "governing doctrine" of the Founding Fathers, who risked their lives, fortunes, and families to be left alone by the British, and to establish a government that would leave its citizens alone.) Brooks and Kristol pined for leaders who would call America "forward to a grand destiny."[17]

What kind of "grand destiny"? Brooks explained in an article elaborating on "national greatness."

> It almost doesn't matter what great task government sets for itself, as long as it does some tangible thing with energy and effectiveness. . . . [E]nergetic government is good for its own sake. It raises the sights of the individual. It strengthens common bonds. It boosts national pride. It continues the great national project.[18]

Brooks and Kristol bemoaned America's lack of a task with which to achieve "national greatness." They got it with 9/11, which necessitated that America go to war.

In an individualistic view of the "national interest," a war is a negative necessity; it is something that *gets in the way* of what individuals in a society should be doing: living their lives and pursuing their happiness in freedom. Not so for the neoconservatives.

Consider the following passage from the lead editorial of the neoconservative *Weekly Standard* the week after 9/11, the deadliest foreign attack ever on American soil. Remember how you felt at that time, and how much you wished you could return to the seemingly peaceful state of 9/10, when you read this:

> We have been called out of our trivial concerns. We have resigned our parts in the casual comedy of everyday existence. We live, for the first time since World War II, with a horizon once again. . . . [There now exists] the potential of Americans to join in common purpose—the potential that is the definition of a nation. . . . There is a task to which President Bush should call us . . . [a] long, expensive, and arduous war. . . . It will prove long and difficult. American soldiers will lose their lives in the course of it, and American civilians will suffer hardships. But that . . . is what real war looks like.[19]

Why is the *Weekly Standard* practically celebrating the slaughter of thousands of Americans? Because the slaughter created "the potential of Americans to join in common purpose—the potential that is the definition of a nation." Even if a "long, expensive, and arduous war" were necessary to defeat the enemy that struck on 9/11—and we will argue that it is not—it is profoundly un-American and morally obscene to treat such a war as a positive turn of events because it generates a collective purpose or "horizon." Observe the scorn with which this editorial treats the normal lives of individuals in a free nation. Pursuing our careers and creative projects, making money, participating in rewarding hobbies, enjoying the company of friends, raising beloved children—these are desecrated as "trivial concerns" and "parts in the casual comedy of everyday existence." The editorial makes clear that its signers think the exalted thing in life is "the potential of Americans to join in common purpose"—not the potential of individual Americans to lead their own lives and pursue their own happiness. This is the language of those who believe that each American is merely a cog in some grand collective machine, to be directed or discarded as the goal of "national greatness" dictates.

Americans sacrificing for the "higher" good of the nation and its "greatness" is what the neoconservatives mean by the "national interest." And in foreign policy, this is the sort of "national interest" they strive to achieve.

An Altruistic Nationalism

Today's neoconservative foreign policy has been formulated and advocated mostly by a younger generation of neoconservatives (though supported by much of the old guard) including the likes of William Kristol, Robert Kagan, Max Boot, Joshua Muravchik, and former deputy secretary of defense Paul Wolfowitz. It holds that America's "national interest" in foreign policy is for America to establish and maintain a "democratic international order"[20] that promotes the long-term security and well-being of all the world's peoples.

Neoconservatives, in keeping with their altruist-collectivist ideals, believe that America has no right to conduct its foreign policy for its own sake—that is, to focus its military energies on decisively defeating real threats to its security, and otherwise to stay out of the affairs of other nations. Instead, they believe, America has a "duty" to, as leading neoconservatives William Kristol and Robert Kagan put it, "advance civilization and improve the world's condition."[21] Just as neoconservatives hold that the individual should live in service to the American collective, so they hold that America should live in service to the international collective. And because America is the wealthiest and most powerful of all nations, neoconservatives say, it has the greatest "duty" to serve. In doing its duty to the world, Kristol and Kagan say, America will further its "national greatness," achieving a coveted "place of honor among the world's great powers."[22]

In this view of nationalism and "national greatness," neoconservatives are more consistently altruistic than other nationalists. Most nationalist nations are altruistic in that they believe their individual citizens are inconsequential, and should be sacrificed for the "higher cause" that is the nation. But they are "selfish" with regard to their own nation; they believe that their nation is an end in itself, that it is right to sacrifice other nations to their nation's needs; thus, the expansionist, conquering designs of fascist Italy and Nazi Germany.

The neoconservatives' brand of "nationalism" does not regard America as an end in itself. It believes that America has a duty to better the condition of the rest of the world (i.e., other nations). It is an *altruistic nationalism*.

Neoconservatives do not put it this way; Kristol and Kagan come out for "a nationalism . . . of a uniquely American variety: not an insular, blood-and-soil nationalism, but one that derived its meaning and coherence from being rooted in universal principles first enunciated in the Declaration of Independence."[23]

One might wonder how neoconservatives square their views with the universal principles of the Declaration—which recognize each American's right to live his *own* life and pursue his *own* happiness and which say nothing about a duty to bring the good life to the rest of the world.

Neoconservatives attempt to reconcile the two by holding that freedom is not a right to be enjoyed, but a duty to be given altruistically to those who lack it. They do not mean simply that we must argue for the moral superiority of freedom and tell the Arabs that this is the only proper way for men to live—and mail them a copy of our Constitution for guidance—but that we give up our lives and our freedom to bring them freedom.

Thus, after 9/11, the neoconservatives did not call for doing whatever was necessary to defeat the nations that sponsor terrorism; rather, they championed a welfare war in Iraq to achieve their longtime goal of "Iraqi democracy." Just a few weeks after 9/11, Max Boot wrote:

> This could be the chance . . . to show the Arab people that America is as committed to freedom for them as we were for the people of Eastern Europe. To turn Iraq into a beacon of hope for the oppressed peoples of the Middle East: Now that would be a historic war aim.[24]

For those familiar with the history of the twentieth century, the international collectivist goals of the neoconservative foreign policy should not seem new; they are nearly identical to those of the foreign policy school of which President Woodrow Wilson was the most prominent member, the school known in modern terms as "Liberal Internationalism" or just "Wilsonianism."

According to Wilsonianism, America must not restrict itself to going to war when direct threats exist; it must not "isolate" itself from the rest of the world's troubles, but must instead "engage" itself and work with others to create a world of peace and security—one that alleviates suffering, collectively opposes "rogue nations" that threaten the security of the world as a whole, and brings "democracy" and "self-determination" to various oppressed peoples around the world. It was on this premise that both the League of Nations and its successor, the United Nations, were formed—and on which

America entered World War I ("The world," Wilson said, "must be made safe for democracy").[25]

The Wilsonian-neoconservative view of America's "national interest" is in stark contrast to the traditional, individualistic American view of America's national interest in foreign policy. Angelo Codevilla, an expert on the intellectual history of American foreign policy, summarizes the difference. Before the twentieth century,

> Americans, generally speaking, wished the rest of the world well, demanded that it keep its troubles out of our hemisphere, and hoped that it would learn from us.
>
> By the turn of the twentieth century, however, this hope led some Americans to begin to think of themselves as the world's teachers, its chosen instructors. This twist of the founders' views led to a new and enduring quarrel over American foreign policy—between those who see the forceful safeguarding of our own unique way of life as the purpose of foreign relations, and those who believe that securing the world by improving it is the test of what [Iraqi "democracy" champion] Larry Diamond has called "our purpose and fiber as a nation."[26]

As to *how* to "secure the world by improving it," Wilsonianism and neoconservatism have substantial differences. Wilsonianism favors American subordination to international institutions and "diplomacy," whereas neoconservatism favors American leadership and more often advocates force in conjunction with diplomacy. Traditional Wilsonians are not pacifists (Wilson, after all, brought America into World War I), but they tend to believe that almost all problems can be solved by peaceful "cooperation" among members of world bodies to paper over potential conflicts or "isolate" aggressive nations that go against the "international community." Neoconservatives openly state that their ambitious foreign-policy goals—whether removing a direct threat or stopping a tribal war in a faraway land—require the use of force.

Some neoconservatives, such as Max Boot, embrace the term "Hard Wilsonianism," not only to capture their intense affinity with Woodrow Wilson's liberal international collectivism, but also to highlight their differences in tactics:

> [A] more accurate term [than "neoconservatism"] might be "hard Wilsonianism." Advocates of this view embrace Woodrow Wilson's championing of American ideals but reject his reliance on international organizations and treaties to accomplish our objectives. ("Soft Wilsonians," aka liberals, place their reliance, in Charles Krauthammer's trenchant phrase, on paper, not power.)[27]

Not only must "power, not paper" (to reverse Krauthammer's expression) be used more often in achieving the desired "international order" than Wilsonians think, say neoconservatives, but America must lead that order. It must not subordinate its decision-making authority to an organization such as the U.N., nor cede to other countries the "responsibilities" for solving international problems.

America must lead, they say, because it is both militarily *and* morally the preeminent nation in the world. America, they observe, has on many occasions come to the rescue of other nations, even at its own expense (such as in World War I or Vietnam)—the ultimate proof of altruistic virtue. (According to the neoconservatives, "Americans had nothing to gain from entering Vietnam—not land, not money, not power. . . . [T]he American effort in Vietnam was a product of one of the noblest traits of the American character—altruism in service of principles.")[28] By contrast, they observe, other nations, including many in Europe, have not even shown willingness to defend themselves, let alone others.

The cornerstone policy of the neoconservatives' American-led, "hard" collectivist foreign policy is the U.S.-led military "intervention": using the American military or some military coalition to correct some evil; give "humanitarian" aid; provide "peacekeeping"; and, ideally, enact "regime change" and establish a new, beneficial "democracy" for the formerly oppressed.

Given the desired "international order" and America's "responsibility" to "improve the world's condition," the obligation to "intervene" goes far beyond nations that threaten the United States. And when America *is* "intervening" in a threatening nation, the "intervention" cannot simply defeat the nation and render it non-threatening; it must seek to benefit the nation's inhabitants, preferably by furnishing them with a new "democracy."

Throughout the past decade and a half, neoconservatives have called for major "interventions" in remote tribal wars in Bosnia, Somalia, Kosovo, Darfur, and Liberia—none of which entailed a direct threat to the United States. And when they have called for responses to real threats, their focus has been on "liberating" the Afghans, Iraqis, and Iranians—not on breaking the hostile inhabitants' will to keep supporting and sponsoring Islamist, anti-American causes.

Endorsing this broad mandate for "intervention," William Kristol and Robert Kagan write, in their seminal neoconservative essay "National Interest and Global Responsibility," that America must be "more rather than less inclined to weigh in when crises erupt, and preferably before they erupt"; it must be willing to go to war "even when we cannot prove that a narrowly construed 'vital interest' of the United States is at stake." In other words, to use a common phrase, America must be the "world's policeman"—and not just any policeman, either: It must be a highly active one. In the words of Kristol and Kagan: "America cannot be a reluctant sheriff."[29]

Despite Wilsonianism and "Hard Wilsonianism's" differences, they agree entirely on a key aspect of the means to their goals: Any mission must involve substantial American *sacrifice*—the selfless surrender of American life, liberty, and property for the sake of other nations.

When Woodrow Wilson asked Congress for a declaration of war to enter World War I, he said:

> We have no selfish ends to serve. We desire no conquest, no dominion. We seek no indemnities for ourselves, no material compensation for the sacrifices we shall freely make. We are but one of the champions of the rights of mankind. We shall be satisfied when those rights have been made as secure as the faith and the freedom of nations can make them. . . .
>
> [W]e fight without rancor and without selfish object, seeking nothing for ourselves but what we shall wish to share with all free peoples.[30]

Similarly, President Bush extolled the (alleged) virtue of "sacrifice for the freedom of strangers" in his decision to invade Iraq. Later that year, in a landmark speech at the National Endowment for Democracy, Bush said:

> Are the peoples of the Middle East somehow beyond the reach of liberty? Are millions of men and women and children condemned by history or culture to live in despotism?. . . I, for one, do not believe it. I believe every person has the ability and the right to be free. . . . Securing democracy in Iraq is the work of many hands. American and coalition forces are sacrificing for the peace of Iraq.[31]

Why must America "sacrifice for the freedom of strangers"? By what right do the problems of barbarians overseas exert a claim on the life of an American twenty-year-old, whose life may be extinguished just as it is beginning?

Both neoconservatives and Wilsonians have a dual answer: It is *morally right* and *practically necessary* for America to sacrifice for the international collective.

The moral component of this is straightforward. In our culture, it is uncontroversial that a virtuous person is one who lives a life of altruism—a life of selfless service to others, in which he puts their well-being and desires above his own. This is the premise behind our ever-growing welfare state and every socialist and semi-socialist country. Max Boot applies this premise logically to sacrificing for other nations: "Why not use some of the awesome power of the U.S. government to help the downtrodden of the world, just as it is used to help the needy at home?"[32]

And this help is not just money—it is also blood. For example, several years ago, when President Clinton finally succumbed to pressure from neoconservatives and liberal internationalists to attack Serbia in an attempt to force its surrender of Kosovo, the neoconservatives condemned him morally—because Clinton decided to forgo sending ground troops, which may have minimized Kosovar casualties, in favor of bombing, which would spare American lives. To quote Max Boot: "It is a curious morality that puts greater value on the life of even a single American pilot—a professional who has volunteered for combat—than on hundreds, even thousands, of Kosovar lives."[33]

This moral argument is crucial to appeals for sacrifice—but it is not sufficient. Imagine if neoconservatives or Wilsonians openly said: "We believe that Americans should be sent to die for the sake of other nations, even though it will achieve no American interest." Americans would rebel against the naked self-sacrifice being demanded.

Thus, a crucial component of the neoconservative call for international self-sacrifice is the argument that it is ultimately a practical necessity—that it is ultimately in our self-interest—that the sacrifice is ultimately not really a sacrifice.

Does National Security Require International Sacrifice?

Nearly every moral or political doctrine in history that has called on individuals to sacrifice their well-being to some "higher" cause has claimed that their sacrifices are practical necessities and will lead to some wonderful long-term benefit, either for the sacrificers or for their fellow citizens or descendants.

For example, calls to sacrifice one's desires for the sake of the supernatural are coupled with the threat of burning in hell and promises of eternal bliss in heaven. (In the militant Muslim form of this, calls to sacrifice one's life along with as many others as possible are coupled with promises of seventy-two virgins.) Environmentalist calls to sacrifice development and industrial civilization for nature are coupled with promises to stave off some ecological apocalypse (currently "global warming") and to reach some future ecological paradise. Calls to sacrifice for the Socialist dictatorship of the proletariat were coupled with claims about the inevitable collapse of capitalism and promises that the sacrificers' children and grandchildren would live in a Utopia where the state had withered away.

The argument always takes the same form. Our well-being depends on "higher cause" X—nature, "God," "Allah," the proletariat—and therefore we must sacrifice for its sake if we are to avoid disaster and procure some necessary benefit. The "higher cause" is always viewed as *metaphysically* superior to the individuals being sacrificed: Religionists view man as helpless in comparison to their supernatural being of choice; environmentalists view man in relation to Mother Nature in much the same way; and collectivists view man as metaphysically inferior to the collective as a whole. If we refuse to subordinate ourselves to this cause, they believe, only disaster can result—and if we do subordinate ourselves, something positive must follow.

Fittingly, both neoconservatism and Wilsonianism promise an ultimate, self-interested payoff to Americans for their acts of international sacrifice: a level of security that is unachievable by any other means. Both promise that when we toil and bleed to "make the world safe for democracy" or to create a "democratic international order," we will ultimately bring about a world in which we achieve new heights of peace and security—in which the collective will of the various "democracies" will make war or terrorism virtually impossible. World War I was called "the war to end all wars."

Instead of the dangerous, threatening world we live in today, the argument goes, a world in which aggressors are willing to threaten us without hesitation, the "international order" would feature an array of friendly, peace-loving "democracies" that would not even think of starting wars, that would inspire backward people of the world to set up similar governments, and that would eagerly act collectively, when necessary, to halt any threats to the "international order." This was the basic argument behind Bush's sending soldiers to bleed setting up voting booths in tribal Iraq, which sacrifice was ultimately supposed to lead to "the end of tyranny"—including international aggression—"in our world."

What if, instead, we refuse to sacrifice for foreign peoples and resolve to use our military only to protect our own security? We will fail, the collectivists say, because our security depends on the well-being of other nations and on "international order." If we let other peoples remain miserable and unfree on the grounds that it is not our problem, they argue, that will give comfort to dictators and breed hatred in populations that will ultimately lead to attacks on the United States.

In their essay "National Interest and Global Responsibility," William Kristol and Robert Kagan write that America should

> act as if instability in important regions of the world, and the flouting of civilized rules of conduct in those regions, are threats that affect us with almost the same immediacy as if they were occurring on our doorstep. To act otherwise would . . . erode both American pre-eminence and the international order . . . on which U.S. security depends. Eventually, the crises would appear at our doorstep. [34]

After 9/11, neoconservatives argued that the case of Afghanistan proved the necessity of "interventions" to resolve foreign crises and spread "democracy." Max Boot writes that many thought that after Afghanistan was abandoned as an ally to fight the Soviets, we could

> let the Afghans resolve their own affairs . . . if the consequence was the rise of the Taliban—homicidal mullahs driven by a hatred of modernity itself—so what? Who cares who rules this flyspeck in Central Asia? So said the wise elder statesmen. The "so what" question has now been answered definitively; the answer lies in the rubble of the World Trade Center. [35]

What should we have done in Afghanistan? Boot says that, in the case of Afghanistan, we should have kept troops there throughout the 1980s and 1990s:

> It has been said, with the benefit of faulty hindsight, that America erred in providing the [mujahedeen] with weapons and training that some of them now turn against us. But this was amply justified by the exigencies of the Cold War. The real problem is that we pulled out of Afghanistan after 1989. . . .
> We had better sense when it came to the Balkans. [36]

In President Bush's second inaugural address, he clearly summarized his agreement with the neoconservatives' position regarding the threat of Islamic terrorism: American security requires us to bring "democracy" to all corners of the earth.

> We have seen our vulnerability, and we have seen its deepest source. For as long as whole regions of the world simmer in resentment and tyranny, prone to ideologies that feed hatred and excuse murder, violence will gather, and multiply in destructive power and cross the most defended borders and raise a mortal threat. There is only one force of history that can break the reign of hatred and resentment and expose the pretensions of tyrants and reward the hopes of the decent and tolerant, and that is the force of human freedom.
> We are led, by events and common sense, to one conclusion: The survival of liberty in our land increasingly depends on the success of liberty in other lands. The best hope for peace in our world is the expansion of freedom in all the world. [37]

But does American security really require that we "sacrifice for the liberty of strangers"? Is every poor, miserable, unfree village on earth the potential source of another 9/11, and is it thus incumbent on America to become not only the world's policeman, but also its legislator?

Absolutely not.

The idea that we depend on the well-being of other nations for our security—or, more specifically, that "the survival of liberty in our land increasingly depends on the success of liberty in other lands"—is given plausibility by the fact that free nations do not start wars and are not a threat to other free nations, including America. But it is false. It evades the fact that innumerable unfree nations are in no way, shape, or form threats to America (e.g., most of the nations of Africa) because their peoples and leaders have no ideological animus against us, or, crucially, because their leaders and peoples *fear* initiating aggression against us.

America does not require the well-being of the whole world to survive and thrive; it is not a mere appendage or parasite of an international organism that cannot live without its host. America is an *independent nation* whose well-being requires not that all nations be free, prosperous, and happy, but simply that they be *non-threatening*. And this can be readily achieved by instilling in them fear of the consequences of any aggression whatsoever against America.

Thomas Sowell, one of America's most astute and historically knowledgeable cultural commentators, cites nineteenth-century England as having such a policy: "There was a time when it would have been suicidal to threaten, much less attack, a nation with much stronger military power because one of the dangers to the attacker would be the prospect of being annihilated. . . ." Sowell elaborates citing the instructive case of the Falkland Islands war:

> Remember the Falkland Islands war, when Argentina sent troops into the Falklands to capture this little British colony in the South Atlantic?
> Argentina had been claiming to be the rightful owner of those islands for more than a century. Why didn't it attack these little islands before? At no time did the British have enough troops there to defend them. . . . [but] sending troops into those islands could easily have meant finding British troops or bombs in Buenos Aires.[38]

If a pip-squeak nation's leader knows that instigating or supporting anti-American aggression will mean his extermination, he will avoid doing so at all costs. If a people know that supporting a movement of America-killing terrorists will lead to their destruction, they will run from that movement like the plague.

Politicians and intellectuals of all stripes continually express worries that some policy or other, and especially the use of the American military, will engender hatred for America, and that such hatred will "radicalize" populations and leaders who will then become greater threats to us. But America need not fear other people's hatred of us. For a nation, movement, or individual to pose a threat to America, some form of hatred or animus is always a necessary condition, but it is *never* a *sufficient* condition. For hatred to translate into attacks on America, it must be accompanied by *hope* of success: hope that the would-be attackers' values, including his movement or cause, will be advanced by anti-American aggression. When all such hope is lost, the respective movements and causes die; their former adherents no longer find glory in dying for them and thus lose interest in doing so. Consequently, the crucial precondition of American security is our declaration, in word and deed, to all nations and movements, that there is no hope for any movement or nation that threatens America.

Let us apply this to the case of Islamic totalitarianism, the state-supported, ideological movement that terrorizes us. If America had memorably punished the Iranian regime once it took fifty Americans hostage in 1979, then other nations would have feared lifting a trigger finger in America's direction. We are a target today because hostile nations do not fear us, but rather have contempt for us, since we have shown time and again that we are a paper tiger who will rarely punish—and never fully punish—aggressor nations.

If we had made clear that any association with Islamic totalitarianism and/or Islamic terrorism would mean a regime's annihilation, it is extremely unlikely that the Taliban would ever have risen in Afghanistan. And if it had, a foreign policy of true American self-interest would have taken care of that threat as soon as it became a threat—as soon as it demonstrated the ability and willingness to attack America. Once the Taliban rose in Afghanistan, openly proclaiming its goal of Islamic world domination, and started providing safe harbor to Islamic terrorists such as Osama bin Laden, it was a threat and should have been immediately defeated. This was especially true once Afghanistan became the launching pad for terrorist attacks against American embassies in Africa and against the USS *Cole*.

It would have been absurdly sacrificial to do as Boot suggests and plant troops in Afghanistan from 1989 on to prevent something bad from happening or to facilitate the "self-determination" of Afghans. Who knows how many American lives would have been sacrificed and how much American wealth would have been wasted in such a debacle—let alone if Boot's principle of "intervening" in "flyspeck regions" had been applied consistently.

The proven way of ending present threats and effectively deterring future threats in any era is to respond to real threats with moral righteousness and devastating power.

America's true national interest in response to 9/11 was to use America's unequaled firepower not to "democratize" but to *defeat* the threatening countries—those countries that continue to support the cause of Islamic totalitarianism—and to make an example of them to *deter* other countries. We should have made clear to the rest of the world that our government does not care what kind of government they adopt, so long as those governments do not threaten us.

There was and is no practical obstacle to such a policy; America's military and technological prowess relative to the rest of the world, let alone to the piddling Middle East, has never been greater. Nor is there any obstacle in terms of knowledge: America's ability to destroy enemy regimes is not some secret of history; everyone knows how we got Japan to surrender and then covet our friendship for sixty-two years and counting.

America could have responded to 9/11 by calling for devastating retaliation against the state sponsors of terrorism, so as to demoralize the Islamists and deter any future threats from thinking they can get away with attacking America. But, under sway of the neoconservatives, it did not. The neoconservatives never even considered it an option—because they believe that going all-out to defeat America's enemies would be immoral.

Consider this typical neoconservative response to 9/11 in the editorial from the *Weekly Standard* immediately following the attacks: "There is a task to which President Bush should call us. It is the long, expensive, and arduous war to replace the government of each nation on earth that allows terrorists to live and operate within its borders." [39]

There is no practical reason why a war between superpower America and piddling dictatorships need be "long, expensive, and arduous." It would be easy to make terrorist nations today feel as terrified to threaten us as the Argentineans felt with regard to nineteenth-century Britain. Potential aggressors against America should be in awe of our power and should fear angering us, but they are not and do not. Why?

Because, per the neoconservatives' prescriptions, America has placed the full use of its military capabilities off-limits. The neoconservatives have taken all-out war—real war—off the table.

The reason is their basic view of the goal of foreign policy: the altruistic "national interest." In this view, the justification of America using its military supremacy is ultimately that it will do so to "improve the world's condition"—not that it has an unqualified right to defend itself for its own sake.

The right to self-defense rests on the idea that individuals have a moral prerogative to act on their own judgment for their own sake; in other words, it rests on the morality of *egoism*. Egoism holds that a nation against which force is initiated has a right to kill whomever and to destroy whatever in the aggressor nation is necessary to achieve victory (see chapter 4). The neoconservatives, true to their embrace of altruism, reject all-out war in favor of self-sacrificial means of combat that inhibit, or even render impossible, the defeat of our enemies. They advocate crippling rules of engagement that place the lives of civilians in enemy territory above the lives of American soldiers—and, by rendering victory impossible, above the lives of *all* Americans.

In Afghanistan, for instance, we refused to bomb the known hideouts of many top Taliban and Al Qaeda leaders for fear of civilian casualties; thus these men were left free to continue killing American soldiers. In Iraq, our hamstrung soldiers are not allowed to smash a militarily puny insurgency; instead, they must suffer an endless series of deaths at the hand of an enemy who operates at the discretion of America. Neoconservatives are avid supporters of such restrictions and of the altruistic theory they are based on: "Just War Theory." To act otherwise would be to contradict the duty of selfless service to others that is allegedly the *justification and purpose* of America using its military might (see chapter 4).

Following the invasion of Iraq—in which American soldiers began the half-measures that eventually enabled pitifully armed Iraqis to take over cities and kill our soldiers by the thousands—neoconservative Stephen Hayes wrote glowingly of the "Just War" tactics of our military.

> A war plan that sought to spare the lives not only of Iraqi civilians, but of Iraqi soldiers. Then, liberation. Scenes of jubilant Iraqis in the streets—praising President Bush as "The Hero of the Peace." A rush to repair the damage—most of it caused not by American bombs, but by more than three decades of tyranny. [40]

Such is the behavior, not of a self-assertive nation committed to defending itself by any means necessary, but of a self-effacing nation that believes it has no right to exist and fight for its own sake.

The idea that America must become the world's democratizer is not the mistaken product of an honest attempt to figure out the most advantageous way to defend America. Neoconservatives have not evaluated our options by the standard of defending America and then concluded that using our overwhelming firepower to defeat our enemies is inferior to timidly coaxing the entire Middle East into a free, pro-American society. Rather, they have chosen policies by the standard of their altruistic conception of the "national interest" and have tried to rationalize this as both consistent with and necessary to America's security from threats. But sacrifice and self-interest are opposites. To sacrifice is to surrender one's life-serving values—to willingly take an action that results in a net loss of such values. By definition, this cannot be practical; on the contrary, it is deadly.

Bloodshed was the necessary result of Wilsonianism in the early twentieth century, just as it is the result of neoconservatism today. Given the destructive history of Wilsonianism (unfortunately unknown to most Americans), the neoconservatives' calls for international self-sacrifice for a "higher" cause that would ultimately somehow secure America should have been ominous. Wilsonianism demonstrated the logical consequences of America sacrificing for some "higher" cause that our well-being allegedly depends on. The sacrifice—Americans toiling and dying for the sake of foreign peoples—is never followed by the alleged payoff—American security.

Thomas Sowell illuminated this point in January 2003, before President Bush had officially decided to go to war for "Iraqi Freedom" but while neoconservatives were clamoring for such a war. For neoconservatives to place themselves "in the tradition of Woodrow Wilson," he wrote, "is truly chilling":

> Many of the countries we are having big trouble with today were created by the Woodrow Wilson policies of nation-building by breaking up empires, under the principle of "self-determination of nations." Such trouble spots as Iraq, Syria, and Lebanon were all parts of the Ottoman Empire that was dismembered after its defeat in the First World War.
>
> The Balkan cauldron of nations was created by dismembering the defeated Austro-Hungarian Empire. That dismemberment also facilitated Adolf Hitler's picking off small nations like Czechoslovakia and Austria in the 1930s, without firing a shot, because they were no longer part of a defensible empire.
>
> The track record of nation-building and Wilsonian grandiosity ought to give anyone pause. The very idea that young Americans are once again to be sent out to be shot at and killed, in order to carry out the bright ideas of editorial office heroes, is sickening. [41]

All of this is true.

But the editorial office heroes disagreed that they were going to bring about new debacles—both in the case of Iraq and in their broader quest to bring about an "international order" of "democracies." This time, international collectivism would work; this time, the sacrifices would be worth it, and the desired "international order" would materialize. The reason it would work this time is that these editorial office heroes were "Hard Wilsonians."

Soft and Deluded Wilsonianism in Iraq

Since neoconservatism counsels military action, not merely in response to threats to America, but also in response to threats to the "international order"—with the aim of improving that "order" and the lives of foreign peoples—it imposes an effectively *unlimited* obligation on Americans to sacrifice for the "international order" until we achieve the neoconservatives' triumph of "international democracy" or Bush's "the end of tyranny in our world." It would seem straightforward that this would involve years upon years of nation-building exercises, and thus years upon years of terrible burdens borne by Americans.

But the neoconservatives claimed that the burdens of their policy would not be all that great. They thought that their desired "international order" could be brought about without too much sacrifice on the part of Americans—sacrifice that would allegedly be paid for many times over by the ultra-secure world we would achieve thereby. "Hard Wilsonianism," they said, was an eminently *practical* policy. Why? Because, they said, with the willingness to use force, and American leadership, "democratic regime change" is far easier than the "cynics" claim—and because successful "interventions" and the spread of "democracy" will deter future aggressors and inspire freedom fighters around the world.

In 2000, Kristol and Kagan wrote of their entire foreign policy of Iraq-like missions, that

> to create a force that can shape the international environment today, tomorrow, and twenty years from now will probably require spending . . . about three and a half per cent of GDP on defense, still low by the standards of the past fifty years, and far lower than most great powers have spent on their militaries throughout history. [42]

They conclude this thought by asking, rhetorically: "Is the aim of maintaining American primacy not worth a hike in defense spending from 3 to 3.5 per cent of GDP?"—as if their policies, fully implemented, would not cost many multiples of that—and as if money, and not the irreplaceable lives lost, was the only value being spent. [43]

Part of the way the neoconservatives and President Bush justified their belief in the ease of "democratic regime change" was to cite the successful American occupation of Japan and Germany. When commentators criticized the viability of Bush's plan to "democratize" Iraq, the Middle East, and ultimately the whole world, the president pointed to the example of Japan, which previous generations of commentators once said was unfit for proper government. Max Boot uses this same example when he writes that "we need to liberalize the Middle East. . . . And if this requires occupying Iraq for an extended period, so be it; we did it with Germany, Japan and Italy, and we can do it again." [44]

But in fact, the examples of Germany and Japan do not vindicate the neoconservative foreign policy; they highlight its crucial vice. Note that these occupations were entirely different than the Iraq "liberation" occupation—

the type prescribed by neoconservatism—both in ends and means. Their purpose was *to render non-threatening the hostile populations of those countries;* their purpose was America's true "national interest," not neoconservative "national greatness." And the most important means to those occupations producing their desired result was the *utter destruction and resulting demoralization* that the Allies brought upon the Germans and Japanese. [45]

Contrast this to the altruistic policy of neoconservatism, which seeks to "liberate," not defeat, hostile regimes. In the Iraq War, we treated hostile Iraqis with kid gloves and made it our mission to let them elect whatever government they chose, no matter how hostile to America or how friendly to Islamic totalitarians. To try transforming an enemy nation without first defeating and demoralizing its complicit inhabitants is to invite those inhabitants both to rise up and rebel against America and to feel no fear in empowering even more anti-American leaders.

Another reason neoconservatives cite for the practicality of their policies is that each "intervention" will have a *deterrent* effect on future threats to America and to other evils—as well as an inspiring effect on good people—so "interventions" become progressively less necessary. Our "intervention" in Iraq, for example, was supposed to deter Iran and Syria and to inspire alleged masses of latent freedom-loving Muslims to democratize their whole region.

The alleged deterrent effect of "interventionism" is one reason Kristol and Kagan write that "a foreign policy premised on American hegemony, and on the blending of principle with material interest, may in fact mean fewer, not more, overseas interventions."[46] Now if an "intervention" means decisively defeating a real threat, then that certainly has a deterrent effect on potential threats, just as appeasement has an emboldening effect. But neoconservatives argue for the deterrent effect of *altruistic* missions fought with pulled punches.

In the 1990s, neoconservatives made this deterrence argument in favor of a policy of "intervention" in the conflicts of Bosnia and Kosovo. Many opponents of the war objected to intervention because these conflicts, involving the slaughter of racial minorities by Serbs, were of no threat to America. But the neoconservatives claimed that in Kosovo

allowing a dictator like Serbia's Slobodan Milosevic to get away with aggression, ethnic cleansing, and mass murder in Europe would tempt other malign men to do likewise elsewhere, and other avatars of virulent ultra nationalism to ride this ticket to power. Neoconservatives believed that American inaction would make the world a more dangerous place, and that ultimately this danger would assume forms that would land on our own doorstep. [47]

So, while Milosevic was no direct threat to the United States, the argument goes, it was necessary to deal with him to deter those who are or might become threats to America.

But how was America's use of its limited military resources to go after a random dictator who poses absolutely no threat to it—treating him as a far greater priority than Iran, North Korea, the Taliban, or the like—supposed to deter Iran or North Korea or the Taliban or bin Laden or Hussein? No such explanation was given, because none was possible. One does not deter a genuine enemy by picking a weak, irrelevant adversary to beat up on while leaving the genuine enemy be. Such conduct emboldens him, because he concludes that we are not strong enough, or courageous enough, to go after him. If Iran is a real threat, then to attack Serbia suggests to our enemies our lack of focus as well as our lack of moral backbone in going after our real enemies. The way to deter potential threats is to make clear that there is nothing to gain and indeed everything to lose from anti-American aggression (including supporting terrorism or spreading Islamic totalitarianism).

To say that welfare missions such as our foray into Kosovo deter terrorist nations is like saying that going on a mission to "liberate" South Africa pre-World War II would have prevented the attack on Pearl Harbor or Hitler's march across Europe.

No practical benefits for American self-defense can materialize from a policy whose central pursuit is American self-sacrifice. If one understands that the neoconservative foreign policy is a self-sacrificial "nationalism"—the goal of which is for Americans to sacrifice, to take a loss for some "higher purpose"—then it should be no surprise that, by the standard of the interests of individual Americans, a war conceived on this philosophy turned out to be a failure. The key thing to understand, however, is that by the standard of neoconservatism, the war has been a success.

Guided by neoconservative altruist-collectivist values, the Bush administration sought and fought *a war of self-sacrifice*—a war that necessarily failed to accomplish the only thing that can end threats to America: the thorough defeat of the enemies that threaten us. This war instead devoted us to the "national greatness" of endless "sacrifice for the [alleged] freedom of strangers."

Given the nature of the Islamic totalitarian threat, a war in Iraq did not have to be self-sacrificial. Iraq, after all, was no Kosovo. It was run by an avowed enemy of the United States who broke his terms of surrender, sponsored anti-American terrorists, and heavily sponsored suicide bombers against our vital strategic ally in the Middle East, Israel.

A war to defeat that regime could have served a valid purpose as a first step in ousting the terrorist-sponsoring, anti-American regimes of the Middle East and thus rendering the region non-threatening. For example, it could be used to create a strategic base for taking on Iran, our most important enemy to defeat. But such a goal would entail rendering enemy regimes *non-threatening*, which is not the same as free or "democratic."

But if one's standard of value is an altruist-collectivist ideal such as the "international order"—or if one seeks to police the "flouting of civilized rules of conduct"—then it is possible to do what President Bush did, which is to make Iraq a top priority, to evade the major threat that is Iran, and to set goals that were not oriented toward American self-defense.[48]

Bush went to war with neoconservative, thus altruistic, ends and means. He thereby necessitated a disaster.

In the run-up to the war, President Bush stated not one but three goals in invading Iraq: 1) ending the threat to the United States posed by Saddam Hussein's support of terrorists, his apparent possession of chemical and biological weapons, and his apparent pursuit of nuclear weapons; 2) "restoring" the "integrity of the U.N.," which Saddam Hussein had allegedly tarnished by violating seventeen U.N. resolutions; and 3) "liberating" Iraq from the evil tyrant Hussein and furnishing the Iraqi people with a peaceful, prosperous new "democracy."

In the view of President Bush and the neoconservatives, this combination of self-interested and altruistic goals was ideal; it was an act of selfless service to the world that would also supposedly protect America. But in fact, it was disastrous, because it did not focus America on identifying and eliminating the actual threat in Iraq; rather, it tore us between the contradictory goals of ending a threat and empowering Iraqis to do whatever they want. Combined with tactics designed to preserve the Iraqis we were there to serve, this contradictory combination guaranteed the fiasco that we are witnessing today.

Is it any wonder that our sacrificial objectives and sacrificial tactics have neither deterred our enemies nor inspired freedom-seeking allies—but instead have inspired large populations to elect our enemies into political power? We have seen a definite trend in the rise of Islamic totalitarianism, the ideology that motivates Islamic terrorists and their strongest supporters—for example, the rise of Hamas in the Palestinian territories, Hezbollah in Lebanon, Ahmadinejad in Iran, and the Muslim Brotherhood in Egypt. Our enemies who were militant before 9/11 are now even more so. Iran and Syria, for instance, continue to support the slaughter of American soldiers in Iraq without fear of consequence, and Iran pursues nuclear weapons to bolster its policy of worldwide Islamic terror.

Given the neoconservative foreign policy's altruistic ends and means, a war based on them would have to be a disaster. (In the run-up to and early aftermath of the Iraq War, the authors went on record on various occasions predicting this.) No president or secretary of defense or number of troops can make a policy of self-sacrifice yield anything but self-destruction.

But another component of the neoconservative foreign policy has made the Iraq War even more self-destructive—a component that made us pursue the particularly absurd altruistic mission we set ourselves regarding Iraqi governance. It is one thing, on the premise of altruism, to provide a foreign people with "humanitarian" aid or even to kill their reigning dictator in hopes that someone better comes along. It is quite another to try to make a primitive, tribal country into a modern "democracy"—and to expect that mission to protect us by inspiring the other primitive, tribal countries in the region to embrace "democracy" as well.

If one knows anything about those to whom we are bringing about "the end of tyranny in our world," if one looks at the endless warring tribes and religious factions raised on a philosophy of faith, mindless obedience, and coercion, and if one knows anything about the meaning and preconditions of freedom—one sees that the "Hard Wilsonian" policy is a prescription for endless welfare wars and countless American casualties, not a mere half percentage point hike of GDP.

To the credit of neoconservatives' opponents, many of them ridiculed the idea of an easily achieved, thriving Iraqi "democracy" that inspired spontaneous "democratic" uprisings in the Middle East. And given the results—the triumph of Islamists in Iraq, Afghanistan, Egypt, Lebanon, and the Palestinian Authority—they were right (see chapter 3).

To understand how the neoconservatives were so deluded about Iraq, we must grasp the essence of their political philosophy. For neoconservatives (who are influenced by the writings of philosopher Leo Strauss), politics is the central force influencing and guiding a culture. Thus, the regime a country has is the dominant cause of the direction its culture takes. Consistent with their view of individuals as metaphysically inferior to the collective, neoconservatives believe that the individual is necessarily an ineffectual product of the regime he is brought up in.

Bad regimes, they argue, inculcate in a people bad behavior and norms. If you take the same people and place them under a good regime (i.e., a "democracy"), they will become radically better people. The regime changes the culture. Thus, it is the governing elite, not the people, who ultimately determine the regime and the culture in a given country. If we replace the elite through regime change and help to establish a better elite that is pro-"democracy," a new, better culture will be born.

Ultimately, according to the neoconservatives, the foundations for any good culture, the sort that a regime must strive to foster, lie in a respect for tradition and a strong role for religion. These are the forces that restrain individuals in every society from pursuing their own "passions" and thus from immorality and anarchy. [49]

By this standard, Iraq was a promising yet troubled country in need of assistance. It was a tradition-based, religion-oriented society that for decades had been ruled by a cruel, inhumane elite—the Baath Party and Saddam Hussein—an elite that had not been chosen by the people. Do away with that elite, cultivate the local traditions and the religious leaders, and Iraq was ripe for "democracy." Once Iraqis experienced the wonders of electing their own leaders, once they participated in writing their own constitution, the neoconservatives postulated, Iraq would be transformed. The euphoria they expressed after the January 2005 Iraqi elections and the subsequent approval of a new constitution expressed their sincere belief that Iraq had fundamentally changed for the better. The new regime and the new practices in "democracy" would bring out the best in the Iraqis. Not only would this approach lead to political freedom in Iraq; it would also lead to economic prosperity through the adoption of free markets and to the peaceful coexistence of Iraq with its neighbors. And—in the ultimate payoff for America—this new Iraq would become our ally in the Middle East; it would help us reshape the region and destroy the threat of terrorism forever.

The neoconservative view of the relationship between individuals and regimes—which President Bush holds in an even stronger form, believing that freedom is "written on the soul of every human being"—also explains the plausibility of the idea that bringing "democracy" militarily to one country will likely set off a chain of "democracies" in other countries due to overwhelming civilian demand—thus lessening the need for future military "interventions." As Bush put it, to raucous applause at the National Endowment for Democracy in late 2003: "Iraqi democracy will succeed—and that success will send forth the news, from Damascus to Tehran—that freedom can be the future of every nation. The establishment of a free Iraq at the heart of the Middle East will be a watershed event in the global democratic revolution." [50]

But the view of individuals and regimes that all of this is based on is false.

The truth is that the entrenched philosophy of a people is fundamental to what type of government those people can live under, and a government based on tradition and religion is in total opposition to freedom. (Contrary to the claims of conservatives, America was founded in complete *opposition* to centuries of religious and statist tradition—opposition that included its revolutionary separation of religion and state.) For example, it would be impossible for Americans, especially eighteenth-century Americans, to accept the rule of Saddam Hussein. Our forefathers did not submit to tyranny; they courageously rebelled against it in the name of individual rights, against far greater odds than Iraqis faced under Hussein. By contrast, today's Iraqis, with the primacy they place on mystical dogma and tribal allegiances, are utterly incapable of the respect for the individual and individual rights that define a free society. Their religion and traditions do not facilitate respect for freedom; they make such respect impossible.

The Iraqis are essentially similar in this regard to the other peoples of the Middle East who are subjugated under terrorist states. It is no accident that the Islamic totalitarian movement that terrorizes us enjoys widespread support throughout the Arab-Muslim world. If it did not, hostile governments would not be able to rally their populations with appeals to that cause.

(As for claims about freedom being "written on the soul of every human being," this is false. There is no inherent belief in either freedom or anti-freedom—though one could make a far stronger case for an innate hostility toward freedom. Freedom is incredibly rare historically—because its root, a rational, individualistic philosophy, has been so rare.)

As a result of the neoconservatives' false view of regimes, they take lightly the colossal task of replacing a barbaric nation with a civilized one—in fact, they do not even acknowledge it as barbaric. The pitiful peoples of oppressed nations are lionized as mere victims of bad actors—victims who must merely be "liberated" to go from members of terrorist states to good neighbors.

The neoconservatives' false belief in the fundamentality of regimes, not philosophy, in human action, is made worse by the political system they advocate: "democracy."

When President Bush and the neoconservatives use the term "democracy," they act as if the term refers more or less to the type of government we have in the United States. Thus, the term "Iraqi democracy," at least prior to its implementation, conjured up images of a nation with civilized courts, rule of law, respect for individual rights (including those of racial minorities), a prosperous, free-market economy, separation of church and state, and so on.

But the literal meaning of "democracy"—and the meaning applied in the actual carrying out of "Iraqi democracy"—is *unlimited majority rule*. "Democracy" refers to the system by which ancient Athenians voted to kill Socrates for voicing unpopular ideas. In 1932, the German people "democratically" elected the Nazi Party, including future chancellor Adolf Hitler. "Democracy" and liberty are not interchangeable terms; they are in fact antithetical.

The distinctively American, pro-liberty principle of government is the principle of *individual rights*—which, to be upheld in a given society, requires a constitution that specifically protects these rights *against* the tyranny of the majority (see chapter 3).

Neoconservatives are unabashed promoters of "democracy," while knowing that it is not America's system of government and that it was opposed by the Founding Fathers of this country. As Joshua Muravchik writes, "This is the enthusiasm for democracy. Traditional conservatives are more likely to display an ambivalence towards this form of government, an ambivalence expressed centuries ago by the American founders. Neoconservatives tend to harbor no such doubts."[51]

The practical justification for "spreading democracy" is that "democracies don't start wars," and thus to promote "democracy" is to promote our long-term security. But that idea is a dangerous half-truth. "Democracies," in the literal sense, *do* attack other countries. To take a modern example, observe the elected Hamas government whose fundamental goal is to exterminate Israel. Or observe the triumph of the Supreme Council for the Islamic Revolution in Iraq and Moktada al-Sadr in Iraq's "democratic" political process.

What gives plausibility to the notion that "democracies don't start wars" is the fact that *free nations* do not start wars. This truth was elaborated by Ayn Rand in her landmark essay, "The Roots of War," reprinted in her anthology *Capitalism: The Unknown Ideal.*[52] But a free society is not simply one that holds elections—it is one that holds elections as a *delimited function* to select officials who must carry out, and cannot contradict, a constitution protecting individual rights.

To the extent that it is necessary for America's national security to occupy a given country, an understanding about the relationship between voting, freedom, and aggression is imperative. Because the neoconservatives and President Bush lacked such an understanding, we have been treated to the spectacle of an Iraqi "democracy" in which Islam "is a fundamental source of legislation" and "No law that contradicts the established provisions of Islam may be established."[53] We have a "democracy" that is dangerously close to being a puppet or clone of the theocracy of Iran—an enemy we will have created on the grounds that "democracies don't start wars."

Holding the false view that freedom equals "democracy," and clinging to the fiction of the noble Mideast Muslims, we have abetted and applauded these freedom haters as they have voted themselves toward terrorist theocracy. And we have promoted elections around the Middle East as the solution to the threats these nations pose, as if the people are civilized and friendly toward America but just "happen" to be under despotic rule. The results of these elections, which have empowered Islamic totalitarians or their close allies in the Palestinian territories, Egypt, and Lebanon, are testament to how deluded the neoconservative advocacy of "spreading democracy" is.

To add offense to this destruction, in responding to criticisms of Mideast "democracy," Bush administration members and neoconservative intellectuals had the gall to counter that American "democracy" has had problems, too. "Working democracies always need time to develop, as did our own," says Bush, who called on us to be "patient and understanding as other nations are at different stages of this journey." Thus, the American "stage" of the Jefferson-Hamilton debates and the Iraqi "stage" of Sadr vigilante executions are rendered equivalent: They are just two peas in a "democratic" pod.

The Realistic Moral Alternative:
A *Morality* of Self-Interest

The basic reason for the failure of the neoconservative foreign policy is that it is a thoroughly altruistic, self-sacrificial foreign policy, and American self-defense is incompatible with self-sacrifice. Importantly, however, this analysis is not limited to the policy of the neoconservatives; it applies equally to the allegedly opposite policy of "realism."

In our earlier discussion of "realism," we focused on that doctrine's view of nations as "rational" actors and its view of "diplomacy" as the foreign policy cure-all. Part of this policy's failure derives from its short-range mentality that views America's "national interest" in the time frame of political terms, a mentality that is always willing to kick the can down the road. But equally important is the policy's thoroughly altruistic moral base. This may seem strange to those familiar with "realism," because one tenet of that doctrine is that a nation should reject moral considerations in foreign policy and instead concern itself solely with its "vital interests." In the "realist" view, moral considerations—moral ideals, moral restrictions, moral judgments of good and evil—get in the way of dealing with "practical reality."

For the "realist," in any given situation, everything is theoretically on the table, to be accepted or rejected depending on whether it will "work" to achieve the "national interest." Moral principles cannot be permitted to get in the way; one must be "pragmatic," not an "ideologue."

But this is nonsense. To pursue "practicality" divorced from morality is impossible. Any claim that a course of action is "practical" presupposes some basic *end* that the course of action aims to achieve. For example, any claim that "diplomacy" with Iran is practical, or that democratic "regime change" is practical, presupposes some basic goal—whether achieving the approval of others, or establishing "stability" in the Middle East, or winning "hearts and minds," or fulfilling our duty to "improve the world's condition," or maintaining the status quo, or eliminating the Iranian threat. The question of what basic ends one should pursue in foreign policy is inescapable to the issue of practicality—and it is a *moral* question.

Because "realism" rejects the need for moral evaluation, and because the need for moral evaluation cannot be escaped, its advocates necessarily take certain goals for granted as "obviously" practical—and reject others as "obviously" impractical. Which goals are good? Goals consistent with altruism and collectivism—like winning over positive "world opinion," or coalition-building as an end in itself.

They will not consider any truly self-interested goals or means of achieving them—for example, ending state sponsorship of terrorism through devastating military action. To propose such an alternative to them would bring a flood of practical rationalizations—"We can't go to war with the whole world"; "What about the allies?"; "That will just 'radicalize' more potential terrorists." But all such objections evade the fact that such wars historically have ended the threats. This fact is ignored by the so-called "realists" because their opposition to such wars is rooted in their acceptance of altruism.

Take the example of former secretary of state Colin Powell, a prominent "realist" about whom we wrote in "'Just War Theory' vs. American Self-Defense" (chapter 4):

> Does he call for America's unequivocal, uncompromising self-defense using its full military might, since that would be eminently practical in achieving America's self-interest? No. Instead, when he ran the State Department, he sought to avoid war, to appease any and every enemy, to court "world opinion," to build coalitions, to avoid civilian casualties—while at the same time somehow to protect America. In other words, he did everything that pacifism and Just War Theory would have him do. While Powell and his ilk may say that they eschew moral analysis in matters of foreign policy and war, altruism nevertheless shapes what they think and seek to do. [54]

Since "realists" cannot conceive of doing what is truly practical in regard to threats, and since they reject explicitly altruistic missions of the neoconservative variety, they are left with only the option of ignoring or appeasing threats. This dereliction of responsibility makes more plausible the neoconservative idea that we need to be the world's policeman—since the most prominent alternative is to be a negligent, passive, doughnut-munching American policeman.

But this is a false alternative.

The antidote to both of these disastrous options is to truly embrace the virtues that the neoconservatives claim to embrace—such as thinking long range, wide range, and morally about America's interests—but to make our moral standard *American self-interest*—that is, the individual rights of Americans. If America is to have a future of freedom and security, this must be the supreme and ruling goal of American defense. (What such a standard means and why it is morally correct was a major theme of chapter 4.) This is the moral perspective needed to defeat Islamic totalitarianism—a moral perspective that truly values American lives and liberty.

So long as we evaluate the question of where to go in foreign policy by the standards of the two leading altruist foreign policies—in terms of how many more troops, or whom to hold talks with, or how many U.N. Resolutions to pass—we will continue to lose. We need to jettison the corrupt moral framework of "realism" and neoconservatism, and adopt one in which American self-defense is the sole concern and standard of value—in which we take a long-range, principled, *selfish* approach to our self-defense.

In the wake of neoconservatism's fall from grace, we must make clear that there is another alternative. Our *true* national interest, our lives and our freedom, depend on it.[55]

PART 3

From Here, Where Do We Go?

In part 2, we saw how the moral ideas at the center of our cultural mainstream have had a deleterious effect on U.S. policy. The American response to 9/11 has been subverted by the crusade for democracy; by the doctrine of Just War Theory; and by the influential viewpoint of neoconservatism—all of which are fundamentally informed by the altruistic view of the good. Miring us in a "no-win" war while vitalizing the Islamists, Bush's policy was a fiasco.

At the close of the Bush era, however, some of his supporters undertook a salvage operation. Rooting around the wreckage left by his policy, they claimed that we were in fact succeeding, that we were poised on the cusp of victory. They pointed to the surge of U.S. troops sent into Iraq, and, with a straight face, asserted that at least now that country was nearing stability. The surge, some maintained, was a tipping point. But neither wishful thinking nor downgraded standards of success can alter the facts.

In chapter 6 we appraise U.S. policy since the surge. The Bush policy, it is argued, was worse than doing nothing at all. In Iraq, Afghanistan, Pakistan, Iran, and across the world, it left Islamists more powerful, and America weaker, than before. The need for a different way forward is urgent.

In chapter 7 we look to the future. With the start of Barack Obama's term in office, we ask how Washington should respond to the continuing threat from the Islamist movement. What direction should our policy take in the years to come? The road to victory—for we can indeed achieve victory—must begin with an overhaul of our foreign policy, an overhaul of its moral foundations.

CHAPTER SIX

Eight Years After 9/11:
An Appraisal

Elan Journo

Is *This* Victory?

During the final year of President George W. Bush's tenure, some doubters who had long ago pronounced his war policy a dismal failure, felt themselves chastened by the facts. Once untiring, the chorus of reproach softened its tone, dialed down its volume, qualified its predictions. Drowning out remnants of that chorus was the re-energized pep squad for the Bush policy. Elbowing their way to center stage, they celebrated what they deemed manifest gains in the Bush "war on terror."

Listen to Sen. John McCain: "I'm not painting to you the most rosy scenario but I am telling you, compared to a year ago, before we started this surge, and with this great general, one of the great generals in American history, General David Petraeus, that we are succeeding in Iraq." The basis for that claim? "I've seen the facts on the ground," he said upon returning from a visit to Iraq.[1] Lending credibility to such assertions, the head of CIA, Michael V. Hayden, told the *Washington Post* a while later that, "On balance, we are doing pretty well," and listed evidence of what he took to be major strides forward: "Near strategic defeat of al-Qaeda in Iraq. Near strategic defeat for al-Qaeda in Saudi Arabia. Significant setbacks for al-Qaeda globally . . . as a lot of the Islamic world pushes back on their form of Islam."[2] By summer, a columnist for the *Wall Street Journal* happily announced: "The Iraq war is over. We've won."[3]

With less than two months to go before the presidential elections, it seemed the American people were coming around to the conclusions of the pep squad, even if they were not all beguiled by its gleeful vibe. According to one poll, reported in the *Washington Post*, "56 percent of registered voters say the United States is making significant strides toward bringing order in Iraq—the highest proportion to say so in nearly three years and nearly double the level in late 2006" (before Bush sent in a surge of U.S. troops to Iraq).[4] Another indicator of the same phenomenon was the staggering comeback of Sen. McCain's bid for the presidency. McCain's early commitment to the war, and then the surge, nearly sank his campaign, when Iraq was in the throes of a brutal civil war. But, in time, fewer Iraqis slaughtered each other; fewer Americans were blown up; some Islamists were evicted block-by-block from their strongholds in some Iraqi provinces. What was once a millstone around McCain's neck became an asset. McCain trumpeted his backing for the war as he pulled ahead to clinch the Republican nomination and compete (albeit unsuccessfully) against Barack Obama.

The applause at how Islamists had been kicked out of Basra and Baghdad neighborhoods continued unabated despite the fact that Afghanistan was in flames. Yes, the cheerleaders assured us in soothing tones, it is worrisome that Islamists were back and wrecking havoc in that country—but hardly reason to think that the Bush policy failed. After all, now that we've got a handle on what fixed Iraq, that same magic can be made to work in Afghanistan, too.

Of course not everyone is willing to raise a champagne toast, or to unfurl the "Mission Accomplished" banner. But the boosters can haul out a dependably effective talking point. They can acknowledge that, yes, perhaps the Bush policy could have been more effective more quickly; more forceful or more gentle; better managed and better executed (depending on your attitude); but on balance we're better off for it, because in eight years there has not been another 9/11.

But *are* we better off for it?

In weighing that question, remember what we are up against. The menace confronting us is larger than Al Qaeda in Iraq, larger than the network of Al Qaeda itself. We face an ideological movement: Islamic totalitarianism. Al Qaeda is one, and a relatively new, faction within that movement (see chapters 1 and 2). The movement's origins date back to the early decades of the twentieth century with the establishment of the Muslim Brotherhood in Egypt; its standard-bearer since 1979 has been the totalitarian regime in Iran. The Islamists wish to establish a global regime that subjugates all under sharia. There is disagreement within the movement on how to achieve that goal—terrorist attacks, revolutionary overthrow, lawful political subversion, running for elected office, or some combination of these. But whatever the means adopted, their common vision necessitates expunging the freedom of individuals and negating the political principles of secular society. So we're in a conflict far broader than Iraq and Afghanistan.

Moreover, Islamists operate on an expansive time horizon. For Americans, the long view in politics is remarkably short. It ranges somewhere beyond the rapid pulse of the cable TV news cycle and, at the outer reaches, the four-year presidential term in office. Rare is the political venture that projects forward (or looks back) on the scale of decades. Rarer still is an administration that thinks on that scale. In the Muslim world, by contrast, people are acutely sensitive to the sweep of historical time. Sermons and political speeches, for instance, are typically laced with allusions to heroes (e.g. Saladin), wars (e.g., the Crusades), and triumphant conquests (e.g., the Muslim capture of Spain) from many hundreds of years ago. Leaders of the Islamist movement, in particular, see themselves as engaged in a war that may have to span many generations into the future before their cause is victorious. Losing a battle may entail pausing temporarily to rest, regrouping and rejoining the fray when the conditions are more auspicious—but it certainly does not mean the war is over. When Islamists talk about avenging the "tragedy" of Al-Andalus, the parts of the Iberian peninsula where Islamic rule was overthrown in 1492, they are serious. [5]

We should keep this context in mind when measuring the success or failure of U.S. policy. The proper benchmark derives from the basic goal of protecting American lives from the Islamist threat. Achieving that goal is our government's moral obligation in its function as defender of our rights. Victory means rendering the Islamist movement and the states that sponsor it non-threatening. (How this should be done is explored in detail in chapters 3–5 and again in chapter 7.) When assessing the results of American policy, we need to take into account the nature of the threat and the tenacity of Islamists in pursuit of their goals. To triumph, therefore, we must stamp out the threat, not merely for today, but for good.

If we take the long view, if we hold as our standard of success the protection of American lives, what should we conclude? What are the results of U.S. policy since 9/11 and since the surge of U.S. troops in Iraq, and what evaluation of them is warranted by the actual facts on the ground?

Afghanistan

Conventional wisdom on the Afghanistan campaign, at least until recently, went like this. The Taliban regime was toppled, quickly. Thousands of Islamists were killed or captured in battle. A new Afghan state, with nominally friendly ties to the West, was founded. The war was seen as the right war, at the right time, for the right reason—and it was acknowledged as a job well done (even if Osama bin Laden and his lieutenants escaped). Then it faded from public awareness, especially with the onset of U.S. military operations in Iraq. It was in 2006, some five years after the war began, that Afghanistan once again made front-page news. The Islamist forces, it turned out, had never really gone away. Yes, many died in combat or were hauled off to Guantanamo. But under Washington's "compassionate" war, with U.S. forces hamstrung by self-denying rules of engagement, the military operation failed to crush the Islamists. It managed only to weaken them, temporarily, and drive them out of some parts of the country (see chapters 3 and 4).

Many simply crossed into the vaguely demarcated borderlands of Pakistan. Directly across from Afghanistan is the area of Pakistan known as the tribal belt, where the government has no real authority. Many fleeing Islamists settled in those primitive, warlord-controlled wastelands. The lawlessness meant they would have little to worry about from Pakistan's military, since it avoids venturing into that area. And the local population was sympathetic, even eagerly supportive, of the Islamists (at the start of the Afghanistan War, there were fund-raising drives to send them money; many locals donated money and jewelry for the sake of jihad).

Basing themselves in the badlands of Pakistan, the Islamists built up their manpower, reconstituted their training camps, and launched their resurgence. Since 2003, they have seized power over parts of southern Afghanistan, only to lose, and then regain control of some villages. While the scope of their dominion has fluctuated, with some parts of the country changing hands several times, the trend is unmistakable: the Taliban are fighting to reassert their Islamic rule over the country.

Their military campaign has grown more aggressive with each passing year. The number of IEDs and roadside bombs climbed from 782 in 2005, to 1,931 in 2006, to 2,615 the following year. Suicide bombings, once unheard of in Afghanistan, have become a commonplace. There were thirty such attacks in the first five years of the war; in the first six months of 2008, there were more than 1,200.[6] And the tally of U.S. casualties has soared. In 2008, the death toll was 155—more than twelve times the number in the first year of the war and almost as many as the total for the first four years, combined. By one reckoning, most of the first 100 U.S. deaths in the war were the result of accidents or illnesses, not combat, and almost half occurred "outside the main theater, across a regional network of supply bases and refueling outposts."[7] But today most deaths occur in combat.

Taliban fighters and their allies have set up checkpoints on some roads, and on others they carry out regular ambushes. The Kabul-Kandahar highway is a critical artery bearing fuel and food trucks heading for the nation's capital. But this supply route has been choked under the heel of resurgent Islamist forces. In one brutal incident, some fifty trucks carrying supplies for the U.S. military were attacked. "The convoy was set on fire," reports the *New York Times,* while "Seven of its drivers were dragged out and beheaded"; in another attack two American soldiers died when their vehicles were hit by mines and rocket-propelled grenades.[8]

One measure of how daring the Islamists have become is evident in an episode that unfolded in the summer of 2008. Intent on freeing comrades who had been captured, a contingent of Taliban fighters mounted a spectacular attack on a prison in Kandahar. Outside the prison gates, one foot soldier parked a fuel tanker, fleeing the scene with a laugh amid a hail of bullets from the guards at the prison. Within moments, the Taliban fired a rocket-propelled grenade at the tanker, blowing it up. That explosion "killed the prison guards, destroyed nearby buildings, and opened a breach in the prison walls as wide as a highway."[9] Some 350 members of the Taliban escaped and rejoined the jihad.

Although American and NATO forces do inflict real damage on the Islamists, fighters from outside the country are enlisting to replace the fallen and to swell the ranks of holy warriors. The success of this rejuvenated and well-financed Afghan jihad has drawn recruits from the Middle East, North Africa, and Central Asia. Recruits arrive on commercial flights to Pakistan and then travel by car or bus into the lawless tribal region on the Afghan-Pakistan border; some—it is unclear how many—go overland through Iran and then up into a different part of Pakistan's border region. These foreign jihadists can enter Afghanistan through what military officials have euphemistically called a "porous border."[10]

Across wide swathes of the country, Islamists are succeeding in imposing their authority by force. They are making considerable progress toward reinstating the Islamist ideal of a political order defined by sharia. Through intimidation or assassinations, Islamists have shut down courts and summarily executed police officers and judges. Schools have been bombarded with rocket fire, for daring to allow girls to attend classes. In Helmand Province, five teachers have been slaughtered and dozens of schools shut down.[11] There is now, writes one scholar, a "parallel Taliban state" within the country, "and locals are increasingly turning to Taliban-run" courts that implement sharia law.[12] The *Wall Street Journal* reports that Islamists now run some two dozen law courts; the institutions of the Taliban shadow government "now handle everything from land disputes to divorces."[13] Gangs of Islamist enforcers—assuming the job once done by the notorious virtue police—harass men who shave their beards and threaten punishment of un-Islamic behavior. Some women, in self-protection, have taken to wearing a head-to-toe veil, the veil once mandated under the Taliban's theocratic regime.

We were told that the Afghan government, the one Washington helped install, would function as a bulwark against Islamists. Under the mandate of Bush's crusade for democracy, the U.S. cleared the way for the Afghans to define their own political destiny. They did. The result was supposed to reflect the popular will. It does. But instead of becoming a U.S. ally against the Islamists, Afghanistan is sliding under their dominion.

Apologists in the West tell us that the Afghan regime lacks the financial resources and expertise to combat the Islamists. Before we can count on the government in Kabul to pull its weight, so the story goes, it will need millions more in economic aid, scores of additional American police and military trainers, and several more years of "reconstruction" and nation-building. But the material weakness of the government obscures a deeper problem. U.S. policy has gone a long way toward creating a regime that is fundamentally impotent to oppose the Islamists on principle—and in fact advances their goal. The reason is that what distinguishes the current government from the Islamists ideologically is only a difference in the degree of their fidelity to the principle of rule under Islam.

With the blessing of Washington (and the United Nations), the Afghan constitution defines the regime as an Islamic Republic (Article 1). Islam is enshrined as the state religion (Article 2), and the supreme source of law: "In Afghanistan, no law can be contrary to the beliefs and provisions of the sacred religion of Islam" (Article 3). The national anthem is required by law to mention Allahu Akbar—meaning "God is greatest" (Article 20). Of course there are perfunctory nods to the idea of rights and legal equality before the law (e.g. Articles 22, 33, 40), including the promise that "freedom of expression is inviolable" (Article 34).[14] But the operative principle in Afghanistan is Islamic law.

Notice the ominous pattern in the following incidents.

Under the country's sharia laws, blasphemy is a crime. One of the first journalists convicted on a charge of blasphemy was Ali Mohaqiq Nasab, editor of a magazine called *Women's Rights*. The prosecutor in the case demanded that Nasab receive the death penalty, but the editor was spared and instead sentenced to jail for two years.[15] A year later, in 2006, news filtered out that an Afghan convert to Christianity, Abdul Rahman, had been denounced as an apostate. He too was threatened with execution, the traditional punishment for those who dare abandon the Muslim faith. After an international outcry, the embarrassed government in Kabul allowed Rahman to be spirited away to safety in Europe. Many people in Afghanistan, including the frothing mobs and clerics who demanded his execution, were cross with the government for letting him flee.[16]

Or consider the persecution of Parwiz Kambakhsh, a twenty-four-year-old Afghan student. In 2008 he was accused of circulating an article regarding the rights of women in Islam and for starting un-Islamic discussions in class. The council of clerics that tried his case decreed capital punishment. Afghanistan's upper house of parliament endorsed that sentence. Crowds took to the streets in support of the verdict; one cleric told the press, "He should be punished so that others can learn from him."[17] It was under heavy pressure from the West (again) that the sentence was reduced on appeal—to twenty years in prison.[18]

When Muslims across the world exploded in a (contrived) outrage over Danish cartoons of Muhammad, Afghanistan was the scene of angry protests. In theory, you might expect Hamid Karzai, the allegedly pro-freedom, pro-Western president of Afghanistan, to come out for the principle of free speech, for the right of individuals to express any ideas however distasteful some may find them. After all, the Afghan constitution does hold that specific right to be "inviolable." But instead he essentially pandered to and endorsed the violent mobs by declaring his view that any insult to Muhammad "is an insult to more than a billion Muslims." [19]

Observe that Karzai (and other so-called "moderates") must placate and appease more ardent proponents of sharia and the Afghan public at large—or else risk seeming to contradict the teachings of Islam. If they flout those teachings, they unavoidably strengthen the reputation of Islamists as the true idealists, the genuinely principled ones. To the extent Karzai and others may try to water down that ideal, to compromise it with talk of rights and freedom, they indict themselves as deviating from the straight path of Allah's will. This weakens whatever credibility they may have, and casts the so-called conservative factions and the Taliban as the authentically principled exponents of Islamic law.

Moreover, there's little that separates the goal of Taliban ideologues and Afghanistan's council of legal scholars, an official advisory body counseling the government. The council, for instance, has urged Karzai to stop foreign-aid groups from (alleged) missionary work for Christianity. When it was in power, the Taliban expelled such groups. The council has urged the president to reintroduce public executions. Under the former Taliban regime and today wherever the Islamists have reasserted their authority, criminals and blasphemers and others deemed un-Islamic are publicly executed (the custom is to dispatch them on Fridays, typically, after midday prayers). The council has demanded that the president prevent local TV stations from broadcasting the enormously popular Indian soap operas and movies. These diversions, say the clerics, are rife with obscenity and scenes of immoral behavior. The Taliban, of course, were brutally effective in shutting down un-Islamic broadcasters and newspapers; in "executing" TV sets and video recorders; in forcibly shuttering video rental stores; in enforcing obedience to religious standards of modesty and propriety.[20]

The inestimable clout of moral legitimacy in Afghanistan lies with the proponents of sharia. So there's no reason to think that, even if it were competent and strong enough, the government could take a principled stand against the resurgent Taliban. (News reports indicate that in at least one incident, an Afghan police chief and another district leader aided Islamist fighters in carrying out an attack on U.S. forces, in which nine Americans died.)[21] Karzai walks among Western leaders and presents himself as one of them, but the foundations of Afghanistan's government rest on the ideal of Islamic law.

Recall that it was Bush's explicit policy to endorse and help establish precisely this kind of regime in Afghanistan, in the name of serving the political conscience of Afghans (rather than U.S. interests) (see chapters 3–5). Islamist leaders (and many Afghans) may lament that the incumbents in Kabul fail to live up fully to the ideal of sharia and that the government is too friendly to the West. But whether the Taliban manage to seize full or only partial control in Afghanistan, their political ideal has already been enshrined in the existing government. And, accordingly, the likelihood is high that Afghanistan will enforce sharia even more strictly in the years to come, and that it will become a large-scale breeding ground and training base for jihadists taking aim at America and the West.

The only winners—and all the more so in the event the current regime collapses—are the Islamists. For this considerable gain, they should thank U.S. policy.

Of course no one in Washington wants to see Afghanistan continue its downward spiral. But what to do? In keeping with the prevailing mindset in U.S. policy circles, the chaos in Afghanistan has been misdiagnosed. The problem is seen not as a consequence of Bush's "compassionate" war, a policy that renounced using all necessary force to defeat the Islamists; it is seen rather as a failure to deliver enough aid, to deploy enough troops, to be even more compassionate in combat. The cure? The common view today is to replicate the alleged success in Iraq: Let's surge in Afghanistan.

But what exactly has happened in Iraq? How should we judge the outcome there?

Iraq

The before-and-after portraits of Iraq reveal that a marked change has taken place in that country since the 2007 surge.

Before the surge, the situation in Iraq was verging on anarchy. During one of the lowest points, morning in Baghdad would bring with it a grisly harvest of bodies shot in the head and bearing the telltale signs of torture—drill holes in the skull, electrocution burns—and some that were desecrated beyond identification. For example, in April 2007, more than 400 unidentified bodies turned up in Baghdad; the next month, the body count climbed to 726. (These figures, it is worth noting, represented a mild *decline* from the rate of ethnic-sectarian executions which were far higher the previous year.)[22] Many more victims were put to death, not in secret under cover of night, but in broad daylight: they were among the thousands torn apart in routine car bombings and suicide attacks.

After the surge, a measure of calm has supplanted the chaos. In April 2008, Gen. David Petraeus reported to Congress that "security in Iraq is better than it was when Ambassador Crocker and I reported to you [in September 2007], and it is significantly better than it was 15 months ago when Iraq was on the brink of civil war and the decision was made to deploy additional US forces to Iraq." Although Petraeus qualified his remarks carefully with an acknowledgement that the progress was "fragile and reversible," his testimony seemed to vindicate the Bush administration's policy.[23]

Statistics told a similar story. The Department of Defense, in a September 2008 report to Congress, reckoned that "security incidents" in Iraq "have remained at levels last seen in early 2004 for nearly three consecutive months." Civilian deaths across the country declined to a level 77 percent lower than one year ago; the lowest "monthly death rate on record occurred in June 2008." Despite a minor uptick in ethnic-sectarian killing during July and August that year, deaths in that category "remained 96 percent below the reported death rate in the same period in 2007."[24]

Bombings never completely died down, but they became infrequent and typically smaller. Nor did the murders end, but they too became rarer.[25] By the end of Ramadan, in the fall of 2008, some Baghdad residents ventured out of their homes. They went to parks, cafes, and ice cream parlors.[26] The same was true in other cities. Within tightly controlled areas, fortified by armed checkpoints and blast walls that line the streets, the people in towns like Samarra could begin resuming normal life. By the week of Thanksgiving, writer Michael Yon offered an assessment that was anything but controversial: "Nobody knows what the future will bring, but the civil war [in Iraq] has completely ended."[27]

But, so what?

Recall why the administration ordered the surge. The purpose was to dig ourselves out of a self-made quagmire. Even by a generous accounting of the facts, Saddam Hussein's Iraq was never a hub of Islamist activity nor a major backer of the Islamic totalitarian movement. But following the Bush crusade to bring "democracy," welfare goods, and a so-called reconstruction to that nation, it became a jihadist playground. The fantastical notion of a pro-Western, pro-freedom Iraqi regime evaporated amid the blazing wreckage of umpteen roadside bombs and the acrid stench of decaying corpses felled in the insurgency (see chapter 3). The surge of thousands of U.S. troops went to fight our way back up from a catastrophic negative, to some point closer to zero—a state of *relative* calm, for the sake of Iraqis.

That this turn of events is celebrated not merely as progress, but as a triumphant achievement, reveals just how the idea of success in war has been emptied of meaning. In 2001, Bush had vowed to "pursue nations that provide aid or safe haven to terrorism." That goal, if achieved, would have brought us closer to an authentic victory. But that legitimate, if imprecisely defined goal, was shoved aside. Replacing it was the grandiose (and perverse) idea of lifting up the Middle East through U.S.-backed elections. Then the goal degraded further to a stable, then to a non-anarchic, Iraq. Now we hear the pep squad rejoicing that insurgents have been quieted, for now, in some backstreets of Baghdad. Nobody would have bought that as a vision of success, in the devastating aftermath of 9/11; nobody should buy it now.

This perniciously myopic take on the situation in Iraq fits neatly with another kind of distortion that colors people's appraisal of the Islamist threat. Recall that initially the Bush administration termed its response a "*global* war on terror" (giving rise, in government documents, to the unlovely acronym GWOT). The single element of truth in that designation is that the scope of the conflict extends far beyond Iraq, or even Afghanistan. But the public's initial recognition of this fact has been undone. For most of Bush's second term in office, "the war" referred exclusively to Iraq. Hence for many people, America's military response to 9/11 came to be judged according to the latest news reports from Iraq. This made it possible, for a while, to evade the problem, or at least shut out of mind the true outlines of its scale (e.g. that Afghanistan was another front).

But if we apply the proper standard of success—the long-range safeguarding of the lives of Americans—there can be only one verdict on the campaign in Iraq: It is a wretched failure.

Let's pause to identify who, exactly, gained political power in U.S.-endorsed elections.

The government of Iraq, reflecting the proclivities of the fractious population, is headed by a Shiite-Kurdish coalition. At its head is the Supreme Council for the Islamic Revolution in Iraq (SCIRI), an outfit that Iran helped to create during the Iran-Iraq War with the goal of establishing an Islamist theocracy to supplant the regime of Saddam Hussein. SCIRI, like another prominent pro-Iranian element in the coalition, Dawa, was based in Iran for much of its existence. SCIRI's armed "militia," the Badr Brigade, received training from Tehran's military. Since the invasion, the Badr Brigade has operated death squads from within the Iraqi police to kill undesirable Sunnis. Fighters belonging to SCIRI ran their own parallel network of secret jails where they carried out horrific tortures reminiscent of the Hussein regime. The jockeying for power and influence between rival Shiite militias has been cutthroat; their mutual hostility perhaps equals their hatred for Sunnis, whom they have worked to decimate. These are the political groups whose rise to power Washington endorsed.[28]

Early on, the kingmaker in government was Moktada al-Sadr, a militantly anti-American Shiite cleric. Sadr is an advocate of Islamist theocracy, and like SCIRI and Dawa, he is allied with the Islamic totalitarian regime of Iran (he threatened that, should America dare lay a finger on Iran, his forces would lash out at U.S. assets and personnel in retribution). Though for now Sadr has stepped back from politics, his ascendancy was in large measure thanks to Washington. At the time of the U.S. invasion, Sadr (or rather his minions) murdered a rival cleric and a warrant was issued for his arrest. U.S. officials decided, however, that it would be better not to arrest Sadr (lest that anger his followers) and instead bring him into the political process.

By some magic hitherto unknown to mankind, that was supposed to temper Sadr's hostility. Even after Sadr's private militia (the Mahdi Army) fought bitterly against U.S. forces, it was decided to leave his militia intact and allow Sadr's bloc to continue wielding power in government. Sadr and his jihadists escaped retribution for their aggression. Unscathed after his clashes with American forces, Sadr was able to cash in on his growing prestige as a formidable opponent of the United States. One illustration of the stature that Sadr has gained among certain sectors of the Iraqi public was on display on the morning that Saddam Hussein was hanged. Amid the jeering of the onlooking guards could be heard the martial refrain "Moktada! Moktada! Moktada!"[29] Exit strongman, enter the militant cleric.

The ideological pedigree of the power holders in Baghdad reflects the behind-the-scenes machinations of an *eminence grise*: the Islamic Republic of Iran. Confirmation of that was evident in a 2008 skirmish in Basra between the Shiite forces of Moktada al-Sadr and those led by the Iraqi government.

The clash dragged on, without a clear victor. That in itself is remarkable enough, but the real story is how the stalemate was resolved. The top leadership of the Iraqi parliament came to negotiate a deal with Sadr's forces. Despite all the might, blandishments, and bribes at their disposal, they got nowhere. To the rescue came Brig. Gen. Qassem Suleimani. He was instrumental to the resolution. It was he who successfully brokered the agreement between the two Iraqi factions, managing a feat no one else in Iraq was able to pull off.

Who is this Suleimani? He is little known to most Americans, and that may be because Suleimani is an officer of Iran's Revolutionary Guard Corps. His name, according to one news report, appears "on U.S. Treasury Department and U.N. Security Council watch lists for alleged involvement in terrorism and the proliferation of nuclear and missile technology." Observe the magnitude of Iran's influence. Practically with the wave of a hand, Tehran can initiate hostilities through its many insurgent proxies in Iraq—and just as easily halt the fighting between two of the rival Islamist forces that it sponsors.[30]

Witness what now passes for progress in Iraq: Baghdad now has a *new* anti-American regime dominated by Islamists that are deep in Iran's pocket.

It is entirely conceivable that Iraq will become an anarchic bog of sectarian warfare when the precarious calm implodes; or an Iranian client/puppet, perhaps even a full-fledged totalitarian regime, where jihadists resume industrial-scale training; or some splintered combination of these. But no better prospect is imaginable, given the ideological-political forces that U.S. policy has loosed and nourished in Iraq.

This dismal assessment will doubtless prompt the objection that the surge has really changed things. Recall the inventory of glittering accomplishments that are attributed to the influx of American troops in Iraq. The consensus is that "Al Qaeda has been defeated," that some Islamists there are on the run or in hiding, that they have been demoralized. So it would seem to follow that in a real sense the military campaign has salvaged an authentic gain that advances our security. But that's wishful thinking.

In the mythic account of the surge, the insurgency spun out of control owing to a lack of U.S. troops (and, in a wrinkle on that, the overly aggressive conduct of troops already in Iraq). For this the remedy was thousands more soldiers, under orders to be kinder, gentler. Chapters 3–5 explored why this is an arrant misdiagnosis of the fundamental problem, a point bolstered by what actually led to the (temporary) diminution in the slaughter. Ignored in the standard account are two significant explanatory factors.

First, the Mahdi Army was a potent engine of violent attacks and murders that were classified under the umbrella term of the insurgency. Around the time that the first battalions of the surge landed in Iraq, Sadr called a cease-fire (or *hudna*, a temporary pause in fighting, on the model of Muhammad's war strategy, to allow for rearming and resumption of fighting at a later, more opportune time). Thanks to that cease-fire, many of the killers are taking a breather, and the death toll has dipped somewhat. General Odierno, the commander of forces in Iraq, estimates that Sadr's move is responsible for 15–20 percent of the reduction.[31] Considering Sadr's prestige and avid following, that estimate may well be on the low end.

The second factor stems from Iraq's endemic sectarian tribalism, and the opportunism of rival factions. Before any effects of additional U.S. troops could be felt, American military leaders had begun an unusual program in the highly volatile Anbar province, the wellspring of the Sunni insurgency. The program, later dubbed the Anbar Awakening, involved bribing Sunni tribes (and a smattering of Shiite ones) to fight against Islamist militias. Tribal elders, who were complicit in the murder of so many Americans, were plied with tens of thousands of dollars in cash. Upwards of 100,000 men, called Sons of Iraq, were eventually enrolled in the program. Many of them had previously laid the roadside bombs that killed our troops and had fought in Islamists ranks, but for about $300 a month they turned their guns against their former allies.

The Sons of Iraq program has so far cost on the order of $250 million. Such handouts were championed by General Petraeus. When he was in charge of Mosul, Petraeus and his men spent some $58 million; when he became commander of forces in Iraq, he encouraged the wider application of this tool. Testifying before Congress, Petraeus explained the rationale: "the salaries paid to the Sons of Iraq alone cost far less than the cost savings and vehicles not lost due to the enhanced security in local communities." (Exactly the same could be said about paying off a mafia protection racket; it certainly looks like a cost savings compared to replacing smashed shop windows and surgery for broken kneecaps; but what happens next month?)

The Awakening was accompanied by a spending spree to buy the good graces of Iraqi civilians. Under a program called the Commander's Emergency Response Program (CERP), which has since been institutionalized across Iraq under the updated policies, soldiers

> walk the streets carrying thousands of dollars to pay Iraqis for doorways battered in American raids and limbs lost during firefights. Sheiks appeal to commanders to use larger pools of money locked away in Humvees and safes at military bases for new schools, health clinics, water treatment plants and generators, knowing that the military can bypass Iraqi and U.S. bureaucratic hurdles.

Some items on this shopping spree: $100,000 worth of dolls; $500,000 of action figures made to look like Iraqi security forces; $12,800 for pools to cool bears and tigers at a Baghdad zoo; $48,000 to buy children's shoes; $14,250 for "I Love Iraq" t-shirts.[32]

Witness the so-called progress in Bush's "war on terror": never mind about defeating the enemy—now we stoop to bribe people *not* to butcher Americans.

By design and in practice, the essence of the surge was not to end the Islamist threat, but to appease hostile Iraqis—to bribe them with children's shoes and wads of cash to be nice to us, and as long as the money flows, to turn against the jihadists. A scheme in which you have to pay people not to attack or kill you is extortion. The United States instigated the practice of appeasement, and now this humiliating scheme is celebrated as a stroke of consummate military genius.

What happens when the torrent of cash dries up? That future problem will sort itself out, we are told, because once stability is achieved, there will be a reconciliation among Iraq's warring ethnic and sectarian factions. The deadly gangland-style shoot-outs in the streets and ugly wrangling in parliament will cease, or so we have been promised. Washington believed that by arming and empowering the Sunni tribes, who constitute the bulk of the Sons of Iraq, it would pave the road for them to feel included in the nation's politics—which the majority Shiites now hold in a vise-grip. Ultimately, the idea is to fold these gangs of former (and current) criminals, supposedly former jihadists, and ordinary Iraqis into the nation's Shiite-dominated police force. Some of that has happened, but the deep-seated, bitter resentment between Sunnis and Shiites in Iraq cannot be wished away. Many Sons of Iraq believe that their real enemy is the Shiite-run government in Baghdad, and with their American-provided arms, they await the day of reckoning.[33]

Washington has thrust itself into the maelstrom of primitive, sectarian conflict that dates back many centuries. The hoped-for "reconciliation" between Iraq's sects, if even possible, may well require seismic theological shifts. One upshot of the Awakening is that we have backed what is essentially the establishment of a quasi-feudal, neighborhood-level warlord society.[34] That social organization is at odds with the central government and the Shiite majority, and awash in money, arms, and vengeance-hungry fighters ready for a showdown. This is to say nothing of the resentment we incur from Shiites who regard our arming and backing of Sunni tribal groups as an endorsement of that sect—members of which, during Saddam Hussein's era, cruelly dominated them. We may yet witness a sectarian clash that erupts with a fury surpassing the mayhem at the peak of the insurgency.

What are we to make of the assertion that at least the jihadists, and particularly Al Qaeda, have been killed; that many have been driven into hiding or out of Iraq; that they have been demoralized?

True, some jihadists have been killed in Iraq, but to trumpet this as success is pure fantasy. It makes as much sense to trumpet the "success" of a doctor who infects his patients, lets thousands of them suffer and succumb to heinous death, until, finally, in a few cases, he palliates the symptoms of the disease he instigated. Prior to Washington's military intervention, Islamists were a minor constituency, brutally suppressed along with other opposition groups, under Saddam Hussein's regime. This is one reason, for example, why SCIRI based itself in neighboring Iran. Since 2003, though, Islamists have built up a larger popular following in the country, while hordes of jihadists, eager for martyrdom, flowed into Iraq to join the insurgency. (By one accounting, most of the suicide operations have been carried out by foreign fighters from Arab countries.)[35]

The insurgency presented holy warriors with a kind of proving ground to perfect their tactics and skills. It also offered them ample opportunity to slaughter U.S. troops; in large part due to Washington's self-denying rules of engagement (see part 2). Empowering the killers, Iran provided financial support, training, weapons, and explosives to Shiite factions, and also backed some Sunni groups. The full extent of Iran's culpability for U.S. deaths in Iraq may be hard to tabulate exhaustively. But it is clear that the insurgency enabled Iran, a regime that lusts after "Death to America," to engineer the deaths of many Americans.

True, some jihadists have gone into hiding, but there's a world of difference between a tactical retrenching (or *hudna*) and defeat. Take the case of Moktada al-Sadr. In the summer of 2008, having apparently relocated to Iran, he announced that his Mahdi Army would restructure. Following the tried and true popularity-boosting strategy of Islamist groups like Hezbollah and Hamas, Sadr's organization would divide its attention. One focus will be social service to the needy (to spruce up its image as a pious organization, following some allegations of graft); the other area of focus will be the righteous, armed "resistance" to un-Islamic and Western elements. No group that has been defeated bothers to realign its popular outreach and streamline its militant operations. To be defeated means to give up one's goals.

Islamists like Sadr who have stepped into the shadows for now seem to be biding their time in hopes that an auspicious occasion will present itself. Perhaps they hope that anarchy will engulf Iraq. That may happen with their nudging or simply as a result of pent-up Sunni-Shiite enmity. Either way, anarchy is fertile ground for Islamists—not only because they can operate with impunity in a lawless state, but also because they can position themselves as the only genuine advocates of social-political order. It was under essentially these conditions that in 1996 the Taliban came to rule Afghanistan; ditto for the Islamist rise to power in Somalia in 2006–07. Sharia law certainly brings order and a kind of security: it replaces mayhem with a brutally severe, totalitarian Islamic control over people's thought and action. But regardless of whether Islamists make a serious comeback in Iraq, we have a great deal to fear from those who have supposedly been demoralized and driven out of the country.

True, some jihadists have lost their zeal, and a few may be truly depressed about their prospects—in Iraq. Although they have suffered a minor setback there, they persist in believing their ideal to be achievable. Many (as noted earlier) have joined the insurgency in Afghanistan, where their prospects look brighter, and the burgeoning jihadist forces menacing Pakistan's borders. Observe how, just as the notion of success in war has been degraded and defined down, so too with the idea of what it means to demoralize the enemy.

The experience of Iraq has left many with greater confidence in their ability to subjugate infidels under the sword. There's reason to question whether Islamists fully expected to get all that far in Iraq, at least in the short run. It may be that they were content to exploit the conflict as an opportunity to maximize the number of American casualties and to hone their skills for use in other theaters of combat. These modest goals they accomplished, spectacularly. In the assessment of two scholars, Daniel Byman and Kenneth Pollack, the Iraq War

> served a Darwinian function for jihadist fighters; those who survived ended up better trained, more committed, and otherwise more formidable than when they began. Unfortunately, the skills they picked up in Iraq—sniper tactics, experience in urban warfare, an improved ability to avoid enemy intelligence, and use of man-portable surface-to-air missiles—are readily transferable to other theaters. The insurgents have also learned how to get through U.S. checkpoints, which are far less formidable on U.S. borders than they are in the war zone of Iraq. The ethos that glorifies suicide bombing has spread as well. The United States and its allies are more likely to face young men and women willing to kill themselves as they kill others, making targets much harder to defend. Most important, the jihadists have learned how to use improvised explosive devices, the greatest killer of U.S. forces in Iraq, and these devices have already shown up in Kuwait.[36]

Suicide bombing, another tactic heavily practiced in Iraq, is now rampant in Afghanistan. The sharing of "best practices" among jihadists is potentially unlimited in its scale and lethal impact. Although person-to-person training may be the traditional mode of transferring combat knowledge, the Web offers Islamists an inexpensive, worldwide communications platform. Through bulletin boards, online videos, and written manuals, they can recruit fighters to their cause and disseminate to them hard-won expertise in mass murder, to be deployed anywhere.

Nothing that the United States has done in Iraq or Afghanistan has given jihadists reason to abandon their desire for such mass-casualty attacks on the West. Washington's policy has in fact left them stronger than before. It has made the ideal of Islamic totalitarianism seem ever more viable—both by empowering and blessing Islamist rule, and by betraying its own timidity in the refusal to crush the jihad. The Islamist equation that fidelity to Islam is the path to existential dominance, while American secularism (read: impiety) means weakness, thus gains added plausibility in their minds.

Ayatollah Khomeini and Osama bin Laden rightly concluded that when America is pushed, it folds. To this lesson can now be added a self-humiliating innovation—outright bribery.

The Broader Conflict

Survey other fronts of the conflict, and the same dispiriting finding emerges: the enemy stands strengthened. Sometimes through direct encouragement from Washington, sometimes by dint of its passive failure to act against them, Islamists have made military and political advances toward their ideal.

For a sober, and reliably understated, assessment of the Islamist threat, leaf through the State Department's annual *Country Reports on Terrorism*. The edition published in 2008 notes that clusters of jihadists are encamped in "parts of East Africa, particularly Somalia, where they pose a serious threat to U.S. and allied interests in the region." Meanwhile "elements of Palestinian Islamic Jihad, Hamas and the Lord's Resistance Army" are settled in nearby Sudan. Al Qaeda itself has grown stronger through a merger with two additional Islamist groups, one based in Algeria, the other in Libya.[37]

Perhaps the most significant new Islamist operational stronghold today is in the tribal belt along the Afghan-Pakistan border.

Pakistan

J. Michael McConnell, the U.S. National Intelligence director, told Congress in early 2008 that in Afghanistan and Pakistan, Al Qaeda is gaining in strength and prepping new recruits who can blend into American society and attack domestic targets. "[T]he group has retained or regenerated key

elements of its capability, including top leadership, operational mid-level lieutenants, and de-facto safe haven in Pakistan's border area with Afghanistan."
That no-man's-land, as we have seen, is "a staging area for al-Qaeda's attacks
in support of the Taliban in Afghanistan as well as a location for training new
terrorist operatives," but it is also a base for preparing and deploying "attacks
in Pakistan, the Middle East, Africa, Europe and the United States." [38]

Taliban factions there have organized training schools for suicide bombers (some as young as ten) and produce and distribute propaganda DVDs to
recruit holy warriors.[39] The plot in 2006 to blow up airliners crossing the At-
lantic has been linked to the Pakistan tribal belt; the ringleader of the London Underground suicide bombers had trained in the area. In the autumn of
2008, Michael V. Hayden, director of the CIA, painted a dire picture. Sum-
ming up the gravity of the situation, he noted: "Today, virtually every major
terrorist threat my agency is aware of has threads back to the tribal areas."

Within Pakistan itself, Islamists "operate relatively freely in cities like
Karachi," according to *Newsweek*, and "pretty much come and go as they
please" in that country. Some Taliban commanders "have moved their wives
and children to Pakistan, where they live in the suburbs of cities like Peshawar and Islamabad. . . . Mullah Shabir Ahmad is a member of the Taliban's
30-man ruling council, or shura. He's moved his family to a modest neigh-
borhood of nearly identical brick and mud-brick houses in Quetta." Ahmad
spends about half the year in Pakistan, "shuttling between Quetta, Karachi,
Peshawar and the tribal belt to raise funds, recruit new fighters and plot
strategy with other commanders."[40]

From this redoubt jihadists orchestrate not only the military drive to
reconquer Afghanistan, but also a push to "Talibanize" large patches of Pakistan—further entrenching their operational hub. The growing imposition of
sharia law has spilled over from the lawless tribal belt into the neighboring
North West Frontier Province. The outer suburbs of cities like Peshawar,
the capital of that province, are already under Islamist control. Jihadist
forces have laid siege to the city, and may in time overpower the feckless
Pakistani authorities.

Like rampant weeds, Taliban-allied groups are firmly taking root on both
sides of the Afghan-Pakistan border. This Talibanization would formalize the
quasi-sovereignty of the de facto sharia ministates that serve as Islamist bases.
India has already suffered at the hands of this burgeoning Islamist menace.
Jihadist forces launched a devastating bomb attack on the Indian Embassy
in Kabul, and there is strong evidence linking jihadists operating from Pakistan to the three-day massacre in 2008 that claimed more than 170 lives in
Mumbai, India.

The more political power that Islamists seize in the Afghan-Pakistan borderlands, the more easily they can plan, train for, and carry out lethal attacks on targets farther afield. The threat emanating from this area, according to one scholar at RAND Corporation, is "comparable to what [the U.S.] faced on Sept. 11, 2001" when the Taliban ruled Afghanistan. The jihadists' "base of operations has moved only a short distance, roughly the difference from New York to Philadelphia."[41]

All of this has happened with the passive, and often active, complicity of the nuclear-armed Pakistani regime. In the 1990s Pakistan's Inter-Services Intelligence agency (ISI) had helped bring the Taliban to power. Gen. Pervez Musharraf's regime (1999–2008) was one of only three to formally endorse and recognize the Taliban's Islamist rule in Afghanistan. After 9/11, Musharraf claimed to be with us, rather than with the terrorists. Telling Washington what it desperately wanted to hear, Musharraf pledged "unstinted cooperation." But our newly anointed "major non-Nato ally" neither eradicated the Islamists nor allowed U.S. forces to do so. Instead in 2006 Musharraf reached a truce with them: in return for the Islamists' "promise" not to attack Pakistani soldiers, not to establish their own Taliban-like rule, and not to support foreign jihadists—Pakistan backed off and released 165 captured jihadists. This appeasing "truce" collapsed soon after and served to empower the jihadists.[42]

Musharraf's successor, Asif Ali Zardari, also vowed solidarity with America and promised to rid Pakistan of Islamists, who have been blamed for the assassination of Benazir Bhutto, a prominent politician and Zardari's wife. But little has changed: the regime took feeble steps against the Islamists but quickly slid back to pursuing appeasing settlements.[43]

The most ominous deal so far was signed into law in April 2009. In return for a cease-fire, Pakistan's national government granted Islamists the authority to enforce sharia law in the Swat Valley, a former tourist haven in northern Pakistan. The deal endorsed and formalized the advances that Islamists had already made: they had effectively conquered much of Swat, bringing residents under the cruel dominion of sharia.[44] For the Taliban, this was clearly a victory. It encouraged them to continue fighting to install Islamic law nationwide. "When we achieve our goal in one place," explained a spokesman for the Taliban, "we need to struggle for it in other areas." The goal, after all, is to "enforce the rule of Allah on the land of Allah." So the Taliban, of course, surged to exert their control over the nearby Buner district. They set up checkpoints, began patrolling villages, and announced the establishment of sharia courts.

The holy warriors advanced to positions within just *sixty* miles of Pakistan's capital city, Islamabad.[45]

Panicked and facing criticism from the West, Pakistan launched a meager military operation—not to defeat, once and for all, the Islamist forces, but only to try to recapture some of the territory that had fallen under Taliban control. The Islamists were brazen; on one occasion they stopped a Pakistani army convoy heading into Swat and forced it to turn back. The convoy duly complied.[46]

Islamabad may somehow manage to abate, temporarily, the galloping Talibanization of Pakistan. But even that is doubtful.

The regime has not only committed itself to the (self-destructive) policy of appeasement; powerful elements within the regime have long shielded and abetted Islamists. Pakistani forces along the border with Afghanistan have reportedly tipped off jihadists of impending U.S. strikes, and at times fired back on behalf of the holy warriors. Islamabad has denied Washington permission to send troops into the region to root out the jihadists—going so far as to shoot at U.S. helicopters nearing its border. Between Pakistan's military establishment and Islamist groups there are strong bonds. When American forces went into Afghanistan in 2001, many Islamists fled the country and alongside them were Pakistani intelligence officers who had worked as trainers for the Taliban regime. Pakistan has actively fostered Islamist fighters not only in Afghanistan, but also in Kashmir (where the Mumbai attackers apparently trained).[47]

Whether some of Pakistan's nuclear arsenal could fall into their hands is an open question. But that possibility is suggested by the scandal concerning A.Q. Khan, a Pakistani scientist. For years Khan illicitly sold nuclear technology and equipment to buyers worldwide (including Iran). When this came to light, Islamabad was breathtakingly tender in its so-called punishment of Khan (confining him to house arrest), and refused to turn him over to its ally, the United States, for questioning. The scandal revealed that Pakistan's nuclear expertise and materials could be had for a price. Maybe the regime was not complicit in Khan's deals, and maybe it has locked down its nukes and prevents anyone from selling access to that technology; but Pakistan might simply hand out some of those weapons, gratis, to the jihadists it has nourished for so long.

The situation in Pakistan is dire. Emblematic of the festering mess is the fact that jihadist commanders not only operate with impunity, they flaunt their confidence: thus Baitullah Mehsud, a prominent Taliban warlord, has led in-person press conferences before the Western media in Pakistan.

The danger from the Islamic totalitarian movement is not just that it *could* attack us, but the fact that its leaders have grown more confident. Islamists owe a debt of gratitude to George W. Bush's foreign policy, which opened the door for them to make political strides—by force and by electoral means. Their rising political fortunes have fueled ambitious hopes of greater advances.

That is especially true in the cases of Hamas and Hezbollah.

Lebanon and Palestinian Territories

Lebanese Hezbollah, it should be remembered, is the vanguard of Iran's proxy war against America and the West. It was a pioneer of suicide bombings against U.S. targets (see chapter 1). Hezbollah is believed to have established cells in Europe, Africa, South America, North America, and Asia, and it has passed on its military expertise to groups like Hamas and various insurgents in Iraq. George Tennet, former CIA director, observed in 2003 that Hezbollah was "a notch above" Al Qaeda, widely reputed as a global force, and Deputy Secretary of State Richard Armitage described the group as the "A Team" of terrorism. Like Al Qaeda and the rest of the Islamic totalitarian movement, the organization (whose name means "the party of Allah") is motivated by the moral-political ideal of a sharia regime.

The Islamic Resistance Movement—more commonly known by its acronym, Hamas—is a direct offshoot of the Muslim Brotherhood in Palestine (see chapters 1 and 7). Hamas grew enormously popular in part because it outstripped rival Palestinian terrorist groups with the ferocity of its attacks, particularly its deployment of suicide bombers. Its charter calls for the liquidation of the state of Israel as a major step in a global campaign to establish Allah's dominion.

These are enemy organizations—ones that the Bush crusade for democracy greatly bolstered. The administration insisted that Hezbollah be allowed to participate in Lebanon's 2005 elections. The Islamist group for the first time gained cabinet posts in the Lebanese government and control of several ministries. In the 2006 Palestinian elections, the White House ensured that Hamas (an avowedly murderous organization) was allowed to run. It won. The jihadists took over the reins of power in the Palestinian territories.

Facilitated by Washington, these political advances immensely boosted the confidence of both groups. By summer 2006, Hezbollah and Hamas instigated a war with Israel, and they came away with a major success.

Like so many wars that have erupted between Israel and its hostile neighbors, the conflict was in part a proxy fight. In many of the Cold War-era conflicts, Arab forces were surrogates for the Soviets, and Israel represented, and got some backing from, America (and the West). In 2006, the U.S.-aligned Israelis faced the Hamas-Hezbollah-Iran axis fighting under the banner of Islamic totalitarianism. So, it was in America's interest to do everything possible to aid Israel in crushing this common foe.

The war's outcome was stunning. Islamists battered Israel, the reputedly superior military force, and fought it to a stalemate. That accomplishment was possible because Israel renounced the military opportunity finally to destroy Hezbollah and Hamas. The clear victim of their aggression, it had the moral right to do so. It also had the capability—and, with Hezbollah missiles crashing down on cities in northern Israel, doing so was an urgent necessity. But Israel fought a self-denying war in the by-now familiar American pattern (see part 2). After years of U.S. pressure to show restraint, Israel demonstrated that it had accepted that selfless ethos, and backed down. It complied with international demands for a negotiated, appeasing settlement.

With that crumbling surrender, Israel destroyed the last remnants of its reputed military invincibility. Hard-earned in earlier clashes, that awesome stature was central to its deterrent power. Islamists now realized that Israel was a target they could plausibly hope to overpower militarily. Moreover, since Islamists (and the Arab world generally) view Israel as an American surrogate, the Israeli surrender also provided another confirmation of Washington's abject moral weakness. The United States was handed a golden opportunity to endorse Israel's eradication of two jihadist groups in the Middle East, but instead it backed off.

Hezbollah and Hamas emerged stronger. For a time, Hassan Nasrallah, the leader of Hezbollah, eclipsed Osama bin Laden as the Muslim world's hero of the moment. Iran, the chief backer of the Islamist axis, also had cause for joy, because the war's outcome burnished its status as a potent force in the region.

Encouraged by their success, the Islamists charged on. By the close of that year, Hezbollah summoned, and got, a crowd of thousands into the streets of Beirut. The goal was to topple the government. One of their major demands was that Hezbollah be given the power to veto all cabinet decisions. Crowds blocked the streets. The protestors camped out in a makeshift tent city in the center of Beirut, for months. Armed clashes flared up a few times. And although the standoff faded from the news in the West, it kept on going. Hezbollah had every reason to believe it had the upper hand.

More than one year later, in early 2008, the beleaguered government tried to exert pressure on the Islamist group. It shut down Hezbollah's vast telecommunications network and removed a video camera that the group had placed to surveil goings-on at Beirut airport. To this Hezbollah responded by venting its indignation: the gun fights that followed looked like the pandemonium last witnessed in Lebanon's horrific civil war. By proving its superior strength, Hezbollah compelled the nominally pro-U.S. government to back down. More than simply calling off its armed forces, however, the government went on to appease Hezbollah by granting the veto it had demanded.

So the Islamist group significantly enlarged its political dominion. Its power now extended beyond a de facto ministate (aka Hezbollaland) in southern Lebanon, to having the final say on the policies of the national government.

During this same period, Hamas also strived to achieve political supremacy within its current purview. The group worked to uproot its chief rival, the Fatah faction, from the Gaza strip. This it achieved through a protracted civil war that annihilated hundreds of Palestinians. With Fatah loyalists killed or kicked out of Gaza, Hamas turned its sights to the West Bank, the other tract of Palestinian-controlled territory. Even as this internecine fighting went on, Islamists in Gaza fired hundreds of Qassam rockets at neighboring Israeli towns. And like Hezbollah, the Palestinian jihadists are busy rearming, training fighters, amassing rockets. The Hamas-Israel war that broke out in December 2008 revealed the extent to which Hamas had grown stronger militarily; despite heavy Israeli retaliation and a ground war, the Islamists nevertheless managed to continue their rockets attacks, penetrating even farther into Israel.

Where the United States should have worked to dismantle Islamist strongholds, it played midwife for two new terrorist ministates in the Levant. The Bush administration *has* succeeded—but only in galvanizing jihadists in Beirut, Gaza City, Tehran, and beyond.

Iran

There is much truth in the sardonic quip that "we fought Iraq, and Iran won."[48] We noted earlier in this essay (and in other chapters) that Iran fomented much of the insurgent chaos in Iraq. The war enabled it to cause the murder of untold numbers of Americans. Furthermore, Iran has gained considerable power within Iraq, through its alliance with the leading Shiite and Kurdish parties. Tehran continues to provide millions in financing, arms, and explosives, as well as training in bomb-making and terrorist tactics, to all manner of holy warriors, in Iraq and elsewhere.

Tehran's relationship with Al Qaeda began before 9/11 and continues still. As the State Department euphemistically explains:

Iran [has] remained unwilling to bring to justice senior al-Qaeda (AQ) members it has detained, and has refused to publicly identify those senior members in its custody. Iran has repeatedly resisted numerous calls to transfer custody of its AQ detainees to their countries of origin or third countries for interrogation or trial. Iran [has] also continued to fail to control the activities of some AQ members who fled to Iran following the fall of the Taliban regime in Afghanistan.[49]

Translation: Taliban and Al Qaeda forces who fled Afghanistan found a refuge in Iran, where they are continuing to orchestrate their jihad.

But Iran's most malignant enterprise, the one that induces a cold sweat in Jerusalem, Paris, London, and Washington, is its avid quest to master nuclear technology. Even by conservative estimates, it may be just a matter of years before Iran could arm itself with a nuclear weapon—or put a doomsday device into the hands of its proxies. Of course, there have been attempts by the United States and its allies to prevent that outcome. In the last seven years, since con-clusive evidence of the Iranian nuclear program came to light, the regime has toyed with Western diplomats. Rightly believing its adversaries to be weak, Iran has stonewalled and defied the feeble United Nations sanctions imposed upon it. The Europeans, with American backing, try again and again to coax the Iranians with all manner of bribes, but the Islamists unflinchingly maintain that there's one "red line" that no deal can ever cross: that is, they will not give up nuclear technology. After the breakdown of each round of talks, Iran is offered yet another second chance—thereby highlighting the West's weakness.

It is quite clear why Tehran can set the terms of negotiations; Iran's lead-ers feel themselves to be in a position of strength. And indeed they are. The headline story of the last eight years is that, amid a so-called "war on terror," we have witnessed the ascendancy of Tehran—the Islamist regime our State Department routinely designates as the most active state-sponsor of terror-ism. Tehran relishes its new position. The regime's president, Mahmoud Ahmadinejad, underscored why Iran feels invulnerable. When the regime opened its uranium conversion facility at Isfahan, he observed, the West threatened military action, but "now, we are operating over 3,000 centri-fuges, and every week [another] new [centrifuge] system is installed." Darting a finger of rebuke at the West, he drew an apt conclusion: "you are making fools of yourselves—for you cannot harm Iran in the slightest."[50]

The ideological movement led by Iran has grown far stronger than it was pre-9/11. From Afghanistan to Iraq; from Pakistan to northern and eastern Africa, Islamists are succeeding in implementing, to varying degrees, their political-cultural vision of sharia rule. They stand vitalized by these inroads and further inspired by Iran's unbending—and undefeated—militancy.

Within the West
Washington's failure to identify and defeat Islamic totalitarianism—indeed, the active U.S. encouragement of it—has spurred a preexisting insidious trend in the cradle of Western civilization.

Within Europe, Islamists are carrying out a multiform jihad to elevate sharia as the supreme principle of society and government. Seeing their ideal ascendant across the globe, they feel entitled to arrogate to themselves greater political power wherever they reside. Their efforts constitute nothing less than a comprehensive thrust to Islamize the continent of Europe (and perhaps eventually North America). They do so not only by familiar violent means, but also by exploiting the West's intellectual self-doubt and weakness. European (and American) accommodation of this campaign has served only to intensify it.

The openly coercive and violent form of this campaign was on display in the rush-hour bombing of commuter trains in Madrid; the suicide bombings on London's underground; the attempted car bombing of nightclubs in London's West End, followed up by a desperate bid to blow up a crowded terminal building at Glasgow airport. Jihadist plots have been uncovered in Germany, Denmark, and across Europe. The point of such attacks is to punish unbelievers for deviation from Islamic precepts—and thus assert what the Islamists hold as the correct social principle.

That was the rationale behind the assault on the film director Theo Van Gogh. One morning in 2004, he was set upon while riding his bicycle to work in postcard-perfect Amsterdam. The attacker, Muhammad Bouyeri, a self-appointed Islamist enforcer, shot him point-blank and slit his throat, almost to the point of decapitation. A lengthy note pinned to Van Gogh's body with two kitchen knives spelled out why he had been executed. His "crime" was to make a critical film about Islam. The note also promised to visit the same punishment upon other "blasphemers" involved in the film, including the Dutch parliamentarian Ayaan Hirsi Ali.

At the trial, Bouyeri was proudly candid about the religious character of his deed: "I did what I did purely out of my beliefs. I want you to know that I acted out of conviction and not that I took his life because he was Dutch or because I was Moroccan and felt insulted." Unrepentant to the last, he spurned the opportunity to seek the mercy of the court, explaining that "If I ever get free, I would do it again."[51]

Bouyeri took it upon himself to silence, forever, a filmmaker who had dared impugn the religion of Islam. This ritual slaying brought to the Netherlands the same kind of religious censorship that characterizes the Arab-Islamic world, where governments censor the press, books, broadcast media, the Internet, and brutally punish "blasphemers." There is no freedom of speech under such regimes; the import of Van Gogh's murder was that there must not be any in Europe, either.

The Islamist assault on free speech began in earnest with Ayatollah Khomeini's 1989 fatwa enjoining "zealous Muslims" worldwide to murder the novelist Salman Rushdie, whose book, *The Satanic Verses*, supposedly blasphemed against Muhammad (see chapter 1). By demanding that free speech be nullified in the West, Khomeini presumptuously asserted that sharia must have global jurisdiction. Decades later that presumption lives on, with added force, among Islamists in Europe.

This was eloquently demonstrated, on a massive scale, in the uproar over the Danish cartoons of Muhammad (see chapter 2). Notice how this crisis was calculated to elevate sharia precepts above—indeed, to negate—the West's principle of free speech. The twists and turns of the backstory have been diligently recorded by Pernille Ammitzbøll and Lorenzo Vidino in the journal *Middle East Quarterly*. From that account it is clear how the Danish clerics who helped instigate the crisis sought to intimidate the Danish government and people into obedience. "We are not threatening anybody," one of the clerics wrote, early on, in a press release, "but when you see what happened in Holland and then still print the cartoons, that's quite stupid"—a threatening allusion to the fate of Theo Van Gogh.[52]

The instigators of the crisis ratcheted up the pressure by soliciting the help of regimes in the Muslim world. With their support and prompting, the riots exploded. The raging of mobs, the burning of flags, the firebombing of embassies—all this was meant to coerce the nations of Europe and North America to bow down to the dictates of sharia. Practically all of them did. In unison.

The U.S. State Department criticized the publication of the cartoons as "offensive to the beliefs of Muslims." With a perfunctory nod to free speech, Washington went on to betray that principle by indicating that perhaps the cartoons were better left unpublished. Leaders in Europe kneeled down and prostrated themselves. President Jacques Chirac of France said that "overt provocations" (i.e. the publication of those cartoons) should be "avoided." "I condemn all obvious provocations which could dangerously fuel passions," he groveled. E.U. foreign minister Javier Solana pleaded that the European Union shared the "anguish" of Muslims "offended" by the cartoons. The E.U.'s justice minister, Franco Frattini, said that the union would establish a "media code" to encourage "prudence." He told the *Daily Telegraph* of London: "The press will give the Muslim world the message: we are aware of the consequences of exercising the right of free expression. . . .We can and are ready to self-regulate that right."[53]

By appeasing Muslim intimidation and outright aggression, leaders of the West handed another victory to the Islamist cause. Since the Van Gogh incident and especially so after the cartoons crisis, Islamists have capitalized on the fear that they have instilled in European hearts. When necessary, the Islamists (like the virtue police in Afghanistan, Iran, Saudi Arabia) still resort to violence, but it is staggering how far they get without lifting a finger.

It is often enough for them merely to hint at reprisals, or simply to express their displeasure, to compel a gallery to shut down an exhibit, to induce an opera company to call off a performance, to intimidate publishers into self-censorship. Take the Dutch film "Fitna," which suggests a causal link between the Koran's teachings and terrorism. In the months prior to its release, the Netherlands was in turmoil. The Grand Mufti of Syria, speaking before the European parliament in Strasbourg, warned that "If there is unrest, bloodshed and violence after the broadcast of the Koran film, [the filmmaker Geert] Wilders will be responsible."[54] So pervasive were the fears of Muslim violence, that Wilders could not find a venue willing to screen it. The Dutch government denounced the film, sight unseen.

The holy war against free speech is the most salient, but hardly the only, manifestation of the quest to Islamize Europe. A growing number of books—such as Bat Ye'or's Eurabia, Bruce Bawer's While Europe Slept, Melanie Phillips's Londonistan, and Robert Spencer's Stealth Jihad—have documented this trend in Europe as well as its spread to North America. In the cities of Europe, for example, we find Muslims self-segregating in their own communities and demanding official recognition for the sovereign authority of sharia law in their areas. France has officially designated about 750 areas as "no-go" zones, many of them Muslim-dominated neighborhoods, where police lack authority.[55]

The ambition behind all this is voiced openly. One Belgian imam, for instance, helpfully explained that "Soon we will take power in this country. Those who criticize us now, will regret it. They will have to serve us. Prepare, for the hour is near."[56] A cleric in the United Kingdom expressed his fervent desire that Britain become an Islamic state, with the flag of Islam raised above 10 Downing Street.[57] That may seem fanciful, but it is an option for which the door has been opened. Note the trial balloon sent up in 2008 by the Archbishop of Canterbury, head of the established Anglican Church: in a lecture at the Royal Courts of Justice, he suggested that elements of sharia should be officially accommodated within British law.[58] Although his comments elicited a tepid backlash, the fact remains that so prominent a figure would even contemplate such a possibility, much less advocate for it publicly. It captures perfectly the direction in which Europe is heading.

Many Muslim demands are accommodated under the prevailing doctrine of multiculturalism, which ostensibly repudiates judgment of values while scorning and negating Western principles. The institutionalized embrace of multiculturalism reflects a self-doubt about the worth of Western values and the principles of secular society. The same self-doubt, married with fear, underlies other forms of capitulation to Islamist demands. Many in the

West recognize, even if they evade the knowledge, that the Islamist assault on freedom and Western values is backed by the threat of violence. Putting this into words, Osama bin Laden warned Europeans against reprinting the Danish cartoons of Muhammad: "If there is no check on the freedom of your words, then let your hearts be open to the freedom of our actions."[59] Thus we are called upon to "respect" Islamic values and accede to their demands—with the understanding that if we comply and demonstrate our submission, the holy warriors will refrain from punishing us. (The bombing of the Danish Embassy in Pakistan, shortly after bin Laden's message, demonstrated the lesson: the Danish media dared reprint the cartoons, and so here was the penalty.)

This fits the model of jihadist conquest in history. Conquered peoples were given the option of conversion, death, or, sometimes, the status of *dhimmis*—humiliated subject-peoples living as second-class citizens at the mercy of Islamic overlords (see chapter 2). Europeans, to an astounding extent, are rapidly selling themselves into dhimmitude.

While the situation in Europe is particularly acute, the craven submission to Islamist coercion is spreading across the West. It is a measure of the power Islamists wield that the chilling effect on free speech applies even to books that aim to *propitiate* Muslims. For example: *The Jewel of Medina*, a historical novel, offers a calculatedly (and, some say, tendentiously) flattering portrayal of the life of Aisha, one of the wives of the prophet Muhammad. Random House, the American publisher, had paid the author a hefty advance for the novel and was about to publish the book, when it got wind of a hint of trouble. One reviewer of the galleys, an American professor who teaches Islamic history, took a dislike to the book. She in turn alerted a Muslim friend, who runs an online message board. A day later, there was much sanctimonious talk on blogs and forums about instigating a campaign against the novel and its publisher. A sense of foreboding, and then utter panic, swept over the executives at Random House. Citing "fear of a possible terrorist threat from extremist Muslims," the publisher scrapped plans to bring out the book.[60]

It is hard to blame Random House for its capitulation. With governments urging people to keep their heads down and their mouths shut—or else they are on their own—many see no alternative but to censor themselves and preemptively submit. Thus we also hear of moves in Australia to ban topless sunbathing—lest Muslim passersby be offended at the sight of the unclothed human form. Or gyms in American cities and universities that mandate women-only hours—to accommodate the sex-segregation demanded by some Muslims. And though the particular steps may seem innocuous in themselves, they signify a piecemeal advance for Islamists.

Part of what has prevented honest people from grasping the nature of this trend is the widespread failure properly to define the enemy. The focus on one particular means ("terrorism"), rather than the fundamental end actuating the Islamist movement, has prevented many people from recognizing the essential commonality between the events unfolding within the West and the terror-war led by Tehran, bin Laden, and their passionate followers. Contributing greatly to the confusion (and evasion) has been the Bush administration's insistence that we're in a "war on terror"—and its refusal to name and defeat the actual enemy.

Whether or not Islamists can attain a worldwide sharia regime, the shameful truth is that they remain undefeated and strengthening. Many of their victims in the West, meanwhile, tremble and placatingly unroll the red carpet for the advance of the conquest-seeking Islamist movement.

The only party in this conflict that has achieved real success is not Washington, but the Islamists.

Disarming Ourselves

The ruinous effects of Bush's policy will be felt for years to come, but not only because it facilitated and empowered the enemy. It is also because that policy has left Americans demoralized and disarmed.

Even before Barack Obama's tenure began, the legacy of Bush's foreign policy had already circumscribed the options believed to be open to us. For many people, the fiasco of Iraq and Afghanistan discredited the use of military power, per se, to advance U.S. security. In other words: we tried war, war failed, so forget war. That option has been swept off the table.

Take the urgent issue of what to do about Iran. There is a shrinking minority of voices calling for a military attack on Iran, but they timidly focus exclusively on the regime's nuclear facilities—while exempting the Islamists in power, who would remain intact to carry on the jihad by existing means. The idea of taking out Iran's nuclear program commands little support in foreign policy circles, and even then only as a distant, undesirable last resort, an implied threat we would rather never carry out. To many minds, the far more congenial approach is to manage the crisis using diplomatic "carrots and sticks."

The mainstream debate today (if it can be called a debate) concerns not whether, but only how, to engage Iran.

This is how Vali Nasr and Ray Takeyh, two advocates of engaging Iran, believe it should play out: America would begin by backing off from our supposedly "provocative naval deployments in the Persian Gulf, easing its efforts to get European and Asian Banks to divest from Iran and inviting Iranian representatives to all regional and international conferences dealing with the Middle East." As part of this process,

> the language of American diplomacy would also have to alter. The administration cannot propose negotiations while castigating Iran as part of an "axis of evil" or the "central banker of terrorism" and forming a regional alliance to roll back Iranian influence.
>
> Once a more suitable environment has been created, the United States should propose dialogue without conditions with the aim of normalizing relations. For too long, proposed talks with Iran have focused on areas of American concern: nuclear proliferation and Iraq. A more comprehensive platform would involve the totality of disagreements between the two countries and also address Iran's regional interests.

The thought is that "just as Iran will meet confrontation with confrontation, it will respond to what it perceives as flexibility with pragmatism."[61] Bill Richardson, a former U.N. ambassador, also favors this approach. In an op-ed for the *Washington Post*, he asserted that "The Iranians will not end their nuclear program because we threaten them and call them names." But, he claims, "They will renounce nukes because we convince them that they will be safer and more prosperous if they do that than if they don't."[62]

How precisely we should package and present the deal depends on whom you listen to. Some stress the importance of signaling our willingness to impose economic sanctions with real bite, preferably through the United Nations; others, such as the conservative Heritage Foundation, urge bypassing the U.N. (where allies of Iran have neutered already weak sanctions) and opting for "sanctions of the willing" that rely on the cooperation of Western nations.

The manner in which America should petition Iran is also debated. When CNN invited five former secretaries of state to offer their advice to the soon-to-be elected 44th president of the United States, they disagreed only on a minor detail—at what level of government to engage Iran—while unanimously endorsing the conclusion that U.S.-Iranian negotiations are the only way forward.[63] Some months later, Joe Biden explained the viewpoint of the Obama team on how to proceed: "We should make it very clear to Iran what it risks in terms of isolation if it continues to pursue a dangerous nuclear program but also what it stands to gain if it does the right thing." Amplifying that point, in his inauguration speech Barack Obama assured Iran "that we will extend a hand if you are willing to unclench your fist."[64]

Through some diplomatic channel and (per Obama) "without preconditions," we would offer Iran juicy incentives ("carrots")—money, aid, trade agreements, diplomatic prestige—that would dissuade it from pursuing a nuclear program. We just have to be creative in concocting an appetizing enough package. Key to this exercise is that we make Iran an offer too good to refuse. "Just talking about better relations is clearly not enough to get Tehran's attention," argues an editorial in the *New York Times*. "What is needed is a credible grand gesture, like sending a high-level envoy to Tehran with a concrete list of diplomatic and economic rewards, including a timetable for restoring full diplomatic relations with the United States—if Tehran is ready to deal."[65] But if Iran balks, we hint at the proverbial "stick" of punishment: for example, economic sanctions and the vaporous threat of military action that in reality we've already shelved.

The chances of Iran taking our carrots and stopping its nuclear program? Slim, according to proponents. Some claim that unless we try, we won't know—and even if we fail, at least we may win some friends. Ambassador Mitchell Reiss, a former senior State Department official under a Republican president, suggested that "Even if [such talks] are a nonstarter for Tehran, I think we score points in the region for trying."[66]

The track record of economic sanctions on Iran—through the U.N. and via U.S. alliances with foreign nations—should offer no solace to the would-be appeasers. Although multi-layered restrictions on U.S. trade with Iran have been on the books for years, such trade goes on nonetheless.[67] More damning still is that, despite all the existing sanctions and its membership in the Nuclear Nonproliferation Treaty, Iran has bought and developed what it needs to run 3,000-plus centrifuges that could produce weapons-grade fuel.

But for the sake of argument, suppose that such measures could buy Iran's agreement to halt its nuclear program. Could this do more than buy us the illusion of security? Iran would have every incentive to go through the motions of compliance, while using the bribes as a revenue stream and talks as a cover for clandestine nuclear operations—repeating the extortion cycle at will. North Korea exploited the same kind of arrangement to stave off economic ruin and arm itself with a nuclear weapon. Evidence from the horse's mouth suggests that Iran is already using this ploy. In a closed-door meeting with the leading clerics, one of Iran's chief negotiators explained to his audience that "When we were negotiating with the Europeans in Tehran we were still installing some of the equipment at the Isfahan [nuclear facility] site. . . . In reality, by creating a tame situation [with talks], we could finish Isfahan."[68]

The popular agitation for a diplomatic deal would in fact have us resign ourselves to a nuclear Iran, while we perform as cash cow and moral cover for its militant ambitions. When all of this blows up in our face—or in downtown Manhattan—we can console ourselves that, well, maybe we scored some points in the region. How comforting.

To say that this policy of appeasing bribery projects timidity is much too charitable; it actively encourages Iran and the legions of jihadists around the world. Pinning our hopes for security on the practice of appeasement makes as much sense as trying to put out a house fire by dousing the flames with gasoline.

The popularity of this idea reflects how far America has sunk in the years since 9/11. In the weeks following these attacks, people were (properly) keen to see their government assert its military power in the service of our lives and freedom. But now, it is the weakest, avowedly self-denying, proposal that America embraces as a rational option for dealing with the enemy. Even if we have yet to admit it to ourselves, we are in retreat.

Eight years after 9/11, and two wars later, this is where Washington's policy has brought us. We find ourselves repeating the destructive pattern that marked the period leading up the attacks on that Tuesday morning (see chapter 1).

For decades prior to 9/11 the United States had evidence, piling up from many sources, of an escalating threat from the Islamist movement. The alarms wailed, the attacks increased, but America remained oblivious.

Today the jihadist threat (as we saw earlier in this chapter) is growing worse: we noted ominous developments—from Afghanistan and Pakistan, to Iran and Europe—that speak for themselves; we heard the dire warnings from the head of the CIA, the National Intelligence Director, and others. And yet Americans fail to take these alarms seriously. Many prefer not to think about the problem and evasively find solace in the so-called successes in Iraq and the non-recurrence of another 9/11—even as Islamists rally and Iran builds nukes.

For decades since our first clash with Islamic totalitarianism, in the 1979 Embassy crisis, Washington's dominant response to Islamist aggression was a multiform policy of appeasement. American reliance on passivity, negligible pro forma retaliation, and outright bribery had the effect of fueling a spiral of Islamist hostility.

Today our leaders have taken the horrendous experience of the Bush wars as grounds to rule out any thought of a self-assertive foreign policy entailing military force. Instead, we find a broad-based cultural drift toward the self-destructive, myopic policy of appeasement.

The return of this pattern should provoke outrage. Americans should demand of their government a genuine alternative—a policy that will in fact protect our freedom and our lives for decades into the future. But no such outrage can be expected from a nation that, like its leaders, has been dispirited. Nor can we expect from Washington a fundamentally different kind of policy. Our leaders look, but refuse to recognize the severity of the problem. They make and implement policy, but drift toward appeasement and evade its inescapably calamitous future results. For, at root, the return of this policy orientation reveals an intellectual-moral bankruptcy.

We desperately need new thinking in our foreign policy, if we are to achieve our security.

CHAPTER SEVEN

The Road to Victory: A Radical Change in U.S. Mideast Policy

Elan Journo

The Precondition for Victory

Although Islamic totalitarianism grows stronger, although jihadists continue to threaten America and the West, although the situation appears hopeless—in fact, we *can* defeat the enemy. We *can* achieve an unqualified victory—a genuine victory, as final and unquestionable as we did in World War II against Japan. We *can* achieve lasting security in the face of the threats emanating from the volatile Middle East. And while it may sound strange, what holds us back is not at root any lack of material strength or resources. Our gravest weakness lies in our foreign policy.

It is ultimately U.S. foreign policy that brought us here. It exposed us to jihadist predations prior to 9/11 (part 1) and mired us in "no-win" wars since then (chapters 3–6). We cannot overcome the problem simply by changing the personnel at the State Department or even the Oval Office. The problem transcends party politics, because it is rooted in the prevailing approaches to foreign policy.

On one side is the so-called realism of pursuing myopic, range-of-the-moment "practicality," an unprincipled approach that leads to appeasing an enemy we refuse to identify. We saw in earlier chapters that this was the pattern of U.S. policy in the decades leading up to 9/11—and that it is returning under the Obama administration. On the other side is the putatively long-range, principled policy exemplified in the Bush administration's response to 9/11. Part 2 of this book showed how this orientation to foreign policy mandates altruistic wars and the empowerment of our enemies. If we take a macroperspective, the options presented to us are these: a principled, idealistic policy that entails sacrificing our security—or a supposedly practical policy that likewise subverts our security.

Let us finally jettison the selfless moral ideas and anti-principled pseudo-practicality that have shaped our Mideast policy, because it is these intellectual underpinnings that have crippled our security in practice. To formulate and implement a principled policy that achieves our actual self-interest, we must begin with an entirely different intellectual framework.

That framework must rest on the moral ideal of rational self-interest. This moral principle, championed by the philosopher Ayn Rand, entails a new conception of what constitutes our self-interest. A foreign policy informed by the principle of egoism, in Rand's words, would be "explicitly and proudly dedicated to the defense of America's rights and national self-interests."[1] Such a policy puts the goal of protecting American lives first—as its exclusive concern and as an inviolable moral principle (see also the discussion in part 2). The vision we uphold is that of the United States living up to its full moral stature: a nation exhibiting the earned confidence that we have the moral right to defend ourselves and to assert our own interests in the Middle East.

What would such a policy look like? In confronting the Islamist movement, what policy is truly in our self-interest—and how would that play out in practice?

The recommendations laid out in this chapter illustrate what it would mean to adopt a foreign policy in the Middle East premised on the ideal of rational egoism. Specifically, we look at the immediate question of how to defeat Islamic totalitarianism, and the ongoing issue of defining and securing America's self-interest in the region.

Defeating the Standard-Bearer

Seven years ago, the People's Mojahedin, a group opposed to Tehran's regime, brought to light evidence that Iran was building a clandestine nuclear plant at Natanz. Officials with the atomic energy agency of the United Nations were sent to investigate. Iran, it turned out, had made significant progress—far more so than previously suspected in what some regarded as exaggerated U.S. intelligence assessments. Michael Rubin and Patrick Clawson, scholars of Iran, describe the foreboding situation.

> [Iran had] 164 centrifuges completed, 1,000 more being built, and a facility being completed to house 50,000 more. In addition, Iran acknowledged that it had not declared more than a ton of uranium of various types it had imported from China in 1991, including some processed uranium, now missing, which

was suitable as feedstock for the centrifuges. [Iran] also announced that it was building a heavy water reactor at Arak, that it was preparing to mine uranium ore, and that it had produced "yellowcake" (the first stage in the transformation from natural uranium to centrifuge feedstock).[2]

The years since then have brought further Iranian advances. By late 2008, the regime boasted that it had put online some 3,000 centrifuges, and it continued stridently to reject demands from Washington and its allies to halt the program. Iran routinely scoffs at attempts to block its progress through U.N. sanctions and other instruments of diplomatic pressure. All of this has dialed up the panic in capitals throughout the Western world. But there is something bizarre and dangerously parochial in the escalating fears about a nuclear-armed Iran.

Of course, we should worry about that ominous prospect. But there's much more going on than Iran's violation of the terms of the (laughably impotent) Nuclear Nonproliferation Treaty. Many people sense, even if few will say it openly, that Iran's pursuit of a nuclear weapon—despite its destructive power—is not the whole story. Notice that other countries, such as France and Britain, have nukes, and that no one in the West worries about it. Fears about Iran going nuclear stem from what we believe the regime is capable of doing.

Let us then widen the artificially narrow, crisis-bound context in which our policy is commonly thought about and formulated. Viewed in a broader context, Tehran's quest for mastery of nuclear technology is one element in a long campaign. This campaign of aggression—sometimes direct, usually through proxies—began with the seizure of the U.S. Embassy in Tehran in 1979 and the captivity of American hostages in Iran for 444 days. The regime's subcontracting forces in Lebanon carried out the car bombing of the embassy in Beirut in 1983. Months later, Islamist forces working hand in glove with Tehran dispatched a suicide bomber, driving a large explosive-filled truck, to attack the barracks where American servicemen were stationed in the Lebanese capital. The U.S. death toll—241 souls—made it "the single deadliest attack for U.S. Marines since the Battle of Iwo Jima" and among the worst post-World War II attacks on Americans.[3] Throughout the 1980s in Lebanon, Islamists took more than 100 Westerners hostage, including twenty-five Americans, torturing some of them to death (see chapter 1).

And on it went. FBI investigations into the 1996 bombing of Khobar Towers, in which seventeen U.S. servicemen lost their lives, found that Iran was pulling the strings behind that attack. Al Qaeda carried out the simultaneous bombings of embassies in Kenya and Tanzania in 1998; the group gained important technical and logistical training vital to carrying out the attacks from the Iranian subcontractor Hezbollah. There's more: the 9/11 Commission found that "senior Al Qaeda operatives and trainers traveled to Iran to receive training in explosives," and that eight to ten of the fourteen Saudi "muscle hijackers" had "traveled into or out of Iran between October 2000 and February 2001."[4]

Data on Iran's concerted aggression is not a secret confined only to those privileged with top-secret clearances. It has been reported in newspapers and magazines and books, in open sources that laymen and policymakers can readily consult. Yet the prevailing attitude toward the regime holds that these past violent acts are unrelated crises, like so many dots that need not be connected. Hence Iran's channeling of explosives and arms and trainers to anti-American insurgents in Iraq—another mode of aggression—is regarded as an independent point of friction, another crisis to be viewed in isolation. Hence the regime's nuclear quest is to be dealt with as a separate, unlinked issue. The splintered approach of hatching ad hoc responses—now to this crisis, now to that one—in the absence of any long-range perspective on the problem does not a policy make. Its main result is to multiply and worsen crises (see chapter 1). Witness, for example, how American policy has so far succeeded only in facilitating Iran's burgeoning (military and political) influence in the region (see chapter 6).

A commitment to defining a policy that flows from the facts and that serves U.S. self-interest requires an integrated perspective. Its starting point is to understand, and keep in mind, the sweep of Iran's past actions and the ideological goals informing its behavior. That is necessary for objectively evaluating the threat from Iran—and defining steps we should take to assure our security across many years and arenas.

Iran's Centrality to the Islamist Movement

Even a highly abbreviated record of Iran's violent acts must be summed up as nothing less than an outright proxy war against us. And this war is integral to the global jihad. Iran aims to advance a goal shared by the many adherents of Islamic totalitarianism: to smite down the infidel West—and principally the "Great Satan"—that stands in the way of fulfilling the vision of a global sharia regime (see chapter 2). For decades the Islamic Republic of Iran has been the jihad's standard-bearer.

A standard-bearer leads the charge and, by virtue of keeping the flag aloft, signals to all who follow him that the battle is advancing. The sight of that flag nourishes hope of victory. It reinvigorates hope amid setbacks and daunting odds. It inspires fighters to redouble their effort and it attracts new recruits to a winning cause. A glimpse of that fluttering banner during the tumult of a clash fires up the serried ranks, tells them to dream big and to march on confident in the eventual triumph of the cause. The role of standard-bearer thus entails something far more than leading the charge at the front line; fundamentally, it serves as an ideological inspiration to the cause.

Consider the prospects and mood of the Islamist movement prior to the Iranian revolution in 1979.

Though groups within the Islamist movement argued about the optimal means to achieve their goal, they agreed on the basic nature of that goal: supplanting existing regimes with new ones in which sharia is the supreme law of the land. The Muslim Brotherhood, founded in Egypt in 1928, sought to overthrow what it saw as the impious rule of man-made, secular law and impose all-encompassing rule under Islamic laws. The path to making religion the supreme principle of politics was jihad, which would be undertaken by the masses, whom the Brotherhood would prepare and educate. (Islamists elsewhere, e.g., Pakistan, came up with essentially the same analysis.) In 1936 there were in Egypt some 150 branches of the Brotherhood; eight years later, 1,500. Membership in those early years has been estimated to fall somewhere between 100,000 and 500,000. With time the number of members and sympathizers burgeoned to the millions. From its base in Egypt, the Brotherhood sent out envoys to set up local chapters in Sudan, Saudi Arabia, Syria, Lebanon, Morocco (among others).[5] In Palestine, for example, the first of many local chapters opened in 1945; two years later, there were some 12,000 to 20,000 active members.[6]

Members of the Brotherhood hatched numerous plots to assassinate political figures in Egypt, hoping thereby to start a popular uprising for Islamic rule. Some plots went nowhere, others were foiled. Five decades after its founding, the Brotherhood had hardly come close to accomplishing its goal. Nor had any of its offshoots, splinter cells, or ideologically allied groups in other countries. Allah's obedient slaves, longing to foist theocratic government upon all mankind, failed even to change the regime under which they lived. Was it Allah's will that they failed? Perhaps. Was there any hope of realizing their ideal? Little to none, apparently, given the brutal government crackdown aimed at crushing the movement in Egypt (when thousands of members were imprisoned).

Everything changed after 1979.

The Iranian revolution sent shock waves across the Muslim world. It proved to followers of the movement that their ideal was achievable. The truly pious could, in fact, prevail over the materially more powerful infidels and apostates. Pictures of Ayatollah Khomeini, the intellectual founder of the new Islamist state, appeared in Cairo and other cities in Egypt.[7] At the time Ayman al-Zawahiri, who went on to become the number two of Al

Qaeda, headed a militant Egyptian organization called Al-Jihad. Inspired by the accomplishments of the faithful in Iran, the organization backed the revolution with leaflets and cassette tapes encouraging other Islamic groups to model themselves after Iran. [8] (Al-Jihad has since merged with Al Qaeda.) One researcher has observed that the

> Iranian revolution contributed to a revival of the political role of mosques in the mobilization of politically-oriented Islamic elements throughout the Islamic world. Some Islamic actors in Egypt were impressed by the proposed Iranian project of Islamic renaissance with its extranational dimensions. For those actors, the Iranian revolution represented a new reality to which all Muslims could relate their history, ideals and the objective of reviving the Islamic Umma [community of believers]. [9]

For the Muslim Brotherhood in particular, this was a world-historic event. Members "frequently cited the Iranian revolution as evidence of the eventual victory of those who followed the path of God." The transformation of Iran's political system "gave the Muslim Brotherhood greater self-confidence." Some Islamist groups urged followers to study (and copy) the revolution's political and organizational tools, such as the use of mass-produced speeches distributed on cassette tapes.[10]

The tumult in Iran reignited the Palestinian cause, which was losing momentum, and transmuted it from a quasi-secular, nationalist struggle to an emphatically religious one (see chapter 2). Within the Palestinian territories, the strategy of the local branch of the Muslim Brotherhood held that the time for jihad was years off in the future. In preparation for that day, the important work was to recruit believers and instill in them a love of jihad and religious rule. And so it went for decades. Khomeini's triumph in Iran, however, quickened the desire of Islamists in Palestine (as elsewhere) to pursue their ideal—not tomorrow, but *now*. Clearly the time for jihad was at hand. That conviction led some members of the Brotherhood to splinter off and launch Palestinian Islamic Jihad, a group explicitly following Khomeini's path. In justifying its enmity toward Israel, the group cited a fatwa from Khomeini indicating that destroying the "'Zionist entity' is a religious duty."[11] Eventually, the Muslim Brotherhood spun off its own jihadist outfit—Hamas—to lead the revived campaign against Israel.

The unprecedented rise in Iran of a new, purely Islamic state galvanized Muslims throughout the Middle East, in Morocco, in Algeria, in Nigeria, in South Africa, in Bangladesh, in Indonesia, across wide swathes of Europe, and behind the Iron Curtain.[12] In an editorial titled "A Thumping Yes to the Islamic Republic," one London-based periodical argued at the time that,

Very early on in the agitation it had become manifest that the Iranian movement was not just a negative movement protesting against the tyrannies of the
Pahlavi monarchy. It represented a profound and vehement assertion of the
long denied Islamic urges of the Iranian people.[13]

Tehran fed that excitement. The regime pumped out propaganda trumpet-
ing its accomplishments, and made good its promise to export the revolution.[14]
Lebanese Hezbollah was its most notable foreign enterprise, with outposts in
South America, Europe, and the Far East. Its attacks on American interests
in Lebanon, described in chapter 1, succeeded in driving out U.S. troops from
the country. Here was another confirmation that devotion to Allah empow-
ers the faithful to vanquish stronger infidel forces. They had done it in the
streets of Tehran, against the impious rule of the Shah, and now they were
humiliating the most powerful infidel nation on earth. "The governments of
the world," Khomeini had announced, "should know that Islam cannot be
defeated. Islam will be victorious in all the countries of the world, and Islam
and the teachings of the Koran will prevail all over the world."[15] For Muslims
witnessing Iran's striving in the path of Allah, this boast had teeth.

By uniting words with violent action, the totalitarian Islamic regime in
Iran distinguished itself as the genuine vanguard for the cause. Domestically,
using radio, billboards, posters, school textbooks, postage stamps, currency—
through every medium—the clerics worked to reshape the society according
to Islamic dictates.[16] Internationally, the regime marched forward to expand
the dominion of Allah's reign on earth (engaging itself, to varying degrees,
in the Bosnian conflict and also the Algerian civil war of 1991, among others).[17] When compared with the monarchies, quasi-secular, nationalist, and
socialist regimes in the Middle East—regimes that invoked Islamic themes
for populist ends—Iran stood out for its authentic devotion and embodiment
of the Islamist ideal. Not only was it a booming ideological voice, it was also
an activist in the service of that ideology.

This contrasted with Saudi Arabia, guardian of two of Islam's sacred
places, Medina and Mecca, and thus the presumptive leader of worldwide
Muslims. The Saudi regime was put on the defensive. It actively sought to
propagate and proselytize for its own brand of Islamic totalitarianism (Wah-
habism) abroad, and impose sharia law domestically. Yet the regime fell short
of equaling Iran's crusading spirit and orchestration of murderous attacks in
the name of God. Elements within the Saudi regime finance Islamic terrorism, and the regime may well outspend Iran in missionary work. But this relative passivity serves to highlight Iran's militancy. The Saudis bankroll thousands of the *madrassas* (religious schools) and mosques where future jihadists
are educated. But Iran energizes and glorifies jihadists. Whereas the Saudi

regime elicits contempt from Islamists, because of its ties to Washington and its Westernized (read: impious) royal family; Iran inspires them.

For the Islamist movement, the theocracy of Iran redefined what's possible. Islamists would go on to chalk up what, to them, were further successes. In 1981 an Egyptian jihadist group assassinated the country's president, Anwar Sadat. By 1989 holy warriors (mujahideen) in Afghanistan had bloodied the invading Soviet army, which eventually pulled out ignominiously. That withdrawal was arguably the result of U.S. and Saudi assistance to the mujahideen; nonetheless, Islamists distilled from that episode another demonstration of the existential power of piety. Later there came the formation of Al Qaeda, bringing together a number of separate Islamist organizations. The Taliban, with Saudi and Pakistani assistance, wrested control of Kabul in 1996 and established its infamous totalitarian regime. Later there came a string of lethal attacks in the Middle East, Europe, and the United States.

What's significant about these developments is not that Iran pulled the strings behind each and every one; it did not. But it was Iran as exemplar, as a functioning, aggressive Islamist state, that has been fundamental to the daring and confidence of jihadists worldwide. Years after its revolution, Tehran's regime continued to be an inspiration (to Sunni and Shiite Muslims) for "upholding Islam against the power of the West."[18] Were it not for the enduring inspirational power of Iran, were it not for the regime's fidelity to the cause of jihad, were it not for its prosecution of that campaign with impunity across decades, the Islamist movement today would be little more than a sulky anti-Western pamphleteering society. (See chapter 1 on the role of the Western appeasement in encouraging Islamists since 1979.)

There's no question, either, that Iran's stature has grown since 9/11 because of Washington's refusal to target the regime as the primary enemy. Tehran's successful expansion of its proxy war to post-invasion Iraq, its military strengthening of Hamas and Hezbollah, its unbending commitment to developing nuclear technology—all serve to strengthen its reputation as the nation that can humiliate and inflict considerable harm upon the mighty United States.

For these reasons, therefore, it is imperative that we recognize the full extent of Iran's threat to our lives and freedom. To put an end to the Islamist movement, to eliminate the immediate threats emanating from the Middle East, we need to begin with Iran. How?

The Way Forward, Informed by History
Considering the corpse-strewn history of Iranian aggression, we must reject the proposal of sitting down with the regime at the negotiating table. Underlying that proposal is the assumption that Tehran could be persuaded to

change its behavior out of a desire for peace and prosperity for its people. But in reality this is a regime that during the Iran-Iraq War sent children and teenagers to march across battlefields: they had to "move continuously forward in perfectly straight rows. It did not matter whether they fell as cannon fodder to enemy fire or detonated the mines with their bodies: the important thing was that [they] continued to move toward the enemy over the torn and mutilated remains of their fallen comrades, going to their deaths in wave after wave." This ghastly practice is today the source not of "national shame, but of growing pride."[19]

Iranian leaders and official media foster and encourage reverence for "martyrdom" operations (suicide attacks). "Today, more than ever," Mahmoud Ahmadinejad said in January 2008, "we must inculcate in the younger generation the culture of *shahada* [martyrdom]. This is a mission of supreme ideological [importance] . . . One who treads the path of martyrdom and brings himself to this extreme attains the pinnacle of human [achievement]. It is a duty incumbent upon [each member of] the public to bring himself, as well as others, to this pinnacle." And there is a movement afoot in Iran today to recruit and train future "martyrs."[20]

Tehran's regime has proven its monumental contempt for the irreplaceable value of human lives. Contrary to the make-believe of Western diplomats, Tehran cannot be dealt with through persuasion. Any attempt at bribery only feeds the belief of Islamists that America is morally bankrupt and defeatable.

Nor would it be in our long-range self-interest to launch a military operation exclusively targeting Iran's nuclear facilities (see chapter 6). Even if that half-hearted measure were successful, it would merely deprive the regime of a potential weapon, for a while. Our problem is not the weapon, but those driven to acquire and use it. Such an operation would do nothing meaningful to halt Iran's backing of Islamist warriors in the proxy war. At best this operation would cause Iran some annoyance, but not deter other forms of the regime's aggression.

Nor could such a meek jab at Iran snuff out the fervor of Islamists. Far from conveying our disgust and contempt for Iran's regime, far from broadcasting our judgment that it is perverse, a limited strike on its nuclear facilities would imply an endorsement of our enemy's right to remain in power and its right to harm us using conventional tactics and arms. What else could it mean that, after years of tolerating Iranian aggression, we bestir ourselves to act *only* in order to pluck from its hands one particular instrument of destruction, leaving the unbowed regime to deploy whatever other instruments it can find to continue its jihad? To the victims of Iran it is irrelevant whether they die from the blast of a conventional or nuclear device; either way, they're dead.

The only practical way forward requires that we recognize Iran's role as the ideological motor of the Islamist movement—and then proceed to crush it.

This is a twofold job. Breaking totally with our policy of timidity, inaction, and appeasement, we must demonstrate an indefatigable commitment to defending the lives of Americans. Fundamentally, that begins with declaring—publicly and proudly—our moral condemnation of Iran and of the Islamist movement that it leads. We need to lay out the facts underlying our reasoning and pronounce the verdict: that the ideology of Islamic totalitarianism is vicious and depraved. In doing so, we project a righteous dedication to our values of individual rights and political freedom and affirm that we will tolerate no threat to the lives and freedom of Americans.

The second element, which presupposes the first, is to live up to that dedication in practice by unleashing all necessary military force to put an end to the Iranian regime and demoralize the Islamist movement. To eliminate the threat from Iran, at minimum our forces should bring down the regime, neutralize its military power, and capture or kill its leadership. Throughout the process, the United States must resolutely affirm the propriety of its own retaliatory action and denounce the ideology at the heart of Iran's regime and its jihad. The regime must be defeated in fact and it must accept and internalize that reality. It must be made to realize that, if Iran ever dares to threaten or take up arms against us, we will again meet that aggression with a crushing military onslaught.[21]

Does this mean another military nightmare like Iraq and Afghanistan? No. In those campaigns, the goal of Washington was not defeating whatever threat we faced from those countries, but to "liberate" Afghans and Iraqis and give them the vote (see part 2). That selfless goal went hand in hand with the altruistic rules of engagement that hamstrung our military. Consider the needlessly brutal ordeal of U.S. combat troops in Iraq. Iraqis throw Molotov cocktails (i.e., flaming gasoline-filled bottles) at your vehicle—but you are prohibited from responding with force. Iraqis, to quote a Pentagon study, "drop large chunks of concrete blocks from second story buildings or overpasses" as you drive by—but you are not allowed to respond. "Every group of Soldiers and Marines interviewed," the study summarizes, "reported that they felt the existing ROE [rules of engagement] tied their hands, preventing them from doing what needed to be done to win the war."[22] It is self-effacing policies like these that encourage insurgents and enable them to flourish, while sinking our troops into quagmires.

We need to unshackle America's brave and capable warriors from the perverse battlefield restrictions that put the lives of enemy fighters and civilians above those of our troops. It is imperative that Washington allow our military tacticians to deploy (or threaten to deploy) any weapon—including nuclear weapons—that they deem necessary to destroy the enemy rapidly and with minimum cost in American lives. Culpability for the regrettable loss of civilian lives belongs entirely to the aggressor. Washington's practice of apologizing for such casualties in Afghanistan and Iraq—like the offer to pay to rebuild mosques destroyed by sectarian infighting—is shameful, and has no place in the prosecution of a war in self-defense[23] (see chapter 4).

By pulling out Iran's military fangs and utterly humiliating it, we would eliminate an existential threat to our security and deal a massive blow to the ideal of Islamic totalitarianism. We should then proceed to drive home the lesson of Iran with the comprehensive demoralization of the movement's followers. What they must understand is that their cause is discredited, that anyone who fights to advance it will be similarly crushed, that the jihad is over. The followers must be made to repudiate the goal of implementing their political-cultural ideal of total sharia rule.

But, it may be asked, might an American strike in fact achieve the opposite result? Would it not further antagonize Muslims across the region, and would it not spur Iranians in particular to "rally round the flag"—and against us? Would it not simply generate more enemies?

No, so long as we demonstrate a resolute drive to crush the enemy and discredit its goals. That's how we achieved victory over Japan in World War II. We devastated that country. The historian John David Lewis has observed:

By the end of 1945 . . . the Japanese had lost it all. Surrounded by an impregnable armada, they lay prostrate before merciless American bombers. The best of their youth had killed themselves in suicide attacks. Their fleet was sunk. More than sixty cities had been firebombed. Two cities had been atombombed. They were militarily defeated and psychologically shattered, and they faced the possibility of a famine that could kill millions.

Yet the result was not to inflame, but to extinguish the Japanese desire for war. With "a zeal as great as that with which they had once armed for battle, the Japanese reformed their nation."

They adopted a new constitution, purged their schools of religious and military indoctrination, and abandoned aggressive warfare. Imperial subjects became citizens; "divine" decrees were replaced with rights-respecting laws; rulers became administrators; feudal cartels became corporations; propaganda organs became newspapers; women achieved suffrage; and students learned the principles of self-reliance and self-government. Hiroshima, formerly the headquarters of a fanatical military force, became a world center for nonviolence. Those who had once marched feverishly for war now marched passionately for peace.[24]

Key to the sixty-plus years of peace that have followed the U.S. victory over Japan was that nation's abandonment of its religious-military ideology, the creed that fueled its all-consuming hunger for supremacy. The same kind of ideological repudiation can, and must be, effected in the strongholds of Islamic totalitarianism.

There is nothing uniquely intractable about the pervasive support for Islamic totalitarianism. Followers of this—and every—creed accept it by choice; it is not implanted before birth, and it can be uprooted. Remember, too, that its emergence as a dominant view in the Muslim world occurred only in the latter half of the twentieth century. Prior to that, a different ideology captivated millions of Muslim minds: pan-Arab nationalism. But that entrenched ideology was utterly discredited, and dislodged from the minds of its followers, through a military defeat.

In its heyday, pan-Arab nationalism was the most potent force in Arab-Muslim politics. A woozy blend of tribalism and statism, it demanded subordination of individuals to an expansive, supra-national quasi-socialist regime. Egypt's military dictator, Gamal Abdel Nasser, famously championed the cause and sought to make his regime the vanguard of the pan-Arabist movement. It was under this banner that Nasser justified the seizure and nationalization of Western assets such as the Suez Canal in 1956; and it was also the battle cry rallying Egypt and its allies to fight against Israel, hoping to clear the way for Arab regional supremacy. Arguably the movement's first, and unequivocal, triumph came in 1958 with the political combination of Egypt and Syria into the United Arab Republic (UAR).

To the news of this political union, Arabs throughout the Middle East reacted with "stunned amazement, which quickly turned into uncontrolled euphoria." The announcement of the UAR, in the words of one journalist at the time, was "the greatest hour in the history of the Arabs since the . . . victories of Salah al-Din [al-Ayubi]," the legendary conqueror fighting under the banner of Islam. In Syria, the new political union drew huge crowds from across the country, who flooded into the streets and public squares of Damascus. "Unable to contain their joy, they sang, listened to impromptu patriotic orations, danced the *dabka* (Syrian folk dance), and made up instant poetic slogans that were rhythmically sung and repeated by all."[25]

The rapture across the Arab world strengthened the belief that pan-Arabism was the unstoppable wave of the future, an eminently realizable ideal. Leaders in neighboring countries witnessed the elation of their people, and feared that this movement would rise up within—or without—their borders to challenge their hold on power (though the UAR was a fragile, short-lived union).

Popular and potent though it was, pan-Arabism no longer commands passionate support. The movement faded, losing its grip on the Arab-Muslim world, because it was discredited. The tipping point was the Arab-Israeli War of 1967, also called the Six Day War.

With that offensive, Egypt and its Arab allies intended to expunge the Zionist "cancer" from the region. Vilifying Israel as an obstacle to the fulfillment of Arab unity, they geared up for a climactic showdown. Military superiority lay on the side of the Arab forces, whose combined resources dwarfed those of Israel. The Arab nations poised themselves finally to re-conquer that minuscule, though highly symbolic, tract of land between the Jordan River and the Mediterranean Sea. Hopes were running high. The Israelis, it was boasted, would be fed to the fish in the sea.

But within the first hours of the clash Israeli bombing raids demolished Egypt's fleet of bombers while the Egyptian aircraft were still on the tarmac. Destroyed also were hundreds of Egyptian and Jordanian tanks and thousands of military vehicles. Egypt's military hardware was decimated (only 15 percent remained). The casualty rates were more than 20-to-1 in Israel's favor; among the Arab forces, Egypt suffered the largest numerical hit, between 10,000–15,000 men, among them 1,500 officers.[26] It is said that retreating Egyptian soldiers in the Sinai Dessert fled with such despairing haste that many abandoned their boots in the sand dunes, and scampered away. In just 132 hours—roughly six days—the Arabs were trounced.

What followed the military defeat, though, was a profound rethinking of the prevailing ideology. Fouad Ajami, a political scientist, observes that "No sooner had the Six Day War ended than a war of a different sort erupted in the Arab world: a conflict over the defeat. Who was responsible for it? What did the defeat say about the basis of Arab society, the quality of the Arab as an individual? How should the Arab world be organized to cope with the defeat and its consequences?"[27]

The search for answers gave rise to a flurry of articles, pamphlets, and books offering explanations of the "disaster." The quantity and range of accounts led one scholar to classify the analyses into five categories; another researcher, a former prime minister of Iraq, saw fit to define twice as many distinct schools of thought on the issue.[28] The answers covered the spectrum—from secularists denouncing the current regimes as insufficiently committed to the revolutionary pan-Arabist ideal; to operational accounts blaming incompetent military leadership; to the all-purpose Islamist account blaming any failure on a lack of piety.

From this ideological ferment, one conclusion bubbled up with dazzling clarity. "While Arabs, in whatever state they lived, continued to recognize their membership in the cultural space called 'the Arab world,' . . . they no longer truly believed in the viability of organic political unity."[29] The event that overthrew that ideal was the 1967 war.

> And what stamped on it this sense of fatality was the fact that it was Egypt under [Nasser] that lost. Egypt's devastating defeat was Arab nationalism's mortal loss, for . . . the fate of Arab nationalism during the struggles, triumphs and reversals of the 1950s and 1960s was inexorably linked to Egypt and its charismatic president. Had it just been Syria or Jordan, or even both, who lost the war, it would not have been the unmitigated disaster for Arab nationalism that the June war turned out to be. But Arab nationalism could not survive the abject humiliation inflicted on its acknowledged prophet, who, through his shrill and overzealous propaganda machine, had promised a fabled triumph in this al-Ma'raka al-Masiriya, the battle of destiny.[30]

Evidently the people of the Arab-Islamic world are just as susceptible to having their cherished ideal overthrown and discredited as were the people of imperialist Japan in the 1940s. So there is every reason to expect that America's defeat of the self-assured Islamic Republic of Iran would similarly rob the Islamist movement of its glamour and potency.

But the collapse of pan-Arab nationalism also provides a cautionary lesson on the peril of half-measures. The '67 war, unlike the defeat of Japan in World War II, was at best an equivocal success for the victims of the pan-Arab movement, Israel and the West. With the rumbling of cannons echoing in the air, Israel rushed to negotiate an appeasing settlement with the Arabs. Acting at the behest of Washington and the U.N., Israel thus repudiated the hard-fought-for fruit of victory: the moral right to demand surrender from, and dictate terms to, the defeated aggressors. That fateful decision prolonged the conflict, because the initiators of the war were not compelled to renounce their militancy. Consequently, though pan-Arabism was waning, Arab nations rearmed and took up the fight again in 1973.

And the ambiguous defeat in '67 created an opening for Islamists to fill the void left by Arab nationalism. The nationalists had offered their own tribalist justification for liquidating Israel, and they failed. But that goal was never renounced. Enter the Islamists. They took up and championed that wildly popular goal and recast it as a religious-moral struggle. This theme has lost none of its resonance today, when Iran's leadership vows to "wipe Israel off the map."

For the United States, the broader lesson is that our military campaign must achieve an unambiguous and righteous discrediting of the Islamist movement's goal. In targeting Iran, we must repudiate all outcomes that entail compromise or that otherwise leave any glimmer of hope, in any mind, that the Islamist ideal is achievable.

An important means of accomplishing that is through the deliberate and vocal propagation of our moral justification for the war.

Demoralizing the Enemy

During the military operations, we can use so-called public diplomacy to drive into the minds in the Islamic world that we know our cause is right, that theirs is wrong, and that we will not stop until they give up. Of course, we subvert our objective if we practice the Bush administration's version of public diplomacy. It is worse than useless to set up a U.S.-backed Arab language television network, Al Hurra, and open it up (as Washington did) to serve as a forum for speeches by Islamists such as Hassan Nasrallah, leader of Hezbollah, and Iran's president Ahmadinejad.[31] What's needed is not more touchy-feely programming and pamphlets about how America embraces all cultural values, regardless of how corrupt they are; or fulsome pledges committing the United States to perpetual, selfless service to the needs of Iraqis and Afghans.

We would need, instead, a campaign of leafleting, television and radio broadcasts, and public statements in all available media explaining that Iran is suffering our wrath precisely because of its role as the leader of the jihad. The message we should convey is that the pain and death suffered in that country is a direct result of the regime's commitment to and efforts to advance the Islamist ideal. We can connect in people's minds the devastation of our war with the creed that they hear enunciated at Friday sermons and that they see glorified in jihadist propaganda videos of Westerners getting beheaded and blown up. Through our messaging, we should identify our stature as superiors who fight for moral ideals that are objectively beneficial to human life. To all who hear and read our messaging, we should convey that from now on they will have to make room for and accommodate our value system, our way of dealing with the world.

The demoralization campaign should continue even after the toppling of the regime. Our primary concern is to render Iran non-threatening. It is up to the people in the defeated regime to rebuild; we bear no moral obligation to help them in any way. It is conceivable that occupying the country and directing the establishment of a non-threatening regime (as we did in Japan) may be in our interest, if doing so entails no sacrifice of U.S. wealth or lives (see chapters 3 and 5). Whoever wishes to build up a new regime, can listen to our broadcasts and take them as a lead for what political ideals are truly worth embracing. The crucial point that should be explained and underlined repeatedly—during and after combat—is that we will return with an overwhelming military response if whatever regime arises postwar decides to become threatening. The audience for this point—which cannot be overstated—is the entire Arab-Islamic world.

We would have no further reason to be concerned with Iran, if it were not a source of oil (ranking among the world's top three holders of proven oil and natural gas reserves). But oil is the lifeblood that courses through the industrial organs of the U.S. economy. American households, businesses, offices, and factories consumed 20.7 million barrels per day in 2007—twenty-four percent of the global petroleum supply—making us the largest consumers of the commodity. More than half (58 percent) of the petroleum we consume is imported.[32] Since oil is so important to the American economy, what policy should we adopt toward the oil reserves buried under the Iranian soil and ocean floor? What policy would be in our self-interest?

In a defeated Iran, the new regime that comes to power may or may not be capitalistic; it may or may not be pro-Western. It is quite possible, indeed more than likely given the region's political culture, that some form of strong-man rule takes hold. Obviously it would be preferable if the regime modeled itself on our system of government as a protector of individual rights. But it would be absurd and self-destructive for the United States to fight a war to remove one belligerent regime in Iran, only to allow another one to use profits from the sale of oil to become a new threat. Nor can we allow our access to oil to fall to the whim of whatever regime takes over postwar.

Our policy should be to demand that the regime ensure the free trade in oil, and that not one penny from that trade be used to finance Islamists. This demand we must back with an ultimatum: unless our twin demands are satisfied, the United States will return with force to open up the flow of oil and to strangle off funding of aggression against us. Morally, this would be within our rights to do—both for the sake of assuring our security and our supply of much-needed oil.

Putting out of reach the petro-dollars that have empowered the Islamists would further demoralize the remaining followers of the movement (not to mention existing tyrants). Starkly and emphatically, this policy signals that America recognizes and proudly pursues its own interests; that we brook no attempt to harm the lives of Americans; that we protect ourselves and the free trade of goods necessary for our prosperity. Islamists and sundry despots will see their unearned source of wealth vanish. Those who hate and wish to destroy our society will see America as a righteous colossus that none dare affront—for the reality of its retaliatory wrath is all too real. And all too frightening.

With the resounding defeat of Iran, we can expect a widespread crumbling of the jihadist movement. Holy warriors will find themselves bereft of their inspiring standard-bearer, deprived of financial means, in despair of realizing their ideal. America—the country they used to believe was an easy mark, a lamb to be handily slaughtered by followers of Allah—will stand on the world stage as a formidable adversary. An implacable force committed on moral principle to its own self-defense and values.

Putting out the Embers of the Jihad

Beyond the necessary first step of confronting Iran, our policy toward the Middle East may require further use (or the threat of) military force. There are two major factors for why this is so.

(1) Many Islamists and the leaders of existing regimes may regard America's new policy as just another flip-flop, the latest fad—albeit a terrifying one—emanating from a country with a record of inconsistency and self-contradictory policies. For them the conclusion may be to keep their heads down, and wait it out until a new policy comes into play, or a new administration comes to power (bringing with it a new policy). To be fully effective, then, our policy must be consistently implemented, as a matter of principle, over time and in different arenas.

(2) The other factor has to do with the results of the Bush crusade for democracy. That policy, as noted in earlier chapters, turned a weak threat into a greater one. Remember that the Islamist movement was never militarily superior, nor ever a tightly regimented force. Note, for example, the multi-year incubation time for the 9/11 plot, and the fact that it depended parasitically on using Western technology, embodied by airliners that were hijacked, to harm us. The movement is also riven by infighting and tactical quarrels. Observe the endless subdivision of cells into new groups, and the splintering disputes among them. That's true also of the Al Qaeda network; for example, the organization's number two, Zawahiri, demurred at its Iraqi lieutenant's tactic of fomenting ethno-sectarian strife. But the so-called "war on terror" left jihadists to augment their military capabilities and empowered them morally and politically through elections. Washington's response to 9/11 emboldened a movement that might otherwise have disintegrated or lost steam.

With Iran defeated, however, we can expect to see lingering pockets of the Islamist movement and pro-jihadist regimes like Saudi Arabia quake in fear and retreat. How long it takes for the material and spiritual discrediting of the Islamist ideal to sink in across the board is hard to predict. We could simply stand by and wait for Islamists to hang up their suicide vests, tear up plans for 9/11-scale attacks, and kill each other off through infighting. But it better serves our goal of protecting American lives to hasten the end of this conflict. Doing that may entail confronting the Islamist movement's lesser, but still dangerous, remnants.

We turn now to a number of flashpoints—Saudi Arabia, Pakistan, Afghanistan, Iraq, Lebanon, Syria, and the Palestinian territories—and explore what a policy committed to America's rational self-interest would counsel.

In these contexts as in the case of Iran, the same principles apply. Specifically, we need to judge the situation objectively, and then proceed to define our response by reference to the facts on the ground and our overarching purpose of emasculating the jihadist movement. The steps outlined here encompass two kinds of recommendations: (1) how to clear out any vestiges of the Islamist movement, and (2) what approach we should adopt in the long run toward the region. Regarding the first category, how many of these steps prove necessary will depend on what's left of the Islamist movement post-Iran; it may be the case that we need to implement a few, some, or (improbably) all of these suggestions.

Saudi Arabia

The Kingdom of Saudi Arabia enjoys an undeserved standing as a loyal U.S. ally. Members of the sprawling al Saud royal family hobnob with Washington's elite, some have vacationed at President Bush's ranch in Crawford, Texas, and we sell the regime advanced military hardware (practically arming its puny military). From the end of the 1991 Gulf War through 2003, American forces stationed in the kingdom shielded it from a neighboring predator, Saddam Hussein. Though this U.S.-Saudi relationship goes back decades, the basis for it is an unscrupulous and thus self-defeating American desire to secure access to Saudi oil. Unscrupulous, because it legitimizes the theocratic kingdom and treats it as if it were squeaky-clean, despite the vitriolic jihadist incitement emanating from the regime. Self-defeating, because in turning a blind eye to the character of Saudi Arabia, Washington has allowed that state's ill-gotten petro-dollars to fund and facilitate the spread of Islamist ideology (if not also the actual arming of jihadists).

Within its borders, the Saudi regime governs by reference to sharia. Youngsters are inculcated, in schools, through state-controlled media, and mosques, with an abiding hatred for Western values such as political freedom. State-endorsed religious leaders regularly deliver anti-American diatribes at Friday sermons. Preachers in mosques, on the Internet, and on television incite Saudis to engage in jihad. And it works.

Saad Ibraham Saad al Bidna was among the holy warriors swept up by U.S. forces and held at Guantanamo for four years. After his release, he explained to an interviewer what set him off on his religious struggle:

> Many may find it difficult to believe, but I was not very devout, though I did pray regularly. But enthusiasm and zeal filled the hearts of many young people, and unfortunately, I followed certain fatwas that were posted on the Internet. [These fatwas] call upon young people to wage jihad in certain regions. They tempt them [by describing] the great reward [they will receive], the status of the martyrs in Paradise and the virgins that await them [there].[33]

It would be a mistake to think that such fatwas are exceptions to the prevailing ideas in the country. Far from it. Listen to the advice offered by Sheik Saleh al-Luhaidan, the chief justice of Saudi Arabia's Supreme Judicial Council: "If someone knows that he is capable of entering Iraq in order to join the fight, and if his intention is to raise up the word of God, then he is free to do so." Going to fight Americans, he said, is religiously permissible. "The lawfulness of his action is in fighting an enemy who is fighting Muslims."[34]

Such pronouncements have the clout of revered authority figures, and reinforce the propaganda of various Islamist outfits recruiting holy warriors. During a 2007 raid on an insurgent human-smuggling cell in Iraq, American forces found stacks of documents and computers with some five terabytes of data. Contained in that data was detailed biographical information on hundreds of recruited fighters. The analysis of the origins of the 700-plus recruits was eye-opening. The largest number by far—305, or forty-one percent—were Saudis. (The second-largest group, amounting to 137, came from Libya.)[35] The regime is fast becoming famous for exporting not just oil, but also jihadists. Evidently these holy warriors are carrying on the tradition established by the 9/11 hijackers, fifteen of whom were Saudis.

Billions of dollars from Saudi Arabia are piped across the world to proselytize for the regime's Wahhabist strain of totalitarian Islam. The Finsbury Park Mosque in London, for example, came into being through the patronage of King Fahd of Saudi Arabia. He gave more than 1.25 million pounds sterling to fund the building. One preacher at that mosque, Abu Hamza, evidently had ties to the Islamist group that claimed credit for attacking the USS *Cole* in 2000. He also bragged of his ties with the Taliban government. In the late 1990s, while Hamza was still preaching at the mosque,

[w]orshippers then began noticing groups of young men staying overnight at the mosque. These included Richard Reid, the "shoe bomber"; a Tunisian, Nizar Trabelsi, who was told to drive a truck loaded with explosives into the U.S. Embassy in Paris; Zacarias Moussaoui, the 9/11 planner; Ahmed Ressam, who was arrested attempting to bomb the Los Angeles airport at the millennium; Anas al-Liby, now on the FBI's most-wanted list and in whose Manchester flat police found al-Qaeda's terror manual in 1998; Abu Doha, wanted in the United States and France for plotting bombings; and others.[36]

Now turn to one Saudi-funded mosque in Birmingham, in the north of England. This is but a flavor of the sermons dished out: "Muslims shouldn't [be] satisfied with living in other than the total Islamic state" explains a preacher at the Green Lane Mosque who calls himself Abu Usamah. How this abstract goal should be realized is concretely spelled out: "We ask Allah to bring about the means and the ways in which the Muslims will get the power and the honour of repelling the . . . [unbelievers], where we can go out and perform the jihad. We ask Allah to bring that time, so we can be participants in that." Preachers at Green Lane Mosque studied at religious seminaries in Saudi Arabia; periodically worshippers listen to the religious teachings of a notable cleric in Saudi Arabia, through a live video hookup that is projected onto the wall of the mosque.[37]

According to the estimate of one expert, Saudi charitable donations range between $3 billion and $4 billion annually, and as much as twenty percent goes abroad. [38] There is ambiguity—conveniently so for the Saudi regime—about the dividing line between government sanctioned "charitable" contributions to the spread of Islamist ideas, and money supplied by private benefactors. Many of the Saudi charities and missionary organizations, which build mosques and madrassas and distribute religious books around the world, enjoy the patronage of members of the ruling royal family. The U.S. Treasury Department identified Al Haramain, a major Saudi charitable organization, as "one of the principal Islamic NGOs providing support for the Al Qaida network and promoting militant Islamic doctrine worldwide."[39] One study reports that "U.S. investigators have linked a former Al Haramain employee to the 1998 U.S. embassy bombing in Tanzania."[40] Nor is it plausible that any organization can be truly private, without government involvement or winking indulgence, in a religious monarchy where there is no political freedom.

Of course, the Saudis promised—and to a modest extent carried out—investigations into the financial workings of Islamic charities. They imposed some restrictions on the financial activities of some charities. And a joint Saudi-U.S. task force has apparently investigated some 1,098 Saudi bank accounts for suspected involvement in terrorist financing, if the regime's claims are to be believed.[41] But these and other perfunctory measures, such as arresting some members of Islamist cells, fall far short of what we should expect from a genuine ally.

Let us, once and for all, sweep aside the delusion that Saudi Arabia is a friend. It is openly hostile. While the regime is not itself a considerable military threat, it is a formidable ideological and financial engine of the jihad.

The Saudis may stop these activities on their own out of fear, or we may have to coerce them into it—but either way, the regime's backing of the jihad must end.

Our policy toward the kingdom should reflect an objective judgment of the regime's moral stature. A vicious, brutal state, it is beneath contempt and spectacularly unworthy of the endorsement implied in being designated an ally of the United States of America. We should therefore put the Saudis in their place, formally denouncing their political system and the pernicious ideas on which it is based. That resounding step alone may well be enough to intimidate the regime to capitulate voluntarily (if only so that the Saudi royal family can cling to power).

Unless Saudi Arabia ceases to proselytize and finance jihadists, Washington has every right to demand that the regime do so, immediately—and then watch for signs of backsliding. To compel its compliance, we would make clear that the regime's defiance will render it subject to our standing ultimatum: dare to threaten us, and suffer ruin. We should present the Saudis with a further non-negotiable demand: like Iran and for the same reasons, the Saudi regime must ensure the free trade of oil and must renounce (and prohibit its subjects from) funding the Islamist cause.

Having shut down the ideological and financial engines of the jihad—Iran and Saudi Arabia—Washington will face an increasingly demoralized movement. Whatever die-hard Islamists remain at this point will be waiting with bated breath for any sign of American weakness, any inconsistency, any exception to our policy of defeating their cause, any iota that can fuel their propaganda theme that the pious Muslim warriors can yet vanquish mightier infidels. But remaining principled in our policy, we should give them no such opening.

Unfortunately, the Bush administration has sullied the notion of a foreign policy shaped by moral principle. In its conception, that meant following a corrupt ideal (namely, the duty to serve others, rather than U.S. self-interest [see part 2]) and the practice of arbitrary, out of context judgments that ignore inconvenient facts. Only our enemies benefit from that so-called moralistic policy.

The point of sticking to our principles is not that we must, in the name of some duty, serve some abstract ideas. The point is that with the right moral principle as our guide to action, we can achieve our self-interested goal of protecting Americans. Resting at the foundation of our foreign policy should be the principle that recognizes our moral right to self-defense. That in turn leads to the requirement that we judge other nations objectively. Without properly evaluating other nations, we cannot distinguish between friends and foes, nor deal with them accordingly. That's essential not only for stamping out the remnants of the Islamist movement, but also for our long-term policy toward to the region.

The U.S. policy toward Pakistan provides an object lesson on the need for objectively judging other regimes.

Pakistan and Afghanistan

The entrenchment of Islamist strongholds along the Afghan-Pakistan border, and increasingly within Pakistan itself, is the result of Washington's unprincipled foreign policy. We saw in chapter 6 that Pakistan was a patron of Islamist groups, notably the Taliban, and that despite Islamabad's pledge that it was an ally of the United States, a mountain of evidence contradicts that claim. Yet for years the Bush administration continued to channel billions of dollars in aid to Pakistan, ostensibly to combat the jihadists, even as the regime openly bribed them and at times abetted their resurgence in Afghanistan. Washington continued to insist that Pakistan was a valued ally, that it was making valiant efforts, that its appeasement of jihadists was a sensible policy.

The mess in Pakistan has come about and festered because, fundamentally, Washington deluded itself about the Pakistan alliance. Eschewing the actual practice of moral judgment, we timidly treated the regime as if it were some angelic, unimpeachably loyal friend that deserved our respect and billions—solely because it said so. Shutting out of mind its true character, we then slathered on a coat of whitewash to obscure its corrupt actions. For its part, Pakistan could safely get away with its racket by doing just enough to give the appearance of being an ally, but no more. There was little to fear, considering the weakness Washington displayed in every aspect of the "war on terror."

But a proper approach then, and now, entails facing the truth. We undercut our long-range goal if we fail to judge, or evade our conclusions about, Pakistan (or any regime). Could we have had a profitable alliance with Pakistan? Quite possibly, but only if we dealt with this purported lesser of two evils as, indeed, evil. That would mean acknowledging the immorality

of Pakistan's past and demanding that it vigorously combat the Islamic totalitarians as proof of repudiating them. We would have to be frank: the regime
should be kept at arm's length, and we should explain openly that we would
welcome and support new, pro-American leaders in Pakistan who actually
embrace freedom.

The meaningful threat of U.S. military force may well be enough to instill fear in Pakistan, so that it will indeed combat the jihadists within its
purview. We would be morally entitled to issue, and if necessary fulfill, that
threat—but we could equally decide to bypass the regime altogether, and do
the job ourselves.

We cannot allow Pakistan to have its borders and eat them too: on the
one hand, it claims territorial sovereignty as the reason for denying U.S.
forces access to Islamists in its tribal borderlands; on the other hand, the regime patently lacks exclusive legal sovereignty in those areas, as witness the
growing Talibanization there. Unless Pakistan tamps down the dregs of the
jihad in those areas, Washington should not forsake that goal in the name of
respecting Pakistan's nonexistent sovereignty in those areas.

With the Islamists' stronghold in the Afghan-Pakistan borderlands destroyed, the United States should tell the government of Pakistan that it,
like the defeated Iran, is subject to our standing ultimatum in that part of the
world. Its passive or active support for Islamists will result in the fate that we
inflicted on Iran. That ultimatum—which our actions contra Iran and Saudi
Arabia will have made tangibly credible—should deter Pakistan.

Clearing out the jihadist training camps and operational centers in the
Afghan-Pakistan borderlands will make it easier to squash whatever remains
of the Taliban-Al Qaeda insurgency in Afghanistan. Here the task is to finish
the job begun in 2001 (see chapters 4 and 6).

Flooding the country with many more U.S. troops is probably unnecessary and indeed would not get us far, unless we unburden our troops from the
absurd, self-destructive rules of engagement that prevent them from using all
necessary force to do their job. Washington's so-called battlefield ethics were
tightened even more in recent years in Afghanistan, and not coincidentally,
the Islamist insurgency grew stronger. For example, "Air Force lawyers vet
all the air strikes approved by the operational air commanders," while "[v]ast
numbers of public, religious and historic sites make up a computer database
of no-strike zones."[42]

Under current policies, bombing raids often have to be canceled, sacrificing the opportunity to kill Islamist fighters, for fear of civilian casualties.
The Islamists are aware of these policies, and exploit them to their advantage. But "the beauty of what we do is we will get them eventually," claims

Lt. Gen. Gary L. North, who favors this approach. "Eventually, we will get to the point where we can achieve—within the constraints of which we operate, which by the way the enemy does not operate under—and we will get them."[43]

Eventually.

It is past time to repudiate "eventually" and embrace "now." As part of underscoring our commitment to wipe out all traces of the Islamist movement, we should suspend these irrational, self-denying rules that protect enemy forces and needlessly prolong the fighting and increase the risks to our troops. Our rules of engagement must put the lives of Americans, and specifically of our own troops, above all else. Morally, if we send men into battle, we are obliged to let them fight to win; sending them onto a battlefield to become cannon fodder is utterly wicked.

As for Afghanistan's regime, it should be brought under Washington's standing policy that promises thorough retaliation to any nation in the region that threatens us. This, not hundreds of millions of dollars in reconstruction aid, is the proper incentive to ensure that the regime restrains itself and the people living within its borders.

Iraq

When a line of domino pieces fall, the first upon the second, the second upon the third, each pushing down the next, the cascade begins to feel inescapable. And indeed Washington should broadcast that point. Seeing America bring down their inspiration, the Islamist regime of Iran, and uproot other jihadist strongholds, such as those in Pakistan and Afghanistan, any holy warrior left within Iraq cannot but feel despondent.

With pro-Islamist elements in the Muslim world feeling hopeless and depressed, jihadists will find it harder to secure safe houses, if they can find any; harder to orchestrate and keep secret whatever plots they hope to carry out, if they still believe they stand a chance of executing such plans. But here again, we should not wait for the appeal and the support networks of the Islamist movement simply to dissolve on their own time frame.

With Iran's Islamist regime gone, gone also will be its meddling in Iraq. Jihadists would no longer have access to Iranian mortars, arms, and improvised explosive devices (IEDs); the Revolutionary Guard Corps and Hezbollah trainers, and tacticians; the piles of Iranian-supplied cash to bankroll operations, recruitment, ammunition, safe houses. Militia groups—whether Sunni or Shiite—who enjoyed Iranian backing in the past will find themselves bereft of the means and confidence to fight Americans. The pro-Iranian Shiite parties in Iraq's governing coalition will find themselves politically orphaned. The absence of Iran's tentacles in Iraq could lead to a fizzling out of the insurgency—something that U.S. forces should accelerate by force of arms, unrestricted by current rules of engagement. But the ending of Iran's influence could also precipitate an outright resumption of the simmering sectarian civil war.

What, then, should we aim to accomplish in Iraq? In the Bush administration's original vision of the war, "success" would mean an outcome that bestows aid and the good life on Iraqis—regardless of what that costs in U.S. lives and regardless of how that affects our security. This is a selfless, and corrupt, goal (see chapters 3 and 5). It behooves us to repudiate Washington's promise to bring Iraq up from third-world-level poverty; that was an improper promise that our leaders have no business committing Americans to.

Nor is it in our self-interest to aim at "stabilizing" Iraq in the sense of shepherding its layers of clans, tribes, sects, and factions to some improbable reconciliation. Nor are we in any position to sit in tribunal and favor one faction over another, to reward one gang of warlords while spurning another (as recent policy has done; see chapter 6). Washington has embroiled itself, willy-nilly, in the convoluted web of Iraq's internal quarrels, and there's no straightforward solution to such a messy situation. A rational foreign policy would never put us in the position of having to extricate ourselves from this kind of impossible morass.

The U.S. priority should be leaving behind a regime that is non-threatening, and in doing so, minimize the cost to Americans and the risk to the lives of U.S. troops. In the name of avenging fallen American soldiers, we should stamp out the remaining traces of the insurgency, and, in the name of protecting all Americans, put Iraq on notice that our region-wide ultimatum applies to it as well; like the declawed regimes of Iran, Saudi Arabia, Pakistan, and Afghanistan, it will face military action if it dares to become a threat to us.

Regarding the oil in Iraq, here again our policy should be to demand that trade in that commodity be left unobstructed. That the puny Iraqi regime would refuse is conceivable, but highly improbable, in view of America's newfound reputation for robust and proud self-assertion. If there were no regime, if anarchy prevailed, it would be morally proper for Washington to liberate the oil fields, but only if that is done expressly for the sake of restarting the trade in oil for our own benefit.

The Levant
Witnessing the United States rise to its full stature as a morally confident giant asserting its interests in the Middle East, the Islamist forces in Lebanon (e.g., Hezbollah) and in the Palestinian territories (e.g. Hamas) will shrivel,

financially and ideologically. Without a stream of dollars from Iran, Saudi Arabia, and other regimes—which have been cowed by American intimidation and/or force—any remaining jihadists in the Levant will have suffered a thorough humiliation, and will have to go scrounging. Syria has facilitated and backed Hamas and Hezbollah (allowing top leaders of Hamas to operate freely and run a headquarters in Damascus). The dawn of the new era in the Middle East will find Syria retreating from its past sponsorship of terrorists. By that point it will be common knowledge that whoever dares to back them will thereby single himself out as a potential target of American wrath.

Remember, too, that the United States has an ally in the area that likewise faces a common foe in the shape of the Islamist movement. No, contrary to the propaganda from the White House, that ally is not the Lebanese government. Washington has morally and financially bolstered Lebanon's government, but this is a regime that allows Hezbollah to run an Islamist state-within-a-state and to launch rocket attacks on Israel. In 2008 Lebanon granted that jihadist group a veto on cabinet decisions. Nor is our ally the fledging Palestinian Authority, once run by the Palestinian Liberation Organization and now by Hamas. Perversely, Washington has injected billions of dollars into the Palestinian Authority, legitimating its murderous campaign against Israel. No, in reality our only genuine ally in that area is Israel.

We should forthrightly acknowledge the nature and scope of this bond. It is in our interest to extend to Israel our moral endorsement of any retaliatory steps it decides to take to uproot and destroy whatever is left of the Islamist terrorist infrastructure in the Palestinian territories and in Lebanon. That includes selling Israel the bombs and military hardware that it needs to defend itself—and, by extension, our interests. And when it is called upon to use those weapons in retaliation, Washington should signal its moral approval, rather than imploring Israel to pull its punches and blackmailing the regime with threats to cut off trade in weapons (as many U.S. administrations have done for years).

By extending our hand in solidarity to Israel, we stress the fact that our intimidating ultimatum toward potential enemies has a positive flip side: if you share our values and desire peaceful coexistence with the United States, you have nothing to fear and stand to gain from our friendship (if deserved). Just as we deploy public diplomacy to broadcast our moral justification for the war against the Islamist movement, so, equally, we should publicly name the standard by which we judge Israel (and other allies) and explain the nature and depth of our alliance.

It is fundamentally by projecting our moral strength and clarity of vision that Washington can successfully advance our national self-interest in the region.

U.S. Security through Principled Policy

If we are to set off on the road to victory, we need to abandon the bankrupt policies that weakened us and strengthened our enemies, and instead properly define and consistently pursue our actual self-interest in the Middle East. The fundamental challenge before us, then, is not strategic or even tactical; it has to do with the basic strata of ideas underlying our foreign policy. We need, in other words, to base our Mideast policy on a new moral foundation; the necessary underpinning for all the practical steps outlined above is the moral ideal of egoism. Unless we make that principle the intellectual framework of our policy, none of these steps is possible.

We need, moreover, to begin formulating our foreign policy with a frank recognition of what we confront in the Middle East. Emphasizing our willingness to resort to military force to assert our interests is necessary in dealing with the region. It is the one language best understood by all political actors. Sad to say, the "politics" within and between states in the region consists of continual struggles to assert domination, or escape submission. A brief taste of the internecine conflicts that have wracked the Arab-Islamic world (not including the series of wars against Israel, or the recent sectarian bloodbath in Iraq):

> Morocco and Algeria have fought, and for years Algeria has financed a proxy, the Polisario movement, to continue its feuding against Morocco. Libya has raided across the Egyptian and Tunisian borders and interfered militarily in Sudan. Syria has twice invaded neighboring Lebanon, and once neighboring Jordan, and it has mobilized against neighboring Iraq. Iraq has threatened Kuwait and Syria and has twice sent forces into Jordan, and under Saddam Hussein has fought one of the longest wars of the [20th] century against neighboring Iran. Jordan, North Yemen and South, and Oman have experienced civil war.[44]

Recall the seemingly routine assassinations of political figures in Lebanon (among the latest of which was Rafik Hariri), and the commonplace state-orchestrated violence against citizens (notably Syria's 1982 massacre of tens of thousands of residents in the city of Hama).[45] By one reckoning (again excluding the conflicts with Israel), "in the past six decades, this region has witnessed no fewer than 22 full-scale wars over territory and resources," a gruesome record that only begins to sketch the contours of the region's politics. A fuller picture would fill in the details of "the uninterrupted string of domestic clashes, military coups, acts of sectarian and ethnic vengeance, factional terrorism, and other internal conflicts that have characterized the greater Middle East, not infrequently attaining impressive heights of cruelty and despoliation."[46]

Islamists are, in this respect, one subgroup within the barbaric political culture of the region. In crushing the Islamist movement and convincing its many followers that the cause is hopeless, we are carrying out the only applicable remedy. In proudly asserting our self-interest and wielding the credible threat of devastating retaliation against aggressors, the United States positions itself in the minds of the Arab-Islamic world as a force that cannot be assailed with impunity, not ever. Our policy must requite force with force—to as ferocious a degree as necessary to deter future assailants. This will buy us the robust shield of credible deterrence, far more desirable than having to draw our military weapons.

What we will accomplish is the emasculation of the current threat—the Islamist movement—and of would-be attackers. Maintaining this policy toward the region, particularly by ensuring the uninterrupted free trade in oil, will keep out of reach the loot necessary to carry out attacks against us. In all likelihood, given the tribalism and authoritarian culture of the region, it will continue to be roiled by armed conflicts and wars between and within states. Washington's policy toward this should be: *Let them fight each other all they want, so long as they leave us alone*. If the Arab-Islamic world is to rescue itself from this primitivism, that day will come when the people of the region embrace the necessary life-enriching values of political and economic freedom (which the vision of America's moral strength and prosperity may incidentally inspire them to do).

We will accomplish another significant goal by our confident assertion of military strength. The meaning of such action is that we cherish (egoistically) our lives and cultural institutions, that we will go to war to defend ourselves and what we value. The moral strength to do that is precisely the same strength needed to oppose the subversive Islamist campaign within the West seeking to impose sharia rule, which we considered in chapter 6. By crushing the movement in the Middle East and demoralizing its followers, we will achieve the same effect on its followers everywhere. No one could thereafter seriously believe that we will allow the supplanting of our cultural values with sharia. What if there are die-hards bent on this cause? Such activists will find themselves up against Westerners who are resolutely unwilling to sacrifice their own freedom.

The recommendations outlined in this chapter are not meant to be, indeed cannot be, exhaustive. They are meant as illustrations of how the principle of egoism would apply to our Mideast policy. By its nature, that principle encompasses many possible applications to many particular contexts—obviously including situations that lie in the future. That's what makes it so enormously valuable as a guide to action: its advice applies to innumerable specific situations. And in a given case, it may endorse several different, equally valid courses of action (for example, in seeking to defeat the enemy militarily, there may be multiple morally valid options concerning which weapons to deploy and in what configuration). Consequently, it takes thought and a great deal of knowledge of a given situation to draw the practical guidance of this principled foreign policy.

For that advice to be profitable, we cannot pick up a few random tips or how-tos, and apply that advice, or not, as the fancy takes us. Unless we implement our policy as a matter of principle—in different contexts and across time—we derive no value from it. To conduct U.S. foreign policy by means of a splintered, moment-by-moment, diplomatic square dance—as we did before 9/11 and as the new administration promises to do again—is to subvert our national interest, now and in the long term. It cannot fail to inspire contempt among our enemies, and on occasion, it will mean that (as we've done in the past) we strengthen them and put weapons into their hands, weapons that eventually they turn against us.

So it is wrenchingly ironic that America's reputation in the world today is that of an ogre that ruthlessly bludgeons anyone who stands in the way of his self-interest. On this perspective, Washington somehow operates, robot-like, on an undeviating script calculated to attain its desires (regardless of how shrilly our presidents, in all sincerity and honesty, avow that our aim is selfless service to the world's needy). But the facts of the matter belie this reputation. If there is one motif that runs through the last decades of our erratic foreign policy, it is an overriding failure properly to conceptualize our self-interest and to pursue it as the morally right thing to do.

Up until now, we have trudged onward, from one crisis to a worse one, under self-imposed chains that have hobbled our policymaking and, consequently, our national security. Those chains, by our own choice, defined a narrow range of motion: self-assertive action for our own sake was seen as morally tainted; serving others, a noble ideal. Defeating our enemies was reviled as folly and (contrary to the evidence) as somehow self-defeating. Subordinating our security to the whims of that den of international reprobates, the United Nations, on the other hand, was somehow good.

Up until now, we have renounced the self-interested goal of defeating Islamic totalitarianism, because our leaders—and so many Americans—do not believe we are morally entitled to annihilate those who would annihilate us.

Up until now, we have deployed policies that implicitly or explicitly negate our absolute moral right to self-defense.

But no longer.

The policy outlined here constitutes a new starting point for America's dealings with the Middle East. Implementing it requires that we embrace the moral propriety of defending our freedom and our lives—and that we do so not apologetically, but rather with our heads held high.

Acknowledgments

I wish to thank Debi Ghate, Vice President of Academic Programs at the Ayn Rand Institute, for recognizing the importance of this project from the outset and for affording me the time to work on it. Peter Schwartz and Craig Biddle read early drafts of some of the material in this book. Dr. Yaron Brook read the manuscript at numerous points in its development and gave extensive editorial suggestions.

Special thanks are due to Dr. Onkar Ghate, Senior Fellow at the Ayn Rand Institute, for his insightful editorial guidance throughout this project. In our discussions over the years, Onkar helped me gain greater clarity, and a broader perspective, on the role of philosophic ideas in American foreign policy.

For assisting with the research, I wish to thank Don Watkins and Jeff Scialabba; Mr. Scialabba also helped prepare the final manuscript for the press.

Finally, I wish to thank my wife, Lindsay, for her loving support and encouragement.

The writing of this book was made possible thanks to the individuals, foundations, and corporations whose financial contributions fund the work of the Ayn Rand Institute.

Notes

Introduction

1. George W. Bush, interview by Matt Lauer, *Today*, MSNBC, 30 Aug. 2004, www.msnbc.msn.com/id/5866571/ (accessed 25 Aug. 2008).

2. "Excerpt from *Lone Survivor*," ArmyTimes.com, 18 June 2007, www.armytimes.com/news/2007/06/navy_sealbook_excerpt_070618w/ (accessed 16 Oct. 2008); John Springer, "He Knew his vote would sign their death warrant," TODAYShow.com, 12 June 2007, www.msnbc.msn.com/id/19189482/ (accessed 16 Oct. 2008).

3. Colin H. Kahl, "How We Fight," *Foreign Affairs* (November/December 2006), www.foreignaffairs.com/articles/62093/colin-h-kahl/how-we-fight (accessed 16 Oct. 2008).

4. Kahl, "How We Fight."

5. Ayn Rand, "The Lessons of Vietnam," in *The Voice of Reason: Essays in Objectivist Thought* (New York: Plume, 1990), 140, 143. Emphasis in the original.

Chapter One

1. Lawrence Wright, *The Looming Tower: Al-Qaeda and the Road to 9/11* (New York: Knopf, 2006), 357–59.

2. *The 9/11 Commission Report* (National Commission on Terrorist Attacks Upon the United States, 2004), www.gpoaccess.gov/911/index.html (accessed 2 Jan. 2009). On the scale of the Commission's investigation, see the preface of the *Report*.

3. Mark Bowden, *Guests of the Ayatollah: The Iran Hostage Crisis: The First Battle in America's War with Militant Islam* (New York: Grove/Atlantic, 2007), 346–51.

4. Matthew L. Wald and James Conaway, "Embassy's Fall in Teheran: Guns Ready but None Fired," *New York Times*, 27 Jan. 1980, 1.

5. In describing the American policy response to the crisis, this chapter draws in part upon the account presented in Harold H. Saunders, "Diplomacy and Pressure, November 1979–May 1980," in Warren Christopher, Harold H. Saunders, et al. *American Hostages in Iran* (New Haven: Yale University Press, 1986).

6. Terrence Smith, "Carter, Denouncing Terror, Warns Iran on Hostages' Safety; Says Blackmail Won't Work," *New York Times*, 16 Nov. 1979, 1.

7. See Harold H. Saunders, "Beginning of the End" in *American Hostages in Iran*.

8. Saunders, "Diplomacy and Pressure," 78–92.

9. Both quotations appear in Saunders, "Beginning of the End," 296.

10. President Carter's news conference, 17 April 1980. As transcribed in John T. Woolley and Gerhard Peters, *The American Presidency Project* (Santa Barbara, CA: University of California (hosted), Gerhard Peters (database), www.presidency.ucsb. edu (accessed 2 Jan. 2009).

11. Patrick Clawson and Michael Rubin, *Eternal Iran: Continuity and Chaos* (New York: Palgrave Macmillan, 2005), 93–96.

12. Constitution of the Islamic Republic of Iran (International Constitutional Law), www.servat.unibe.ch/law/icl/ir00000_.html (accessed 28 Sept. 2008).

13. Bowden, *Guests of the Ayatollah*, 563.

14. Ronald Reagan's remarks at the annual convention of the National Association of Evangelicals, 8 March 1983. As transcribed in Woolley and Peters, *The American Presidency Project*.

15. *Dammerell v. Islamic Republic of Iran*, No. 01-2224, (D.D.C. 29 March 2005).

16. Judge Royce C. Lamberth, *Peterson v. Islamic Republic of Iran*, Civil Action No. 01-2094 (Memorandum and Order), 30 May 2004, 16.

17. Lamberth, *Peterson*, 17, 12.

18. Anthony Loyd, "Tomb of the unknown assassin reveals mission to kill Rushdie," *Times Online*, 8 June 2005, www.timesonline.co.uk/tol/news/world/article531110.ece (accessed 25 Aug. 2007).

19. Lamberth, *Peterson*, 6.

20. Ronald Reagan's news conference of 22 February 1984. As transcribed in Woolley and Peters, *The American Presidency Project*.

21. Bernard Lewis, "A War of Resolve," *Wall Street Journal*, 2 Feb. 2002, www. opinionjournal.com/editorial/feature.html?id=105001985 (accessed 7 Sept. 2007). Quoting bin Laden from a 24 May 1996 ABC interview with John Miller.

22. Robert M. Gates, *From the Shadows: The Ultimate Insider's Story of Five Presidents and How They Won the Cold War* (New York: Touchstone, 1997), 351.

23. Gates, *From the Shadows*, 352.

24. Gates, *From the Shadows*, 354.

25. George H. W. Bush's Inaugural Address, 20 Jan. 1989. As transcribed in Woolley and Peters, *The American Presidency Project*.

26. Quoted in Daniel Pipes, *The Rushdie Affair: The Novel, the Ayatollah, and the West*, 2d ed. (New Brunswick: Transaction Publishers, 2003), 27.

27. Khomeini quoted in Efraim Karsh, *Islamic Imperialism: A History* (New Haven: Yale University Press, 2006), 217.

28. Thomas L. Friedman, "Bush Finds Threat to Murder Author Deeply Offensive," *New York Times*, 22 February 1989, www.nytimes.com/1989/02/22/world/bush-finds-threat-to-murder-author-deeply-offensive.html (accessed 25 Aug. 2007).

29. Pipes, *The Rushdie Affair*, 167–71.

30. Louis J. Freeh, "Khobar Towers," *Wall Street Journal*, 25 June 2006, www.opinionjournal.com/extra/?id=110008563 (accessed 7 Sept. 2007).

31. Philip Shenon and David Johnston, "U.S.-Saudi Inquiry Into 1996 Bombing Is Falling Apart," *New York Times*, 21 June 1998, www.nytimes.com/1998/06/21/world/us-saudi-inquiry-into-1996-bombing-is-falling-apart.html (accessed 4 Sept. 2007).

32. Haleh Esfandiari quoted in Clawson and Rubin, *Eternal Iran*, 129.

33. Clawson and Rubin, *Eternal Iran*, 131.

34. James C. McKinley, "Bombings in East Africa: The Overview; Bombs Rip Apart 2 U.S. Embassies in Africa; Scores Killed; No Firm Motive or Suspects," *New York Times*, 8 August 1998, www.nytimes.com/1998/08/08/world/bombings-east-africa-overview-bombs-rip-apart-2-us-embassies-africa-scores.html (accessed 4 Sept. 2007).

35. James Bennet, "U.S. Cruise Missiles Strike Sudan and Afghan Targets Tied to Terrorist Network," *New York Times*, 21 August 1998, partners.nytimes.com/library/world/africa/082198attack-us.html (accessed 23 Oct. 2008).

36. See Daniel Pearl, "New Doubts Surface Over Claims That Plant Produced Nerve Gas," *Wall Street Journal*, 28 August 1998, online.wsj.com/article/SB904255274222359500.html (accessed 23 Oct. 2008); Steven Lee Myers, "After The Attacks: the Overview; U.S. Offers More Details On Attack in the Sudan," *New York Times*, 24 August 1998, www.nytimes.com/1998/08/24/world/after-the-attacks-the-overview-us-offers-more-details-on-attack-in-the-sudan.html (accessed 23 Oct. 2008); William Claiborne, "Targets Described As Primitive," *Washington Post*, 22 August 1998.

37. John F. Burns, "The Warship Explosion: The Overview; Toll Rises to 17 in Ship Blast, as U.S. Hunts Suspects," *New York Times*, 14 October 2000, www.nytimes.com/2000/10/14/world/warship-explosion-overview-toll-rises-17-ship-blast-us-hunts-suspects.html (accessed 4 Sept. 2007).

38. John F. Burns, "How a Mighty Power Was Humbled by a Little Skiff," *New York Times*, 28 October. 2000, www.nytimes.com/2000/10/28/world/how-a-mighty-power-was-humbled-by-a-little-skiff.html (accessed 4 Sept. 2007).

Chapter Two

1. Quoting Edward Said in Patricia Cohen, "Response To Attack Splits Arabs In the West," *New York Times*, 29 September 2001, www.nytimes.com/2001/09/29/arts/response-to-attack-splits-arabs-in-the-west.html (accessed 28 Oct. 2008).

2. "London bomber: Text in full," *BBC*, 1 September 2005, news.bbc.co.uk/2/hi/uk_news/4206800.stm (accessed 21 June 2008).

3. "Last words of a terrorist," *The Observer*, 30 September 2001, www.guardian.co.uk/world/2001/sep/30/terrorism.september113 (accessed 10 Mar. 2006).

4. Quoted in Efraim Karsh, *Islamic Imperialism: A History* (New Haven: Yale University Press, 2006), 210–11.

5. Sayyid Qutb, *Maalim fi-l-Tariq* (Ramallah: Dar al-Kutub-al-Thaqafiya, 1987), 60–61. As quoted in Karsh, *Islamic Imperialism*, 212.

6. Sayyid Qutb, *Milestones* (New Delhi: Islamic Book Service, 2006), 63.

7. Qutb, *Milestones*, 63.

8. Qutb, *Milestones*, 72.

9. Abul Ala Mawdudi, *Political Theory of Islam* (Lahore: Islamic Publications, 1961), 26, 30; Mawdudi, *al-jihad fi Sabil Allah* (Beirut: Dar al-Fikr, 1960), 35. As cited in Karsh, *Islamic Imperialism*, 208.

10. Ayatollah Ruhollah Khomeini, "Islamic Government," in *Islam and Revolution 1: Writings and Declaration of Imam Khomeini*, ed. Hamid Algar (Berkeley: Mizan Press, 1981), 27.

11. Khomeini, "Islamic Government," 55–56.

12. Ayatollah Ruhollah Khomeini, "Islam is not a religion of Pacifists" (1942) in *The Legacy of Jihad: Islamic Holy War and the Fate of Non-Muslims*, ed. Andrew G. Bostom (Amherst, N.Y.: Prometheus Books, 2008), 226.

13. Ayatollah Ruhollah Khomeini, "Speech at Feziyeh Theological School" (24 August 1979), in *The Legacy of Jihad*, 227.

14. Qutb quoted in Paul Berman, *Terror and Liberalism* (New York: W. W. Norton, 2003), 101.

15. Koran, Sura 9.111. As cited in Karsh, *Islamic Imperialism*, 19.

16. Ayatollah Ruhollah Khomeini, "On the Nature of the Islamic State" (1979) in *The Legacy of Jihad*, 229.

17. Paul Marshall, *Radical Islam's Rules: The Worldwide Spread of Extreme Sharia Law* (Lanham, Md.: Rowman & Littlefield, 2005), 48.

18. John F. Burns, "New Afghan Rulers Impose Harsh Mores Of the Islamic Code," *New York Times*, 1 October 1996, www.nytimes.com/1996/10/01/world/new-afghan-rulers-impose-harsh-mores-of-the-islamic-code.html (accessed 10 Mar. 2006).

19. Marshall, *Radical Islam's Rules*, 13.

20. Yaroslav Trofimov, *Faith at War: A Journey on the Frontlines of Islam, from Baghdad to Timbuktu* (New York: Henry Holt and Co., 2005), 8.

21. Paul A. Marshall, *The Talibanization of Nigeria: Sharia Law and Religious Freedom* (Washington, D.C.: Center for Religious Freedom, 2002), 17.

22. Farhad Rajaee, *Islamic Values and World Views: Khomeini on Man, the State and International Politics* (Lanham, Md.: Universities of America Press, 1983), 82–83, as cited in Karsh, *Islamic Imperialism*, 217.

23. Daniel Byman, *Deadly Connections: States that Sponsor Terrorism* (New York: Cambridge University Press, 2005), 92.

24. For bin Laden see, for example, "Transcript of Osama bin Laden videotape," *CNN.com*, 13 December 2001, archives.cnn.com/2001/US/12/13/tape.transcript/ (accessed 10 Mar. 2006); Zawahiri quoted in Thomas Joscelyn, "Iraq Is the Central Front," *Weekly Standard* 12, no. 43 (30 July 2007), www.weeklystandard.com/Content/Public/Articles/000/000/013/900tybar.asp (accessed 2 Jan. 2009); Sheik Omar Abdel Rahman quoted in Jonathan Schanzer, "Breeding Ground: Fundamentalists Pervert Teaching of Islam," *Investor's Business Daily*, 24 September 2001,

schanzer.pundicity.com/106/breeding-ground-fundamentalists-pervert-teaching (accessed 10 Mar. 2006?); Moussaoui quoted in Neil A. Lewis, "Moussaoui, Testifying
Again, Voices Glee Over Witnesses' Accounts of Sept. 11 Grief," *New York Times*,
14 April 2006, www.nytimes.com/2006/04/14/us/nationalspecial3/14moussaoui.html
(accessed 12 Aug. 2006).

25. George W. Bush's remarks at an Iftaar dinner, 19 November 2001. As transcribed in John T. Woolley and Gerhard Peters, *The American Presidency Project*
(Santa Barbara, CA: University of California (hosted), Gerhard Peters (database),
www.presidency.ucsb.edu (accessed 2 Jan. 2009).

26. George W. Bush's remarks at the Islamic Center of Washington, 17 September
2001. As transcribed in Woolley and Peters, *The American Presidency Project*.

27. Bernard Lewis, *The Crisis of Islam: Holy War and Unholy Terror* (New York:
Random House, 2004), 138.

28. George W. Bush's remarks to the National Endowment for Democracy, 6 October 2005. As transcribed in Woolley and Peters, *The American Presidency Project*.

29. John L. Esposito, *Islam: The Straight Path*, 3rd ed. (New York: Oxford University Press, 1998), 88.

30. This survey of Islam's pillars relies on Esposito, *Islam*, 88–93.

31. Qutb, *Milestones*, 47.

32. Koran, Sura 9:29 quoted in Robert Spencer, *Onward Muslim Soldiers: How
Jihad Still Threatens America and the West* (Washington, D.C.: Regnery, 2003), 6.

33. Koran, Sura 9:19–20 quoted in Spencer, *Onward Muslim Soldiers*, 123.

34. Hasan al-Banna, "The Message of the Teachings" (Young Muslims Canada
Online Library, 1997), web.youngmuslims.ca/online_library/books/tmott/ (accessed
2 Jan. 2009).

35. Muhammad ibn Umar al-Waqidi, *Kitab al-Maghazi*, vol. 3 (London: Routledge
& Kegan, 1962), 1113, cited in Karsh, *Islamic Imperialism*, 4.

36. Carole Hillenbrand, *The Crusades: Islamic Perspectives* (Edinburgh: Edinburgh
University Press, 1999), 92, cited in Karsh, *Islamic Imperialism*, 19.

37. David Cook, *Understanding Jihad* (Berkeley: University of California Press,
2005), 6.

38. Karsh, *Islamic Imperialism*, 21.

39. In chapter two of *Understanding Jihad*, Cook offers a robust scholarly defense of
this point. See also the treatment of the issue in Bostom, *The Legacy of Jihad*.

40. Amir Khusrau, *Kuazain-ul-Futuh*, cited in K.S. Lal, "Jihad Under the Turks
and Jihad Under the Mughals," in Karsh, *Islamic Imperialism*, 457.

41. Amir Khusrau, *Ashiqa* (Aligarh, 1917), 46, cited in K.S. Lal, "Jihad Under the
Turks and Jihad Under the Mughals," in Karsh, *Islamic Imperialism*, 457.

42. Babur Nama, cited in K.S. Lal, "Jihad Under the Turks and Jihad Under the
Muhgals," in *The Legacy of Jihad*, 459.

43. Ayatollah Ruhollah Khomeini, "Islam is Not a Religion of Pacifists" (1942);
"Speech at Feyziyeh Theological School" (August 24, 1942), in *The Legacy of Jihad*,
226, 227.

44. Ali Benhadj quoted in Berman, *Terror and Liberalism*, 119–120.

45. Abdallah Azzam, "Martyrs: The Building Blocks of Nations," as quoted in Cook, *Understanding Jihad*, 129.

46. Bernard Lewis, *The Shaping of the Modern Middle East* (New York: Oxford University Press, 1994), 122.

47. Emmanuel Sivan, *Radical Islam: Medieval Theology and Modern Politics*, Enlarged Edition (New Haven: Yale University Press, 1990), 6–13.

48. Sivan, *Radical Islam*, 14.

49. Sivan, *Radical Islam*, 10.

50. Quoted in Sivan, *Radical Islam*, 24.

51. Karsh, *Islamic Imperialism*, 209.

52. Bernard Lewis, *The Crisis of Islam*, 159; see also Bruce Lawrence, ed., *Messages to the World: The Statements of Osama bin Laden* (New York: Verso, 2005), 167.

53. Qutb, quoted in Berman, *Terror and Liberalism*, 69.

54. Berman, *Terror and Liberalism*, 69.

55. Qutb, *Milestones*, 59.

56. Lewis, *The Shaping of the Modern Middle East*, 72.

57. Ibrahim Khalas, *Jaysh ash-Sha'b*, 25 April 1967, quoted in Jabir Rizq, *Al-Ikwhan al-Muslimun w' al-Mu'amara 'ala Suriya* (Cairo: Dar al-I'tisam, 1980), 111. As cited in Daniel Pipes, *The Rushdie Affair: The Novel, the Ayatollah, and the West*, 2nd ed. (New Brunswick: Transaction Publishers, 2003), 75.

58. Pipes, *The Rushdie Affair*, 75.

59. See Elan Journo, "Exposing Anti-Muslim 'Conspiracies'," *The Objective Standard* 1, no. 1 (Spring 2006), www.theobjectivestandard.com/issues/2006-spring/anti-muslim-conspiracies.asp (accessed 2 Jan. 2009).

60. Neil Mackay, "Anatomy of a Global Crisis: How the Fire Spread," *Sunday Herald* (Scotland, UK), 2 February 2006, www.sundayherald.com (accessed 6 Aug. 2006).

61. Pernille Ammitzbøll and Lorenzo Vidino, "After the Danish Cartoon Controversy," *Middle East Quarterly* (Winter 2007), www.meforum.org/1437/after-the-danish-cartoon-controversy (accessed 2 Jan. 2009).

62. Hassan M. Fattah, "At Mecca Meeting, Cartoon Outrage Crystallized," *New York Times*, 2 February 2006, www.nytimes.com/2006/02/09/international/middleeast/09cartoon.html (accessed 2 Feb. 2006).

63. From an article in the December 2000 issue of the Taliban English-language magazine *The Islamic Emirate*. As cited in Trofimov, *Faith at War*, 204.

64. *The Arab Human Development Report 2002: Creating Opportunities for Future Generations* (Regional Bureau for Arab States/UNDP, Arab Fund for Economic and Social Development), as quoted in Lewis, *The Crisis of Islam*, 115–16.

65. Lewis, *The Crisis of Islam*, 116, citing the 2002 *Arab Human Development Report*.

66. Trofimov, *Faith at War*, 275.

67. Robin Wright, "The Mind of Hezbollah," *Seattle Times*, 23 July 2006, seattletimes.nwsource.com/html/opinion/2003143646_sundayhezbollah23.html (accessed 24 July 2006).

68. Daniel Pipes, "A New Round of Anger and Humiliation: Islam after 9/11," in

Our Brave New World: Essays on the Impact of September 11, ed. Wladyslaw Pleszcynski (Stanford: Hoover Institution Press, 2002), 41–61, www.danielpipes.org/417/a-new-round-of-anger-and-humiliation-islam-after-9-11 (accessed 2 Jan. 2009).

69. Trofimov, *Faith at War*, xv.

70. Sheik Muhammad Rafaat Othman, a scholar of Islamic law at al-Azhar University in Cairo; Gameela Ismail, "A Merger of Mosque and State," *Newsweek*, 15 October 2001, US edition. See also Pipes, "A New Round of Anger."

71. See polls cited in Pipes, "A New Round of Anger."

72. Pamela Constable, "Afghans' Uneasy Peace With Democracy," *Washington Post*, 22 April 2006, www.washingtonpost.com/wp-dyn/content/article/2006/04/21/AR2006042101747.html (accessed 22 Apr. 2006).

73. Adrienne Koch and William Peden, eds., *The Life and Selected Writings of Thomas Jefferson* (Modern Library, 1998), 399.

74. Daniel Pipes, "Who Is the Enemy?" *Commentary*, January 2002.

75. See *Report on the Official Account of the Bombings in London on 7th July 2005* (London: The Stationary Office, 11 May 2006), 13, www.official-documents.gov.uk/document/hc0506/hc10/1087/1087.pdf (accessed 12 Aug. 2006) and Peter Whoriskey and Dan Eggen, "7 Held in Miami in Terror Plot Targeting Sears Tower," *Washington Post*, 23 June 2006, www.washingtonpost.com/wp-dyn/content/article/2006/06/22/AR2006062201546.html (accessed 23 June 2006).

76. Gilles Kepel, *Jihad: The Trail of Political Islam* (Cambridge, Mass.: Belknap Press, 2003), 123. In describing the impact of Iran's revolution, I draw in part on the work of Kepel.

77. *Wal Fadjri* 1 (13 Jan. 1984), 2. Editorial signed by the founder, Sidy Lamine Nyass. As quoted in Kepel, *Jihad*, 131–32.

78. Byman, *Deadly Connections*, 84–85.

79. Koran, Sura 8:65, quoted in Sayyid Qutb, *Islam and Universal Peace* (Plainfield, Ind: American Trust Publications, 1993), 10.

Chapter Three

1. George W. Bush's remarks to the American Legion, 24 Feb. 2006, as transcribed in John T. Woolley and Gerhard Peters, *The American Presidency Project* (Santa Barbara, CA: University of California [hosted], Gerhard Peters [database]), www.presidency.ucsb.edu/ws/index.php?pid=65267 (accessed 2 Jan. 2009).

2. The administration has referred to it both as a "forward strategy *of* freedom" and as a "forward strategy *for* freedom." For instance, in the 20 January 2004, State of the Union, and in President Bush's remarks to the American Legion on February 24, 2006. Both transcribed at Woolley and Peters, "The American Presidency Project," www.presidency.ucsb.edu/ws/index.php?pid=29646 and http://www.presidency.ucsb.edu/ws/index.php?pid=65267 (accessed 2 Jan. 2009).

3. George W. Bush speaking at the 20th Anniversary of the National Endowment for Democracy, 6 November 2003, as transcribed in Woolley and Peters, *The American Presidency Project*, www.presidency.ucsb.edu/ws/index.php?pid=844 (accessed 2 Jan. 2009).

4. Jonathan Wright, "Most Arab Leaders Survive to See Another Summit," *Reuters*, 27 March 2006, www.nytimes.com (accessed 27 Mar. 2006).

5. "Mideast Climate Change," *New York Times*, 1 March 2005, www.nytimes.com/2005/03/01/opinion/01tue1.html (accessed 1 Mar. 2005).

6. Tyler Marshall, "Changes in Mideast Blunt Bush's Critics," *Los Angeles Times*, 7 March 2005, published in the *Boston Globe*, www.boston.com/news/world/middleeast/articles/2005/03/07/changes_in_mideast_blunt_bushs_critics/ (accessed 2 Jan. 2009).

7. Ari Z. Weisbard, "Militants at the Crossroads," *The Nation*, 24 April 2003, www.thenation.com/doc/20030512/weisbard (accessed 2 Jan. 2009).

8. Jeffrey Bartholet, "How Al-Sadr May Control U.S. Fate in Iraq," *Newsweek*, 4 December 2006, www.msnbc.msn.com/id/15898064/site/newsweek/displaymode/1098 (accessed 4 Dec. 2006); "Pentagon: Militia more dangerous than al Qaeda in Iraq," *CNN.com*, 12 December 2006.

9. Michael R. Gordon and Dexter Filkins, "Hezbollah Said to Help Shiite Army in Iraq," *New York Times*, 28 November 2006, www.nytimes.com/2006/11/28/world/middleeast/28military.html (accessed 29 Nov. 2006).

10. George W. Bush remarks on Middle East, 24 June 2002, as transcribed in Woolley and Peters, *The American Presidency Project*, www.presidency.ucsb.edu/ws/index.php?pid=73320 (accessed 2 Jan. 2009).

11. Ramsay Short, "Key job for 'terrorist' Hizbollah in Lebanon's new cabinet," *Telegraph.co.uk*, 20 July 2005, www.telegraph.co.uk/news/worldnews/middleeast/lebanon/1494451/Key-job-for-terrorist-Hizbollah-in-Lebanons-new-cabinet.html (accessed 17 Jan. 2007).

12. Efraim Karsh, *Islamic Imperialism: A History* (New Haven: Yale University Press, 2006), 209.

13. Joshua Muravchik, "Jihad or Ballot-Box?," *Wall Street Journal*, 13 December 2005, reprinted at www.aei.org/publications/filter.all,pubID.23577/pub_detail.asp (accessed 2 Jan. 2009).

14. Michael Slackman, "Egyptians Rue Election Day Gone Awry," *New York Times*, 9 December 2005, www.nytimes.com/2005/12/09/international/africa/09egypt.html (accessed 9 Dec. 2005).

15. "Operation Enduring Freedom," *iCasualties.org*, icasualties.org/oef/.

16. Carlotta Gall, "Taliban Threat Is Said to Grow in Afghan South," *New York Times*, 3 May 2006, www.nytimes.com/2006/05/03/world/asia/03afghan.html (accessed 5 Mar. 2006); Carlotta Gall, "Attacks in Afghanistan Grow More Frequent and Lethal," *New York Times*, 27 September 2006, www.nytimes.com/2006/09/27/world/asia/27afghan.html (accessed 9 Oct. 2006); Carlotta Gall and Abdul Waheed Wafa, "Taliban Truce in District of Afghanistan Sets Off Debate," *New York Times*, 2 December 2006, www.nytimes.com/2006/12/02/world/asia/02afghan.html (accessed 4 Dec. 2006).

17. Associated Press, "British MI5 tracking 30 terror plots," *msnbc.com*, 10 November 2006, www.msnbc.msn.com/id/15646571/ (accessed 28 Nov. 2006).

18. Dimitri K. Simes, "No more crusades in the Middle East," *Los Angeles Times*, 9

January 2007, articles.latimes.com/2007/jan/09/opinion/oe-simes9 (accessed 10 Jan. 2007).

19. Anthony H. Cordesman, "Al Qaeda's Small Victories Add Up," *New York Times*, 3 June 2004, www.nytimes.com/2004/06/03/opinion/al-qaeda-s-small-victories-add-up.html (accessed 10 Jan. 2007).

20. Kennan quoted in Lawrence Kaplan, "Springtime for Realism," *New Republic*, 21 June 2004.

21. Michael Rubin, "Right War, Botched Occupation," *USA Today*, 27 November 2006, reprinted at www.aei.org/publications/pubID.25190/pub_detail.asp (accessed 10 Jan. 2007).

22. Max Boot, "Defending and Advancing Freedom: A Symposium," *Commentary* (November 2005).

23. Victor Davis Hanson, *The Soul of Battle: From Ancient Times to the Present Day, How Three Great Liberators Vanquished Tyranny* (New York: The Free Press, 1999), 2.

24. For a fuller consideration of what's required to defeat the enemy, see chapter 7 and also John David Lewis, "'No Substitute for Victory': The Defeat of Islamic Totalitarianism," *The Objective Standard* 1, no. 4 (Winter 2006), www.theobjectivestandard.com/issues/2006-winter/no-substitute-for-victory.asp (accessed 2 Jan. 2009).

25. MacArthur and the writer, Theodore Cohen, are quoted in Joshua Muravchik, *Exporting Democracy: Fulfilling America's Destiny*, revised paperback edition (Washington, D.C.: AEI Press, 1992), 101–2.

26. George W. Bush's remarks to the American Legion, 2 February 2006.

27. George W. Bush's State of the Union Address, 20 January 2004.

28. Alexander Hamilton, John Jay, and James Madison, *The Federalist Papers*, ed. Clinton Rossiter (New York: Mentor, 1999), 49.

29. Associated Press, "Bush Doesn't See Longtime U.S. Presence in Iraq," *foxnews. com*, 19 October 2004, www.foxnews.com/story/0,2933,135868,00.html (accessed 20 Oct. 2004).

30. George W. Bush's remarks at the American Enterprise Institute annual dinner, 26 February 2003, as transcribed in Woolley and Peters, *The American Presidency Project*, www.presidency.ucsb.edu/ws/index.php?pid=62953 (accessed 2 Jan. 2009).

31. Thom Shanker and Eric Schmitt, "A Nation at War: Air Offensive; American Planners Stick With the Scalpel Instead of the Bludgeon," *New York Times*, 27 March 2003, www.nytimes.com/2003/03/27/world/nation-war-air-offensive-american-planners-stick-with-scalpel-instead-bludgeon.html (accessed 11 Dec. 2006).

32. For more on the self-destructive rules of engagement governing U.S. forces, see Brook and Epstein, "'Just War Theory' vs. American Self-Defense."

33. George W. Bush's remarks at the American Enterprise Institute annual dinner, 23 February 2006.

34. George W. Bush's State of the Union Address, 31 January 2006, as transcribed in Woolley and Peters, *The American Presidency Project*, www.presidency.ucsb.edu/ws/index.php?pid=65090 (accessed 2 Jan. 2009)

35. George W. Bush's address to the nation on the War on Terror in Iraq, 10 Jan. 2007. As transcribed in Woolley and Peters, *The American Presidency Project*, www. presidency.ucsb.edu/ws/index.php?pid=24432 (accessed 2 Jan. 2009).

36. George W. Bush addresses the United Nations General Assembly, 10 November 2001. As transcribed in Woolley and Peters, *The American Presidency Project*, www.presidency.ucsb.edu/ws/index.php?pid=58802 (accessed 2 Jan. 2009).

37. Amy Belasco, *The Cost of Iraq, Afghanistan, and Other Global War on Terror Operations Since 9/11* (Congressional Research Service - Library of Congress, October 15, 2008), 11.

38. Churchill quoted in Michael Walzer, *Just and Unjust Wars*, 3rd ed. (New York: Basic Books, 2000), 261.

39. George W. Bush's Inaugural Addresses, 20 January 2005, and 20 January 2001. As transcribed in Woolley and Peters, *The American Presidency Project*, www.presidency.ucsb.edu/ws/index.php?pid=58745 and www.presidency.ucsb.edu/ws/index. php?pid=25853 (accessed 2 Jan. 2009).

40. *Holy Bible, King James Version* (American Bible Society, 1999), The Gospel according to St. Matthew.

41. George W. Bush's State of the Union Address, 28 January 2003. As transcribed in Woolley and Peters, *The American Presidency Project*, www.presidency.ucsb. edu/ws/index.php?pid=29645 (accessed 2 Jan. 2009).

42. President Bush's Address before a joint session of Congress on the U.S. response to the terrorist attacks of September 11, 20 Sept. 2001. As transcribed in Woolley and Peters, *The American Presidency Project*, www.presidency.ucsb.edu/ws/index.php?pid=64731 (accessed 2 Jan. 2009).

43. George W. Bush addresses the nation, 7 October 2001. As transcribed in Woolley and Peters, *The American Presidency Project*, www.presidency.ucsb.edu/ws/index.php?pid=65088 (accessed 2 Jan. 2009).

44. Emphasis in the original. *National Strategy for Victory in Iraq* (National Security Council, Nov. 2005), 4, www.washingtonpost.com/wp-srv/nation/documents/Iraqnationalstrategy11-30-05.pdf (accessed 10 Jan. 2007).

45. See for example, "Blair Says Hope Can Fight Terror," *BBC News*, 8 July 2005, news.bbc.co.uk/1/low/uk_politics/4664391.stm (accessed 10 July 2005).

46. George W. Bush's address to the nation on the War on Terror in Iraq, 10 January 2007.

47. Nicholas D. Kristof, "Talking With the Monsters," *New York Times*, 10 October 2006, select.nytimes.com/2006/10/10/opinion/10kristof.html (accessed 10 Oct. 2006).

48. We here offer a non-exhaustive discussion of the subject; for a detailed treatment of it, see chapter 7 and also Peter Schwartz, *The Foreign Policy of Self-Interest: A Moral Ideal for America* (Irvine, Calif.: Ayn Rand Institute Press, 2004).

Chapter Four

1. George W. Bush, address before a joint session of Congress on the U.S. response to the terrorist attacks of September 11, 20 September 2001. As transcribed in

John T. Woolley and Gerhard Peters, *The American Presidency Project* (Santa Barbara, CA: University of California (hosted), Gerhard Peters (database), www.presidency. ucsb.edu/ws/index.php?pid=64731 (accessed 2 Jan. 2009).

2. Angelo M. Codevilla, *No Victory, No Peace* (Lanham, Md.: Rowman & Littlefield, 2005), 39, 97–98.

3. Codevilla, *No Victory, No Peace*, 39.

4. Michael Walzer, *Just And Unjust Wars* (New York: Basic Books, 2000), 174.

5. Walzer, *Just and Unjust Wars*, 155–56.

6. Jean Bethke Elshtain, *Just War Against Terror: The Burden of American Power In a Violent World* (New York: Basic Books, 2003), 57.

7. Walzer, *Just And Unjust Wars*, xi.

8. David E. Sanger, "Beating Them To the Prewar," *New York Times*, 28 September 2002, www.nytimes.com/2002/09/28/arts/beating-them-to-the-prewar.html (accessed 29 Sept. 2002).

9. Walzer, *Just And Unjust Wars*, 127.

10. Elshtain, *Just War Against Terror*, 65.

11. Elshtain, *Just War Against Terror*, 66.

12. Elshtain, *Just War Against Terror*, 69.

13. Elshtain, *Just War Against Terror*, 70.

14. David E. Sanger, "Pakistan Found to Aid Iran Nuclear Efforts," *New York Times*, 2 September 2004, www.nytimes.com/2004/09/02/international/middleeast/02iran.html (accessed 2 Sept. 2004).

15. There is a small, insignificant minority of Machiavellian realists who consciously reject altruism, but their alternative is to say that there are no moral limits on what the United States (or any nation) can do. Such a view is a sanction to barbarism by any nation, and genuinely horrifies those with a legitimate concern for justice.

16. Robert Mayhew, ed., *Ayn Rand Answers: The Best of Her Q & A* (New York: New American Library, 2005), 97.

17. Mayhew, *Ayn Rand Answers*, 95.

18. Associated Press, "Bush Doesn't See Longtime U.S. Presence in Iraq," published on *Foxnews.com*, 19 October 2004, www.foxnews.com/story/0,2933,135868,00.html (accessed 2 Jan. 2009).

19. The writers would like to thank Dr. Onkar Ghate, Senior Fellow of the Ayn Rand Institute, for his invaluable editorial assistance with this essay.

Chapter Five

1. George W. Bush, speaking during the presidential debate in Winston-Salem, North Carolina, 11 October 2000. As transcribed in John T. Woolley and Gerhard Peters, *The American Presidency Project* (Santa Barbara, CA: University of California (hosted), Gerhard Peters (database), www.presidency.ucsb.edu/ws/index.php?pid=29498 (accessed 18 May 2009).

2. George W. Bush, speaking during the presidential debate in Winston-Salem, North Carolina, 11 October 2000.

3. George W. Bush's State of the Union Address, 31 January 2006. As transcribed in Woolley and Peters, *The American Presidency Project*, www.presidency.ucsb.edu/ws/index.php?pid=65090 (accessed 18 May 2009).

4. William Kristol and Robert Kagan, "Introduction: National Interest and Global Responsibility," in *Present Dangers: Crisis and Opportunity in American Foreign and Defense Policy* (San Francisco: Encounter Books, 2000), 4.

5. Joseph Bottum, "A Nation Mobilized," *Weekly Standard* 7, no. 2 (24 September 2001), 8.

6. George W. Bush addresses a joint session of Congress regarding the U.S. response to the terrorist attacks of September 11, 2001, 20 Sept. 2001. As transcribed in Woolley and Peters, *The American Presidency Project*, www.presidency.ucsb.edu/ws/index.php?pid=64731 (accessed 18 May 2009).

7. Jim Lehrer, "How Wide a War?," *NewsHour*, 26 September 2001, www.pbs.org/newshour/bb/terrorism/july-dec01/wide_war.html (accessed 14 May 2009).

8. George W. Bush remarks at the 20th Anniversary of the National Endowment for Democracy, 6 Nov. 2003. As transcribed in Woolley and Peters, *The American Presidency Project*, www.presidency.ucsb.edu/ws/index.php?pid=844 (accessed 14 May 2009).

9. Charles Krauthammer, "The Neoconservative Convergence," *Commentary*, July/August 2005, 26.

10. "Bush calls end to 'major combat,'" *CNN.com*, 2 May 2003, www.cnn.com/2003/WORLD/meast/05/01/sprj.irq.main/ (accessed 18 May 2009).

11. "Parody," *Weekly Standard* 8, no. 31 (21 April 2003), 40.

12. Reuel Marc Gerecht, "The Restoration of American Awe," *Weekly Standard* 8, no. 34 (12 May 2003); Frank Barnes, "The Commander," *Weekly Standard* 8, no. 37 (2 June 2003).

13. Barry Goldwater, *Conscience of a Conservative* (Washington, D.C.: Regnery, 1994), 11.

14. Irving Kristol, *Reflections of a Neoconservative: Looking Back, Looking Ahead* (New York: Basic Books, 1983), 116; Irving Kristol, *Two Cheers for Capitalism* (New York: Signet, 1979), 119, as quoted in C. Bradley Thompson, "The Decline and Fall of American Conservatism," *The Objective Standard* 1, no. 3 (Fall 2006), www.theobjectivestandard.com/issues/2006-fall/decline-fall-american-conservatism.asp (accessed 4 Apr. 2009).

15. Irving Kristol, "Socialism: An Obituary for an Idea," in *Reflections of a Neoconservative: Looking Back, Looking Ahead* (Basic Books, 1983), 116–17.

16. Ayn Rand, "The Fascist New Frontier," in *The Ayn Rand Column*, ed. Peter Schwartz, 2nd ed. (New Milford, Conn.: Second Renaissance Books, 1998), 98–99.

17. William Kristol and David Brooks, "What Ails Conservatism: The case for national greatness," *Wall Street Journal*, 15 September 1997, www.opinionjournal.com/extra/?id=110007216 (accessed 18 May 2009).

18. David Brooks, "A Return to National Greatness: A Manifesto for a Lost Creed," *Weekly Standard*, 3 March 1997.

19. Bottum, "A Nation Mobilized," 8.

20. Kristol and Kagan, "Present Dangers," 4.

21. Kristol and Kagan, "Present Dangers," 23.

22. Kristol and Kagan, "Present Dangers," 23.

23. Kristol and Kagan, "Present Dangers," 23.

24. Max Boot, "The Case for American Empire," *Weekly Standard*, 15 October 2001, 30.

25. Woodrow Wilson's address to a joint session of Congress requesting a declaration of war against Germany, 2 April 1917. As transcribed in Woolley and Peters, *The American Presidency Project*, www.presidency.ucsb.edu/ws/index.php?pid=65366 (accessed 18 May 2009).

26. Angelo M. Codevilla, "Some Call it Empire," *Claremont Review of Books*, Fall 2005, www.claremont.org/publications/crb/id.842/article_detail.asp (accessed 18 May 2009).

27. Max Boot, "What the Heck is a 'Neocon'?," *Wall Street Journal*, 30 December 2002, www.opinionjournal.com/editorial/feature.html?id=110002840 (accessed 14 May 2009).

28. Mark Gerson, *The Neoconservative Vision: From the Cold War to the Culture Wars* (Lanham, Md.: Madison Books, 1997), 181.

29. Kristol and Kagan, "Present Dangers," 15.

30. Woodrow Wilson's address to a joint session of Congress requesting a declaration of war against Germany, 2 April 1917.

31. George W. Bush's remarks to the National Endowment for Democracy, 6 November 2003.

32. Max Boot, *The Savage Wars of Peace: Small Wars And The Rise of American Power* (New York: Basic Books, 2002), 350.

33. Boot, *The Savage Wars of Peace*, 326.

34. Kristol and Kagan, "Present Dangers," 16.

35. Boot, "The Case for American Empire," 27–28.

36. Boot, "The Case for American Empire," 27.

37. George W. Bush's Inaugural Address, 30 January 2005. As transcribed in Woolley and Peters, *The American Presidency Project*, www.presidency.ucsb.edu/ws/index.php?pid=58745 (accessed 20 Apr. 2009).

38. Thomas Sowell, "Pacifists versus Peace," *Real Clear Politics*, 21 July 2006, www.realclearpolitics.com/articles/2006/07/pacifists_versus_peace.html (accessed 14 May 2009).

39. Bottum, "A Nation Mobilized."

40. Stephen Hayes, "Beyond Baghdad," *Weekly Standard* 8, no. 31 (21 April 2003), www.weeklystandard.com/Content/Public/Articles/000%5C000%5C002%5C524denxh.asp (accessed 18 May 2009).

41. Thomas Sowell, "Dangers ahead—from the Right," *Jewish World Review*, 6 January 2003, www.jewishworldreview.com/cols/sowell010603.asp (accessed 22 Apr. 2009).

42. Kristol and Kagan, "Present Dangers," 15.

43. Kristol and Kagan, "Present Dangers," 15.

44. Boot, "What the Heck is a 'Neocon'?"

45. For an excellent elaboration on this point, see John David Lewis, "'No Substi-

tute for Victory:' The Defeat of Islamic Totalitarianism," *The Objective Standard* 1, no. 4 (Winter 2006), www.theobjectivestandard.com/issues/2006-winter/no-substitute-for-victory.asp (accessed 2 Jan. 2009).

46. Kristol and Kagan, "Present Dangers," 13

47. Joshua Muravchik, "The Neoconservative Cabal," *Commentary*, September 2003.

48. Kristol and Kagan, "Present Dangers," 16.

49. For a discussion of this point, see Irving Kristol, "An Autobiographical Memoir," in *Neoconservatism: The Autobiography of an Idea* (Chicago: Ivan R. Dee, 1999), 8.

50. George W. Bush remarks at the 20th Anniversary of the National Endowment for Democracy, 6 November 2003.

51. Muravchik, "The Neoconservative Cabal."

52. Ayn Rand, "The Roots of War," in *Capitalism: The Unknown Ideal* (New York: Signet, 1986).

53. Full Text of the Iraqi Constitution, courtesy of the Associated Press, 12 October 2005, Article 2, www.washingtonpost.com/wp-dyn/content/article/2005/10/12/AR2005101201450.html (accessed 18 May 2009).

54. Brook and Epstein, "'Just War Theory' vs. American Self-Defense."

55. The writers would like to thank Dr. Onkar Ghate, Senior Fellow of the Ayn Rand Institute, for his invaluable editorial assistance with this essay.

Chapter Six

1. Associated Press, "McCain says U.S. succeeding in Iraq," *USA Today*, 24 March 2008, www.usatoday.com/news/politics/election2008/2008-03-24-mccain-iraq_N.htm (accessed 11 Apr. 2008).

2. Joby Warrick, "U.S. Cites Big Gains Against Al-Qaeda," *Washington Post*, 30 May 2008, www.washingtonpost.com/wp-dyn/content/article/2008/05/29/AR2008052904116_pf.html (accessed 1 June 2008).

3. Bret Stephens, "My Bet With Francis Fukuyama," *Wall Street Journal*, 5 August 2008, online.wsj.com/article/SB121789262234511729.html (accessed 5 Aug. 2008).

4. Jon Cohen, "More Voters Perceive Progress in Iraq," *Washington Post*, 11 September 2008, www.washingtonpost.com/wp-dyn/content/article/2008/09/10/AR2008091003808.html (accessed 11 Sept. 2008).

5. See, for example, *Messages to the World: The Statements of Osama Bin Laden*, ed. Bruce Lawrence (New York: Verso, 2005), 92; Ben Macintyre, "Was Madrid a barbarous revenge for the lost paradise of al-Andalus?," *Times Online*, 13 March 2004, www.timesonline.co.uk/tol/comment/columnists/ben_macintyre/article1044733.ece (accessed 1 Dec. 2008).

6. Data reported in Anthony H. Cordesman, "The Afghan-Pakistan War: New NATO/ISAF Reporting on Key Trends," 10 February 2009, Center for Strategic and International Studies, Washington, D.C., archived at www.csis.org/burke/reports/ (accessed 14 May 2009).

7. Statistics from icasualties.org and Kirk Semple and Andrew W. Lehren, "500: Deadly U.S. Milestone in Afghan War," *New York Times*, 6 August 2008, www.nytimes.com/2008/08/07/us/07afghan.html (accessed 7 Aug. 2008).

8. Carlotta Gall, "Insurgency's Scars Line Afghanistan's Main Road," *New York Times*, 13 August 2008, www.nytimes.com/2008/08/14/world/asia/14highway.html (accessed 14 Aug. 2008).

9. Carlotta Gall, "Taliban Gain New Foothold in Afghan City," *New York Times*, 27 August 2008, www.nytimes.com/2008/08/27/world/asia/27kandahar.html (accessed 27 Aug. 2008).

10. See, for example Eric Schmitt, "Militant Gains in Pakistan Said to Draw Fighters," *New York Times*, 10 July 2008, www.nytimes.com/2008/07/10/world/asia/10terror.html (accessed 10 July 2008); Jane Perlez, "Petraeus, in Pakistan, Hears Complaints About Missile Strikes," *New York Times*, 14 November 2008, www.nytimes.com/2008/11/04/world/asia/04pstan.html (accessed 15 Nov. 2008).

11. David Rohde, "An Afghan Symbol for Change, Then Failure," *New York Times*, 5 September 2006, www.nytimes.com/2006/09/05/world/asia/05afghan.html (accessed 2 Jan. 2009).

12. Barnett R. Rubin, "Saving Afghanistan," *Foreign Affairs*, January/February 2007.

13. Yochi J. Dreazan and Siobhan Gorman, "Taliban Regains Power, Influence in Afghanistan," *Wall Street Journal*, 20 November 2008, online.wsj.com/article/SB122713845685342447.html (accessed 20 Nov. 2009).

14. Afghanistan Constitution (International Constitutional Law), 26 January 2004, www.servat.unibe.ch/icl/af00000_.html (accessed 21 Nov. 2008).

15. Abdul Waheed Wafa and Carlotta Gall, "Afghan Court Gives Editor 2-Year Term for Blasphemy," *New York Times*, 24 October 2005, www.nytimes.com/2005/10/24/international/asia/24afghan.html (accessed 25 Oct. 2005).

16. Pamela Constable, "Afghans' Uneasy Peace With Democracy," *Washington Post*, 22 April 2006, www.washingtonpost.com/wp-dyn/content/article/2006/04/21/AR2006042101747.html (accessed 3 May 2006).

17. Jerome Starkey, "Afghan protest: 'He just shared an article with friends. What's the problem?'," *The Independent*, 1 February 2008, www.independent.co.uk/news/world/asia/afghan-protest-he-just-shared-an-article-with-friends-whats-the-problem-776784.html (accessed 2 Jan. 2009).

18. Laura King, "Afghan student gets 20 years instead of death for blasphemy," *Los Angeles Times*, 22 October 2008, articles.latimes.com/2008/oct/22/world/fg-afghanistan22 (accessed 2 Jan. 2009).

19. Sebastian Rotella, "Anger Over Cartoons of Muhammad Escalates," *Los Angeles Times*, 3 February 2006, articles.latimes.com/2006/feb/03/world/fg-muhammad3 (accessed 5 Feb. 2006).

20. Reuters, "Afghan Clerics Warn Karzai Against Missionaries," *New York Times*, 6 January 2008, www.nytimes.com/2008/01/06/world/asia/06afghan.html (accessed 6 Jan. 2008).

21. Eric Schmitt, "Afghan Officials Aided an Attack on U.S. Soldiers," *New York*

Times, 3 November 2008, www.nytimes.com/2008/11/04/world/asia/04military.html (accessed 4 Nov. 2008).

22. Richard A. Oppel Jr., "Number of Unidentified Bodies Found in Baghdad Rose Sharply in May," *New York Times*, 2 June 2007, www.nytimes.com/2007/06/02/world/middleeast/02iraq.html (accessed 2 June 2007).

23. Associated Press, "Text of Petraeus remarks at Iraq hearing," *USA Today*, 8 April 2008, www.usatoday.com/news/world/iraq/2008-04-08-petraeus-remarks_N.htm (accessed 24 Nov. 2008).

24. *Measuring Stability and Security in Iraq*, Report to Congress, in accordance with the Department of Defense Appropriations Act 2008 (Section 9010, Public Law 109-289; Section 9204, Public Law 110-252), September 2008, www.defenselink.mil/home/features/Iraq_Reports/ (accessed 2 Jan. 2009).

25. Yousif Bassil and Jomana Karadsheh, "Fifteen corpses found in Baghdad mass grave," *CNN.com*, 18 November 2008, www.cnn.com/2008/WORLD/meast/11/18/iraq.main/index.html (accessed 19 Nov. 2008).

26. Sam Dagher, "Defying a Spate of Bombings, Baghdad Has a Party," *New York Times*, 4 October 2008, www.nytimes.com/2008/10/04/world/middleeast/04webiraq.html (accessed 5 Oct. 2008).

27. Michael Yon, "Iraq's New Dawn," *New York Post*, 24 November 2008, www.nypost.com/seven/11242008/postopinion/opedcolumnists/iraqs_new_dawn_140418.htm (accessed 2 Jan. 2009).

28. It is suggestive that SCIRI (Supreme Council for the Islamic Revolution in Iraq) has dropped the R from its name, claiming that a revolution to establish an Islamic state in Iraq is no longer necessary.

29. Dexter Filkins, "Who Wins in Iraq? Moqtada al-Sadr," *Foreign Policy*, March/April 2007.

30. Warren P Strobel and Leila Fadel, "Iranian who brokered Iraqi peace is on U.S. terrorist watch list," *McClatchy Newspapers*, 31 March 2008, www.mcclatchydc.com/227/story/32141.html (accessed 2 Jan. 2009).

31. Michael Duffy, "The Surge At Year One," *Time*, 31 January 2008, www.time.com/time/magazine/article/0,9171,1708843,00.html (accessed 3 Feb. 2008).

32. Dana Hedgpeth and Sarah Cohen, "Money as a Weapon," *Washington Post*, 11 August 2008, www.washingtonpost.com/wp-dyn/content/article/2008/08/10/AR2008081002512.html (accessed 15 Aug. 2008).

33. Nir Rosen, "The Myth of the Surge," *Rolling Stone*, 6 March 2008, www.rollingstone.com/politics/story/18722376/the_myth_of_the_surge (accessed 2 Jan. 2009).

34. Steven Simon, "The Price of the Surge," *Foreign Affairs*, May/June 2008.

35. Daniel L. Byman and Kenneth M. Pollack, "Iraq's Long-Term Impact on Jihadist Terrorism," *Annals of the American Academy of Political and Social Science*, Terrorism: What the Next President Will Face (July 2008), www.brookings.edu/articles/2008/07_terrorism_byman.aspx (accessed 28 Sep. 2008).

36. Byman and Pollack, "Iraq's Long-Term Impact on Jihadist Terrorism."

37. *Country Reports on Terrorism 2007* (United States Department of State Pub-

lication: Office of the Coordinator for Counterterrorism, April 2008), www.state. gov/documents/organization/105904.pdf (accessed 2 Jan. 2009).

38. J. Michael McConnel, *Annual Threat Assessment of the Director of National Intelligence* (Senate Select Committee on Intelligence, 5 Feb. 2008), graphics8.nytimes. com/packages/pdf/national/20080205_testimony.pdf (accessed 6 Feb. 2008).

39. See Jane Perlez, "Taliban Leader Flaunts Power Inside Pakistan," *New York Times*, 2 June 2008, www.nytimes.com/2008/06/02/world/asia/02pstan.html (accessed 3 June 2008); and Nicholas Schmidle, "Next-Gen Taliban," *New York Times Magazine*, 6 January 2008, www.nytimes.com/2008/01/06/magazine/06PAKISTAN-t.html (accessed 10 Jan. 2008).

40. Ron Moreau, "Where the Jihad Lives Now," *Newsweek*, 20 October 2007, www.newsweek.com/id/57485 (accessed 20 Oct. 2007).

41. Mark Mazzetti and David Rohde, "Amid U.S. Policy Disputes, Al Qaeda Grows in Pakistan," *New York Times*, 30 June 2008, www.nytimes.com/2008/06/30/ washington/30tribal.html (accessed 15 July 2008).

42. "Pakistan vows to help U.S. 'punish' attackers," *CNN.com*, 13 September 2001, transcripts.cnn.com/2001/WORLD/asiapcf/central/09/13/pakistan.support/ index.html (accessed 2 Jan. 2009); The President's News Conference With President Pervez Musharraf of Pakistan, 22 Sept. 2006, as transcribed at John T. Woolley and Gerhard Peters, *The American Presidency Project* [online]. Santa Barbara, CA: University of California (hosted), Gerhard Peters (database). Available from World Wide Web: www.presidency.ucsb.edu/ws/?pid=23696 (accessed 2 Jan. 2009); Massoud Ansari, "Omar role in truce reinforces fears that Pakistan 'caved in' to Taliban," *Daily Telegraph*, 29 September 2006. See also "The Return of the Taliban," WGBH/ PBS, transcript posted online 3 October 2006, www.pbs.org/wgbh/pages/frontline/ taliban/etc/script.html (accessed 2 Jan. 2009).

43. "Pakistan Takes Steps Towards Shari'a State In Seven Districts," *Middle East Media Research Institute (MEMRI)*, 16 May 2008, Special Dispatch - No. 1933 edition, memri.org/bin/latestnews.cgi?ID=SD193308 (accessed 2 Jan. 2009), citing May 11, 2008 newspaper reports; Jane Perlez and Pir Zubair Shah, "Cease-Fire by Pakistan in Attacks on Militants," *New York Times*, 31 August 2008, www.nytimes. com/2008/09/01/world/asia/01pstan.html (accessed 4 Sep. 2008).

44. See, for example, Richard A. Oppel Jr. and Pir Zubair Shah, "In Pakistan, Radio Amplifies Terror of Taliban," *New York Times*, 24 January 2009, www.nytimes. com/2009/01/25/world/asia/25swat.html (accessed 14 May 2009).

45. Pamela Constable, "Extremist Tide Rises in Pakistan," *Washington Post*, 20 April 2009, www.washingtonpost.com/wp-dyn/content/article/2009/04/19/ AR2009041901731_pf.html (accessed 20 Apr. 2009)

46. Asif Shahzad, "Taliban Bar Pakistan Army Convoy as Tensions Grow," Associated Press, 25 April 2009, www.google.com/hostednews/ap/article/ALeqM5hkiM xbHNH0BqgpWA2ZG6VD6wVTmAD97PJIVG3 (accessed 27 Apr. 2009).

47. Mark Mazetti and Eric Schmitt, "C.I.A. Outlines Pakistan Links With Militants," *New York Times*, 30 July 2008, www.nytimes.com/2008/07/30/world/ asia/30pstan.html (accessed 1 Aug. 2008); David E. Sanger and David Rohde,

"U.S. Pays Pakistan to Fight Terror, but Patrols Ebb," *New York Times* (online edition), 20 May 2007, www.nytimes.com/2007/05/20/world/asia/20pakistan.html (accessed 2 Jan. 2009); Seymour M. Hersh, "The Getaway," *The New Yorker*, 28 January 2002.

48. Nicholas D. Kristof, "Hang Up! Tehran Is Calling," *New York Times*, 21 January 2007, select.nytimes.com/2007/01/21/opinion/21kristof.html (accessed 2 Jan. 2009).

49. *Country Reports on Terrorism 2007.*

50. Ahmadinejad quoted in Y. Mansharof and A. Savyon, "Escalation in the Positions of Iranian President Mahmoud Ahmadinejad – A Special Report," *Middle East Media Research Institute (MEMRI)*, 17 Sept. 2007, Inquiry and Analysis - No. 389, www.memri.org/bin/articles.cgi?Area=ia&ID=IA38907&Page=archives (accessed 3 May 2008).

51. Anthony Browne, "Muslim Radical Confesses to Van Gogh Killing in Court Tirade," *The Times*, 12 July 2005, online edition, www.timesonline.co.uk/tol/news/world/article543212.ece (accessed 12 July 2005).

52. Raed Hyahel, in *Morgenavisen Jyllands-Posten*, 9 October 2005, as cited in Pernille Ammitzbøll and Lorenzo Vidino, "After the Danish Cartoon Controversy," *Middle East Quarterly*, Winter 2007.

53. U.S. State Department cited in Associated Press, "Muslim outrage spreads; U.S. calls cartoons 'offensive,'" *USA Today*, 3 February 2006, www.usatoday.com/news/world/2006-02-03-muslimanger_x.htm (accessed 3 Feb. 2006); Chirac, Frattini cited in David Rennie, "EU commissioner urges European press code on religion," *Telegraph.co.uk*, 2 February 2006, www.telegraph.co.uk/news/worldnews/europe/denmark/1510007/EU-commissioner-urges-European-press-code-on-religion.html (accessed 15 June 2008); Solana, Annan cited in "Joint UN, European Union, Islamic Conderence Statement Shares 'Anguish' of Muslim World at Muhammad Caricatures, but Condemns Violent Response" (United Nations: Department of Public Information, 2 July 2006), www.un.org/News/Press/docs/2006/sg2105.doc.htm (accessed 2 Jan. 2009).

54. Henryk Broder, "How a Film Triggered a Global Panic," *Spiegel Online*, 20 March 2008, International edition, www.spiegel.de/international/europe/0,1518,542255,00.html (accessed 30 Mar. 2008).

55. For a list of the French *Zones Urbaines Sensibles*, see i.ville.gouv.fr/divbib/doc/chercherZUS.htm; for information on similar "no-go" areas in other countries, see Daniel Pipes, "The 751 No-Go Zones of France," 14 November 2006, updated 16 March 2008, www.danielpipes.org/blog/2006/11/the-751-no-go-zones-of-france.html (accessed 18 May 2009).

56. Quoted in Koenraad Elst, "The Rushdie Rules," *Middle East Quarterly*, June 1998, www.meforum.org/395/the-rushdie-rules (accessed 14 May 2009).

57. Daniel Pipes, "Eurabian Nights," *The National Interest Online*, 1 March 2007, www.nationalinterest.org/PrinterFriendly.aspx?id=13710 (accessed 15 June 2008).

58. Archbishop Rowan Williams, "Civil and Religious Law in England: a Religious Perspective," 7 February 2008, delivered at the Royal Courts of Justice, www.archbishopofcanterbury.org/1575 (accessed 5 June 2008).

59. BBC News, "New 'Bin Laden tape' threatens EU," 30 March 2008, news.bbc. co.uk/go/pr/fr/-/2/hi/europe/7306002.stm (accessed 30 Mar. 2008).

60. Asra Q. Nomani, "You Still Can't Write About Muhammad," *Wall Street Journal*, 6 August 2008, online.wsj.com/article/SB121797979078815073.html (accessed 14 Aug. 2008).

61. Vali Nasr and Ray Takeyh, "What We Can Learn From Britain About Iran," *New York Times*, 5 April 2007, www.nytimes.com/2007/04/05/opinion/05NasrTakeyh. html (accessed 5 Apr. 2008).

62. Bill Richardson, "Diplomacy, Not War, With Iran," *Washington Post*, 24 Feb. 2007, www.washingtonpost.com/wp-dyn/content/article/2007/02/23/AR2007022301595. html (accessed 25 Feb. 2007).

63. CNN.com, "Transcript of September 15, 2008 roundtable discussion with five former secretaries of state at George Washington University," 20 September 2008, transcripts.cnn.com/TRANSCRIPTS/0809/20/se.01.html (accessed 2 Jan. 2009).

64. Joseph R. Biden Jr., "Republicans and Our Enemies," *Wall Street Journal*, 23 May 2008, online.wsj.com/article/SB121150000249615875.html (accessed 3 Jan. 2009); Obama's Inauguration speech transcribed by *New York Times*, 20 January 2009, www.nytimes.com/2009/01/20/us/politics/20text-obama.html (accessed 20 Jan. 2009); see also "Obama tells Al Arabiya peace talks should resume," transcript of an interview by Hisham Melham on Al Arabiya TV, hosted at www.alarabiya. net/articles/2009/01/27/65087.html (accessed 28 Jan. 2009);

65. "Too Easy to Refuse," *New York Times*, 28 January 2008, www.nytimes. com/2008/01/28/opinion/28mon1.html (accessed 28 Jan. 2009).

66. Kristof, "Hang Up! Tehran Is Calling."

67. See for example, "Iran Sanctions: Impact in Furthering U.S. Objectives Is Unclear and Should Be Reviewed," United States Government Accountability Office, GAO-08-58, December 2007, www.gao.gov/new.items/d0858.pdf; Christopher S. Stewart, "The Axis of Commerce," *Portfolio*, September 2008 (online edition), www. portfolio.com/news-markets/international-news/portfolio/2008/08/13/US-Trades-With-Iran-Via-Dubai (accessed 10 Sept. 2008).

68. Philip Sherwell, "How we duped the West by Iran's nuclear negotiator," *Telegraph.co.uk*, 4 March 2006, www.telegraph.co.uk/news/worldnews/middleeast/ iran/1512161/How-we-duped-the-West-by-Irans-nuclear-negotiator.html (accessed 5 Mar. 2006).

Chapter Seven

1. Ayn Rand, "The Wreckage of the Consensus," in *Capitalism: The Unknown Ideal* (New York: Signet, 1986), 226.

2. Patrick Clawson and Michael Rubin, *Eternal Iran: Continuity and Chaos* (New York: Palgrave Macmillan, 2005), 141.

3. *Hezbollah's Global Reach*, Joint Hearing before the Subcommittee on International Terrorism and Nonproliferation and the Subcommittee on the Middle East and Central Asia of the Committee on International Relations (House of Repre-

sentatives, 109th Congress, September 28, 2006), pdf edition, 5, www.foreignaffairs. house.gov/archives/109/30143.pdf (accessed 5 Sept. 2007).

4. *The 9/11 Commission Report* (National Commission on Terrorist Attacks Upon the United States, 2004), pdf edition, 61, 240, www.gpoaccess.gov/911/index. html (accessed 2 Jan. 2009).

5. These figures are cited by Robert Spencer in *Onward Muslim Soldiers: How Jihad Still Threatens America and the West* (Washington, D.C.: Regnery, 2003), 219–20, and *Stealth Jihad: How Radical Islam is Subverting America without Guns or Bombs* (Washington, D.C.: Regnery, 2008), 15. Both refer to Brynjar Lia, *The Society of the Muslim Brothers in Egypt: The Rise of an Islamic Mass Movement 1928–1942* (Ithaca, UK: Ithaca Press, 1998), 153–54.

6. Ziad Abu-Amr, *Islamic Fundamentalism in the West Bank and Gaza: Muslim Brotherhood and Islamic Jihad* (Bloomington and Indianapolis: Indiana University Press, 1994), 3.

7. Walid M. Abdelnasser, "Islamic organizations in Egypt and the Iranian revolution of 1979: the experience of the first few years," *Arab Studies Quarterly* (Spring 1997), findarticles.com/p/articles/mi_m2501/is_n2_v19/ai_20046832/ (accessed 2 Jan. 2009).

8. Lawrence Wright, *The Looming Tower: Al-Qaeda and the Road to 9/11* (New York: Knopf, 2006), 47.

9. Abdelnasser, "Islamic organizations in Egypt," citing Nader Entessar, "Egypt and the Persian Gulf," *Conflict*, vol. 9, 116–17.

10. Abdelnasser, "Islamic organizations in Egypt."

11. Abu-Amr, *Islamic Fundamentalism in the West Bank and Gaza*, 102, citing Elie Rekhess, "The Iranian Impact on the Islamic Jihad Movement in the Gaza Strip" (paper submitted to a conference entitled "the Iranian Revolution and the Muslim World," Tel Aviv, Israel, Jan. 1988), 10.

12. Gilles Kepel, *Jihad: The Trail of Political Islam* (Cambridge, Mass.: Belknap Press, 2002), 130–35; see also Vanessa Martin, *Creating An Islamic State: Khomeini and the Making of New Iran* (New York: I. B. Tauris, 2000), 188–96.

13. Martin, *Creating An Islamic State*, 189, citing *Impact International*, April 13–26, 1979.

14. Kepel, *Jihad*, 130–35.

15. Khomeini quoted in Robin Wright, *Sacred Rage: The Wrath of Militant Islam* (New York: Touchstone, 2001), 21.

16. Clawson and Rubin, *Eternal Iran*, 101.

17. Ilan Berman, *Tehran Rising: Iran's Challenge to the United States* (Lanham, Md.: Rowman & Littlefield, 2005), 14–15.

18. Martin, *Creating An Islamic State*, 196.

19. Matthias Küntzel, "Ahmadinejad's Demons: A Child of the Revolution Takes Over," *New Republic*, 24 April 2006, www.matthiaskuentzel.de/contents/ ahmadinejads-demons (accessed 22 Apr. 2009).

20. M. Nissimov, Y. Mansharof, and A. Savyon, "Iranian Women's Magazine Shut Down for Publishing Investigative Article on Martyrdom Movement," *Middle East*

Media Research Institute (MEMRI) Inquiry and Analysis, no. 439 (22 May 2008), www. memri.org/bin/articles.cgi?ID=IA43908 (accessed 22 Apr. 2009).

21. On what it means for a regime to accept defeat, see John David Lewis, "'Gifts from Heaven': The Meaning of the American Victory over Japan, 1945," *The Objective Standard* 2, no. 4 (Winter 2007/08), www.theobjectivestandard.com/issues/2007-winter/american-victory-over-japan-1945.asp (accessed 2 Jan. 2009).

22. *Fourth Report of the Mental Health Advisory Team (MHAT-IV)*. *Operation Iraqi Freedom 05-07: Final Report* (Office of the Surgeon Multinational Force-Iraq and Office of the Surgeon General United States Army Medical Command, November 17, 2006), www.globalpolicy.org/security/issues/iraq/attack/consequences/2006/1117mhatreport.pdf (accessed 4 May 2007).

23. Thom Shanker, "Gates Apologizes for Afghan Deaths," *New York Times*, 18 September 2008, www.nytimes.com/2008/09/18/world/asia/18gates.html (accessed 18 Sept 2008); Robert F. Worth, "Blast at Shiite Shrine Sets Off Sectarian Fury in Iraq," *New York Times*, 23 February 2006, www.nytimes.com/2006/02/23/international/middleeast/23iraq.html (accessed 27 Aug. 2008); George W. Bush, "Statement by the President," Office of the Press Secretary, 22 February 2006, iraq.usembassy.gov/iraq/20060222_mosque_bombing.html (accessed 11 May 2009).

24. Lewis, "'Gifts from Heaven.'"

25. Adeed Dawisha, *Arab Nationalism in the Twentieth Century: From Triumph to Despair* (Princeton: Princeton University Press, 2003), 200–201. The journalist cited by Dawisha is Riad Taha, *Qissat al-Wuhda al-Infisal: Tajribat Insan 'Arabi Khilal Ahdath 1955-1961* (Beirut: Dar al-Afaw al-Jadida, 1974), 101.

26. See the chapter titled "Aftershocks: Tallies, Postmortems, and the Old/New Middle East," in Michael B. Oren, *Six Days of War: June 1967 and the Making of the Modern Middle East* (New York: Oxford University Press, 2002).

27. Fouad Ajami, *The Arab Predicament: Arab Political Thought and Practice since 1967*, 2d ed. (New York: Cambridge University Press, 1999), 30.

28. Raphael Patai, *The Arab Mind*, revised edition. (New York: Hatherleigh Press, 2002), 273–74.

29. Dawisha, *Arab Nationalism in the Twentieth Century*, 253.

30. Dawisha, *Arab Nationalism in the Twentieth Century*, 282.

31. Helene Cooper, "Unfriendly Views on U.S.-Backed Arabic TV," *New York Times*, 17 May 2007, www.nytimes.com/2007/05/17/washington/17hurra.html (accessed 22 May 2007); see also Joel Mowbray, "Mad TV: U.S. taxpayers subsidize terrorist propaganda and Holocaust denial in the Arab world," *Wall Street Journal*, 1 May 2007, www.opinionjournal.com/editorial/feature.html?id=110010011 (accessed 10 Jan. 2008).

32. "Energy in Brief: How dependent are we on foreign oil?," *Energy Information Administration: Official Energy Statistics from the U.S. Government*, 22 Aug. 2008, tonto. eia.doe.gov/energy_in_brief/foreign_oil_dependence.cfm (accessed 5 Oct. 2008).

33. Fares bin Hazam, "Online Fatwas Incite Young Muslims to Jihad," *Middle East Media Research Institute (MEMRI) Special Dispatch, no. 1335 (26 Oct. 2006),*

memri.org/bin/articles.cgi?Page=archives&Area=sd&ID=SP133506 (accessed 14 May 2009); interpolations in the quotation are by MEMRI.

34. Lisa Myers and the NBC Investigative Unit, "More evidence of Saudi double-talk?," *msnbc.com*, 26 April 2005, www.msnbc.msn.com/id/7645118/ (accessed 7 Oct. 2008).

35. Richard A. Oppel Jr., "Foreign Fighters in Iraq Are Tied to Allies of U.S.," *New York Times*, 22 November 2007, www.nytimes.com/2007/11/22/world/middleeast/22fighters.html (accessed 7 Oct. 2008).

36. Melanie Phillips, *Londonistan* (New York: Encounter Books, 2006), 16.

37. "Undercover Mosques: The Transcripts," Muslim Public Affair Committee UK (MPACUK), 15 Jan. 2007, www.mpacuk.org/index2.php?option=com_content&task=view&id=3266 (accessed 2 June 2008).

38. Alfred B. Prados and Christopher M. Blanchard, *Saudi Arabia: Terrorist Financing Issues* (Congressional Research Service - Library of Congress, December 8, 2004), pdf edition, CRS-15, 17, www.fas.org/irp/crs/RL32499.pdf (accessed 14 May 2009).

39. "JS-1703: Additional Al-Haramain Branches, Former Leader Designated by Treasury as Al Qaida Supporters Treasury Marks Latest Action in Joint Designation with Saudi Arabia" (Office of Public Affairs, 2 June 2004), www.ustreas.gov/press/releases/js1703.htm (accessed 14 May 2009); as cited in Prados and Blanchard, *Saudi Arabia: Terrorist Financing Issues*, CRS-17.

40. Prados and Blanchard, *Saudi Arabia: Terrorist Financing Issues*, citing "JS-1108: Treasury Announces Joint Action with Saudi Arabia In The Fight Against Terrorist Financing" (Office of Public Affairs, 22 January 2004), www.treas.gov/press/releases/js1108.htm (accessed 14 May 2009).

41. Alfred B. Prados and Christopher M. Blanchard, *Saudi Arabia: Terrorist Financing Issues* (Congressional Research Service - Library of Congress, 14 Sept. 2007), pdf edition, fas.org/sgp/crs/mideast/RL32499.pdf (accessed 14 May 2009).

42. Thom Shanker, "Civilian Risks Curbing Strikes in Afghan War," *New York Times*, 23 July 2008, www.nytimes.com/2008/07/23/world/asia/23military.html (accessed 22 July 2008).

43. Shanker, "Civilian Risks Curbing Strikes in Afghan War."

44. David Pryce-Jones, *The Closed Circle: An Interpretation of the Arabs* (Chicago: Ivan R. Dee, 2002), 10.

45. Pryce-Jones, *The Closed Circle*, 11.

46. Amir Taheri, "Is Israel the Problem?," *Commentary*, February 2007.

Select Bibliography

Abu-Amr, Ziad. *Islamic Fundamentalism in the West Bank and Gaza: Muslim Brotherhood and Islamic Jihad*. Bloomington and Indianapolis: Indiana University Press, 1994.

Ajami, Fouad. *The Arab Predicament: Arab Political Thought and Practice since 1967*. 2nd ed. New York: Cambridge University Press, 1999.

Algar, Hamid. *Islam and Revolution 1: Writings and Declaration of Imam Khomeini*. Berkeley: Mizan Press, 1981.

Berman, Ilan. *Tehran Rising: Iran's Challenge to the United States*. Lanham, Md: Rowman & Littlefield, 2005.

Berman, Paul. *Terror and Liberalism*. New York: W. W. Norton & Company, 2003.

Boot, Max. *The Savage Wars of Peace: Small Wars And The Rise of American Power*. New York: Basic Books, 2002.

Bostom, Andrew G., ed. *The Legacy of Jihad: Islamic Holy War and the Fate of Non-Muslims*. Amherst, N.Y.: Prometheus Books, 2008.

Bowden, Mark. *Guests of the Ayatollah: The Iran Hostage Crisis: The First Battle in America's War with Militant Islam*. New York: Grove/Atlantic, 2007.

Byman, Daniel. *Deadly Connections: States that Sponsor Terrorism*. New York: Cambridge University Press, 2005.

Christopher, Warren, Harold H. Saunders, et al. *American Hostages in Iran*. New Haven: Yale University Press, 1986.

Clawson, Patrick, and Michael Rubin. *Eternal Iran: Continuity and Chaos*. New York: Palgrave Macmillan, 2005.

Codevilla, Angelo M. *No Victory, No Peace*. Lanham, Md.: Rowman & Littlefield, 2005.

Cook, David. *Understanding Jihad*. Berkeley: University of California Press, 2005.

Dawisha, Adeed. *Arab Nationalism in the Twentieth Century: From Triumph to Despair*. Princeton: Princeton University Press, 2003.

241

Elshtain, Jean Bethke. *Just War Against Terror: The Burden of American Power In a Violent World*. New York: Basic Books, 2003.

Esposito, John L. *Islam: The Straight Path*. 3rd ed. New York: Oxford University Press, 1998.

Gates, Robert M. *From the Shadows: The Ultimate Insider's Story of Five Presidents and How They Won the Cold War*. New York: Touchstone, 1997.

Gerson, Mark. *The Neoconservative Vision: From the Cold War to the Culture Wars*. Lanham, Md.: Madison Books, 1997.

Goldwater, Barry. *Conscience of a Conservative*. Washington, D.C.: Regnery, 1994.

Hamilton, Alexander, John Jay, and James Madison. *The Federalist Papers*. Clinton Rossiter, ed. New York: Mentor, 1999.

Hanson, Victor Davis. *The Soul of Battle: From Ancient Times to the Present Day, How Three Great Liberators Vanquished Tyranny*. New York: The Free Press, 1999.

Karsh, Efraim. *Islamic Imperialism: A History*. New Haven: Yale University Press, 2006.

Kepel, Gilles. *Jihad: The Trail of Political Islam*. Cambridge, Mass.: Belknap Press, 2002.

Koch, Adrienne, and William Peden, eds. *The Life and Selected Writings of Thomas Jefferson*. New York: Modern Library, 1998.

Kristol, Irving. *Two Cheers for Capitalism*. New York: Signet, 1979.

———. *Reflections of a Neoconservative: Looking Back, Looking Ahead*. New York: Basic Books, 1983.

———. *Neoconservatism: The Autobiography of an Idea*. Chicago: Ivan R. Dee, 1999.

Kristol, William, and Robert Kagan, eds. *Present Dangers: Crisis and Opportunity in American Foreign and Defense Policy*. San Francisco: Encounter Books, 2000.

Lawrence, Bruce, ed. *Messages to the World: The Statements of Osama bin Laden*. New York: Verso, 2005.

Lewis, Bernard. *The Shaping of the Modern Middle East*. New York: Oxford University Press, 1994.

———. *The Crisis of Islam: Holy War and Unholy Terror*. New York: Random House, 2004.

Marshall, Paul, ed. *Radical Islam's Rules: The Worldwide Spread of Extreme Sharia Law*. Lanham, Md.: Rowman & Littlefield, 2005.

Martin, Vanessa. *Creating An Islamic State: Khomeini and the Making of a New Iran*. New York: I. B. Tauris, 2000.

Mayhew, Robert, ed. *Ayn Rand Answers: The Best of Her Q & A*. New York: New American Library, 2005.

Muravchik, Joshua. *Exporting Democracy: Fulfilling America's Destiny*. Revised paperback edition. Washington, D.C.: AEI Press, 1992.

Oren, Michael B. *Six Days of War: June 1967 and the Making of the Modern Middle East*. New York: Oxford University Press, 2002.

Patai, Raphael. *The Arab Mind*. Revised edition. New York: Hatherleigh Press, 2002.

Phillips, Melanie. *Londonistan*. New York: Encounter Books, 2006.

Pipes, Daniel. *The Rushdie Affair: The Novel, the Ayatollah, and the West*. 2d ed. New Brunswick, N.J.: Transaction Publishers, 2003.

Pryce-Jones, David. *The Closed Circle: An Interpretation of the Arabs.* Chicago: Ivan R. Dee, 2002.

Qutb, Sayyid. *Islam and Universal Peace.* Plainfield, Ind.: American Trust Publications, 1993.

——. *Milestones.* New Delhi: Islamic Book Service, 2006.

Rand, Ayn. *Capitalism: The Unknown Ideal.* New York: Signet, 1986.

——. *The Voice of Reason: Essays in Objectivist Thought.* Leonard Peikoff, ed. New York: Plume, 1990.

Schwartz, Peter, ed. *The Ayn Rand Column.* 2d ed. New Milford, Conn.: Second Renaissance Books, 1998.

——. *The Foreign Policy of Self-Interest: A Moral Ideal for America.* Irvine, Calif.: Ayn Rand Institute Press, 2004.

Sivan, Emmanuel. *Radical Islam: Medieval Theology and Modern Politics.* New Haven: Yale University Press, 1990.

Spencer, Robert. *Onward Muslim Soldiers: How Jihad Still Threatens America and the West.* Washington, D.C.: Regnery, 2003.

——. *Stealth Jihad: How Radical Islam is Subverting America without Guns or Bombs.* Washington, D.C.: Regnery, 2008.

Trofimov, Yaroslav. *Faith at War: A Journey on the Frontlines of Islam, from Baghdad to Timbuktu.* New York: Henry Holt and Co., 2005.

Walzer, Michael. *Just and Unjust Wars.* 3d ed. New York: Basic Books, 2000.

Wright, Lawrence. *The Looming Tower: Al-Qaeda and the Road to 9/11.* New York: Knopf, 2006.

Wright, Robin. *Sacred Rage: The Wrath of Militant Islam.* New York: Touchstone, 2001.

Index

Abdel Rahman, Omar, 29
Afghanistan, vii, 4, 19, 41, 45; anti-
  Soviet jihad in, 21, 58, 133, 194;
  Islamist resurgence in, 57, 75, 154,
  155–58, 168, 172, 204, 209; post-
  Taliban regime in, 67, 80, 158–60,
  210; Taliban rule of, 27–29, 85,
  135, 168, 171; U.S.-led war in
  (aka Operation Enduring Freedom;
  2001), viii, xi, 51, 67, 72, 86, 94–95,
  98–99, 104, 118, 129, 133, 137, 155,
  162. See also altruism (morality of
  selflessness); Bush, George W.; Just
  War Theory
Ahmadinejad, Mahmoud, 142, 176,
  194, 201
Ajami, Fouad, 199
Albright, Madeline, 18
Al Fajr, 42
Algeria, 36, 169, 193
Algiers Accord, 10
Al Haramain, 206
Al Hurra, 201
Al-Jihad, 192
Al Qaeda: 3–5, 19, 26, 29, 30, 56, 82,

111, 137, 153–55, 167, 169, 170,
  173, 190–92, 194, 203, 209
Al Qaeda in Iraq (AQI), 55, 153, 154
altruism (morality of selflessness),
  69–77, 90–91, 94, 95, 100–105,
  113, 121, 124–32, 136, 137,
  140–43, 147–49, 187, 188, 196.
  See also Christianity; collectivism;
  Communism; fascism; Islam; Just
  War Theory; Left; nationalism;
  neoconservatism; realism (in foreign
  policy); socialism; Wilsonianism
Ammitzbøll, Pernille, 178
Anbar Awakening, 165, 166
Annan, Kofi, 99
appeasement, x, 6, 8–20, 49, 77, 79, 85,
  92–94, 105, 107, 116, 117, 120, 140,
  148, 159, 166, 171, 172, 174, 178,
  181–85, 187, 194, 200, 208
Arab-Islamic world: cultural antipathy
  to liberty and individualism, 64–65,
  145; Islam and intellectual life in,
  41–47, 63–64, 109, 143, 155, 156,
  174, 177, 198–203; political culture
  in, 213, 214; reactions to 9/11, 44,

About the Contributors

Dr. Yaron Brook, the president and executive director of the Ayn Rand Institute, has written and lectured widely on Middle Eastern history, U.S. foreign policy, and Islamic terrorism. He is a regular commentator on CNBC and Fox News, and speaks to college and professional audiences around the world.

Alex Epstein is an analyst at the Ayn Rand Institute focusing on economic and political issues. His writing has appeared in numerous publications, including the *Detroit Free Press, Houston Chronicle, San Francisco Chronicle, Atlanta Journal-Constitution*, Canada's *National Post*, and the *Washington Times*.

Elan Journo is a fellow at the Ayn Rand Institute specializing in foreign policy. Mr. Journo has spoken at numerous college campuses, including USC, Georgia Tech, Berkeley, and Stanford. His writing has appeared in, among others, the *Los Angeles Times, Philadelphia Inquirer, Chicago Sun-Times*, and the *Globe and Mail* of Canada.

Breinigsville, PA USA
09 March 2010
233808BV00001B/2/P